BY TUBE BEYOND EDGWARE

Tony Beard

Capital Transport

First published 2002
ISBN 185414 246 1

Published by Capital Transport Publishing, 38 Long Elmes, Harrow Weald, Middlesex

Printed by CS Graphics, Singapore

Author's Note

Members of staff at the Archive and Records Management Service at 55 Broadway are painstakingly cataloguing the contents of the vaults where documents originating mainly from the upper floors of the building have been stored. A recent triumph of the staff there, Kathryn Thomas, Teresa Doherty, Philip Wood and Vikki Towey, has been in listing all files associated with Frank Pick. The examination of some of the myriad documents has provided hitherto unpublished information regarding the extension of the Morden to Edgware tube line towards Watford.

I began my researches at the London Metropolitan Archives, investigating the minutes of the LPTB and LTE. Although quite thorough, the information contained in the supporting documents posed more questions than it answered. Fortuitously, Peter Bancroft's book covering some of the records of London Transport in the Public Record Office was published at the time I began my researches at Kew. Here was to be found a wealth of information, files originating from various government departments giving greater detail to my copious research notes.

The House of Lords Record Office provided another piece to the jigsaw, as did the library at London's Transport Museum. Here, Simon Murphy and Hugh Robertson continued to find interesting photographs in the LT collection, some of which are reproduced in this book.

In addition to those previously mentioned, I would also like to record my sincere thanks to others who have also helped me in my researches, namely Peter Waxman of the Mosquito Aircraft Museum; Dorothy Skelley for her wartime reminiscences of Aldenham; Peter Moore of the 2RT2 Bus Preservation Group; Alan Jackson, Mike Horne, J Graeme Bruce, Desmond Croome and Peter Nichols for reading the draft and finally my wife Lynne who provided tremendous support. The beautiful front cover painting is by Barry Pearce.

Illustrations are © Capital Transport Publishing except:

Aerofilms Ltd 16, 17, 100/101, 132/133, 134/135

Laurie Akehurst collection 113

House of Lords Record Office 9

Alan A. Jackson 119, 125, 131 lower

LT Archive and Records Management 20, 56, 63, 81 lower

LT Museum 1, 26/27, 30/31, 53, 57, 61, 64/65, 68/69, 71, 72, 76/77 upper, 79, 82, 83, 84/85, 88/89, 90, 91, 93, 96, 97, 111, 114, 115, 116, 117, 121, 122, 127, 128/129, 130, 131 upper

London Underground Ltd 78, 80, 81 top, 94, 95

Photomatic 124, 126

Contents

Title page **Work completed at Edgware station by 14th February 1940 in connection with the extension of the Northern Line to Bushey Heath.**

CHAPTER ONE

Rails over the Heights

The geography of London presented innumerable problems for the early Victorian railway builders. The descending slopes of the Chiltern Hills that comprise the northern extent of the basin in which the capital is located afford a natural obstacle with few wind gaps available for the projection of new lines. The escarpments run out at a clay plateau extending from which are long spikes of high ground, the most popular being known as the Northern Heights of Finchley, Hornsey and Hampstead.

The London and Birmingham Railway reached Euston in 1837, the line being driven through a 1,182 yard tunnel to reach Camden to avoid the southern edge of the Heights as it set sights for the Metropolis. However, the Great Northern was obliged to create a series of cuttings in which the line continued its descent southwards from Potters Bar avoiding the eastern flank of the Heights in the process. Similar side-stepping tactics to those used by the London and Birmingham were demanded of the constructors of the Midland Railway to St Pancras, the last of the main lines so affected by the Northern Heights until the Manchester, Sheffield and Lincolnshire (later Great Central) in the 1890s.

Such action, whilst providing gradients that would not seriously challenge the capabilities of steam locomotives of the period, denied a railway service to towns and villages situated in the rising ground of north London. Two of the most notable omissions were Finchley and Edgware; the latter situated on the southern side of the Barnet/Bushey ridge and mainly consisting of a healthy farming community and a declining succession of coaching inns.

The earliest proposal to link Edgware with the existing rail network was promoted in 1861, but failed when Parliament decided that there was insufficient finance to build it. The next attempt to project a railway to Edgware came in 1862 when the Edgware, Highgate and London Railway Company (EHLRC), with an authorised capital of £220,000, succeeded in obtaining powers. The 8¾ mile route of the company's line commenced at a junction with the Great Northern Railway (GNR) just north of Seven Sisters Road (later Finsbury Park) station.

The intermediate stations would be located at Hornsey Lane for Hornsey; Highgate, near to the Woodman and Wellington inns; East Finchley (Church End) and at Page Street for Hendon and Mill Hill. The Act also required that the station at Edgware should be built as a terminus with such facilities as accommodation for 'not less than' twelve carriages and a shed capable of accommodating two engines.

The Edgware Highgate and London entered into an agreement with the Great Northern Railway Company on 9th December 1862. By providing one third of the share capital (i.e. £73,300), the GNR could expect to exert its influence on the construction of the line by filling three out of the eight seats on the joint Committee. Six months from its date of opening and for a period of 999 years, the Great Northern Railway would assume complete responsibility for the maintenance and operation of the line. The GNR would receive half of the gross receipts less Government duty and terminus charges.

Eager to emulate the successful passage of the Edgware, Highgate and London through Parliament, an independent enterprise consisting of local landowners with the title Watford and Edgware Junction Railway Company deposited a Bill in Parliament on 9th November 1863. This was the first attempt of many to promote the construction of a railway to link Edgware with Watford and was planned as a natural extension of the previously authorised line from Seven Sisters Road.

Deposited plans indicate that the Watford and Edgware would not have made an end-on connection at Edgware. Instead, a junction would be formed in the approach roads allowing the station to provide both terminal and through facilities. The sites for intermediate stations on the proposed extension were London Road (for Stanmore) to which the line had been purposely directed, Brockley Hill (for Elstree), Caldecott Hill and Bushey. Strong support for providing Stanmore with a railway service came from John Kelk, owner of nearby Bentley Priory, and then currently involved in the construction of Alexandra Palace.

At Watford a junction would be formed with the Watford and Rickmansworth Company's line at a point approximately one third of a mile north of a bridge that carried the main street of Watford over the railway. The Bill also sought powers to build a line about a quarter of a mile in length to establish a more northerly link with the Watford and Rickmansworth and thus form a triangular junction. This would allow trains from either direction to gain direct access to the route of the Watford and Edgware and trains from that line to run on to the London & North Western Railway (LNWR). In consequence, some thought had already been given to the possibility of excursion traffic to Alexandra Park that might originate from this area. Nevertheless extreme care was required to overcome an objection made by the LNWR regarding the loss of passenger revenue. Consequently the Watford and Edgware was described as being for the convenience of local traffic; the through fare to Watford from Kings Cross never to be set lower than that from Euston.

The Watford and Edgware Bill was subject to the scrutiny of a Select Committee which convened in March 1864 to hear evidence. Seymour Clark, Manager of the Great Northern Railway, stated that an extension to Watford had been contemplated since the projection of the Edgware Highgate and London, and gave his company's full support to the new railway. He concurred with the supporters of the Bill that the area to be served by the line would become a very pleasant neighbourhood and numerous stations would be required to accommodate the needs of the district. Clark was asked the reason for his company failing to promote an extension to Watford as soon as the Edgware Highgate and London line was proposed. He responded that the EHLR was an independent company and had only been considered capable of building the line as far as Edgware.

The main thrust of questioning concentrated on the facilities provided at Watford. By bringing the course of the Watford and Edgware trackbed below the main line of the London & North Western Railway, use could be made of the Rickmansworth and Watford's High Street station; the London & North Western's Watford Junction station being located about a mile from the town centre. However the Rickmansworth and Watford was operated by the LNWR which had previously objected to any connections with the Watford and Edgware and subsequent use of the High Street station. When this was put to Clark he stated that if the Rickmansworth and Watford were free to make its own decisions, then it would be in its own interest to allow the junction to be made.

It was also established that should the Bill succeed, there would be two stations near Watford with the name Bushey. Clark confirmed that the proposed Watford and Edgware station of that name would be a quarter of a mile from the village whereas that on the London & North Western Railway was at least twice that distance. A later disclosure revealed that the existing LNWR Bushey station was located in an area where many new houses had been built and was providing an adequate service for this new centre of population.

Further details regarding the Watford and Edgware Railway emerged when one of the two engineers responsible for the new line gave evidence. The estimate placed on the complete 6½-mile railway was £150,000. A single-track configuration would be used but the land acquired would accommodate a double track when demanded by an increase in traffic; all overbridges and the only underbridge having been planned for this eventuality. Gradients were considered easier than those of the Edgware and Highgate where they averaged

Facing page **This map of Middlesex shows the route proposed in the 1864 Bill to link Watford and Edgware by a railway line, its construction, according to the cartographer, considered as being 'in progress'. Note that the junction at Edgware is south of the station which allows the station to provide both terminal and through facilities. An amendment in 1866 sought powers to construct a line from a north-facing junction at Mill Hill on the Midland Railway that would parallel the line to Edgware and form a connection with the line to Watford beyond the station.**

1 in 65, those between Watford and Edgware being, at worst, 1 in 71 making a division of through trains unnecessary. No major earthworks were contemplated, with the exception of one cutting which would be excavated to a depth of 58 feet at its highest point. In the absence of running powers into the station at Watford High Street, some consideration had been given to the new line stopping short and terminating at a new station, although this possibility had not been included in the total cost of construction.

In conclusion the Committee agreed to the provisions contained in the Bill, with the exception of the running powers and the use of the station at Watford. Nevertheless this recommendation went unheeded, the Bill gaining full parliamentary approval allowing the acquisition of land to commence, which it did.

A series of changing fortunes seems to have influenced the development of railways serving townships in the Northern Heights. In the same year as the Watford and Edgware Railway Bill was passed, the Edgware and Highgate successfully obtained an Act for the construction of a branch to the new Alexandra Palace. The line would form a junction beyond the tunnel to the north of Highgate station, additional finance for the project having been acquired. In 1865 the company gained the parliamentary consent for the extension (never to be built) of its Alexandra Palace line to join the Great Eastern Railway.

It was now the turn of the WEJR to propose an extension. With construction work on the railway yet to begin, that company deposited a Bill in November 1865 for a line from just north of the EHLR station at Edgware to connect with the authorised London Extension of the Midland Railway just north of its bridge under Colin Deep Lane. But in May 1866 three directors of the WEJR were replaced with an equal number from the GNR and the Bill was withdrawn.

During April 1866 the EHLR was involved a three-way conflict with the GNR and Midland companies to develop further railways in the area and from which it emerged victorious; the town of Barnet being the main objective. During the Select Committee stage it was reported that work on the line to Edgware was nearing completion with double track having been installed as far as the junction for Alexandra Park. Some provision had also been made for the installation of double track along the entire length of the line, extensive retaining walls apparently having been constructed for the purpose. A further report stated that work was underway with the company's railway through the grounds of Alexandra Park but this was not the case. In 1868, a Bill to abandon the powers to construct the line into the park was obtained, invoking objections from a number of interested parties. It eventually fell to the Great Northern Railway to build the line although work did not commence until 1871, when it was known with some certainty that Alexandra Palace would be built.

The Edgware Highgate and London was transferred to the Great Northern Railway by Act of Parliament dated 15th July 1867; financial difficulties contributing greatly to the company's brief existence. The following month the line to Edgware was complete. As part of the take-over package, the Watford and Edgware also passed to the GNR, which demonstrated its reluctance to intrude on LNWR territory by successfully promoting the Watford and Edgware Junction Railway Abandonment Act of 1870. In its submission, the GNR recorded that whilst it was aware that some lands on the extension had been purchased or contracted for, construction work had yet to be started and that the LNWR already provided a train service between Watford and London. The company therefore considered the extension a waste of financial resources and requested that it be relieved of the duty to build it.

The GNR line to Edgware was not free of criticism from its daily commuters. As soon as the line opened for business in 1867, a petition was received urging the Great Northern to instigate a reduction in fares from its Finchley and Hendon station (later Finchley Church End) to bring them into line with the tariff in force at Southgate and Colney Hatch station (now New Southgate) on the GN main line. A further petition that year requested the continuance of the 6.45am train from Kings Cross, no doubt for the benefit of night workers, whilst another in 1873 pressed for improved train services. The following year complaints centred on delays suffered by the up morning trains, and in 1876 the residents of Finchley campaigned for a reduction in the Sunday service on the line.

In November 1878, a Bill was deposited by the Watford, Edgware and London Railway

Boroughs returning Two Members

Boroughs returning One Member

Boundaries of Boroughs

Division of Counties

RAILWAYS & NAMES OF STATIONS — PINNER

TELEGRAPH LINES & STATIONS — WATFORD

RAILWAYS IN PROGRESS

TUNNEL

WATFORD STA.

RICKMANSWORTH STA.

H E R T F O

NORTH WESTERN RAILWAY (MAIN LINE)

from Tring & Aylesbury

Harefield

North Wood

Potters Street Hill

Pinners Hill

Ruislip Wood

Ruislip Common

Pinners Wood

Wood Hall

PINNER STA.

Harrow Weald Com.

Weald Wood

Bentley Ho.

Bushey Heath

Crabtree Orchard

The Grove

Bowling Green

Elstree or Idlestrey

Brockley Hill

Edgware Bury

Bell Mount

Gt. Stanmore

Harrow Point Hill

Pinner Green

Pinner Park

Pinner

East End

Ascot

West End

Weald Stone

Harrow Weald

Old Church

Cannons Park

Pipers Green

Lawrance House

Headstone Fm.

Cheyney St.

Pinner Marsh

Ruislip

High Grove

East Field

Pinner Field

Hooking Green

Kenton Lane F.

Stanmore Marsh

Whitchurch

Lit. Stanmore

Edgware STA.

Ruislip Field

Roxborough Field

HARROW STA.

Mapit Field

Bracken Bridge Hill

Green Hill

Roxborough Lane

Harrow on the Hill

Tyburn Lane

Kenton

Woodcocks Hill

Kenton Field

Red Hill

Roe Bud Lane

Newton Field

the Back Lanes

Bues La.

Roxeth Green

Sheep Crud F.

Hill Logs Farm

Preston

Ascot Bushes

Stroud Gate

Crouch Field

Oxendon F.

Bush Farm

Kingsbury Gr.

The Hyde

Priors Field

Hollow Field

Wood End Green

Sudbury Gro.

The Hill House

Down Barn Hill

Cut Lane

Northolt Lane

Love La.

Court

Forty Green

Sill Br.

G O R E H U N D

with the aim of reviving some interest in the route abandoned nine years earlier. Roughly following the path of the 1864 Bill but with the addition of a London-facing connection to the Midland at Mill Hill, the Bill was withdrawn before it reached the Committee stage, a similar fate befalling an identical Bill submitted in 1884. In September 1886 a letter was sent to the directors of the Great Northern Railway from the Mayor of High Wycombe. His request, on behalf on the townspeople of High Wycombe and Beaconsfield, was for an improved train service to London. Initially the London & North Western Railway had been approached, but due to an agreement with the Great Western Railway, the LNWR was not in a position to undertake the project.

With a population of 12,000 in High Wycombe, an increasing number in its suburbs and an important chair and timber trade, the GNR was asked to consider extending its Edgware line to the Buckinghamshire town. The suggested route through Pinner, Harefield and Chalfont St Giles would cover a district totally without a railway service and bereft of obstacles that might cause major engineering problems. Indeed one large landowner had made provision in his will that he would give the land required free of all charge, with the exception of erecting fences, 'if the Great Northern will make a double line to High Wycombe'. The directors of the GNR considered the request on 1st October and agreed to inform the Mayor that it could not be entertained.

The next serious attempt to secure powers to build a line between Edgware and Watford took place in 1895 with the deposit of the Watford, Edgware and London Railway Bill. Following initial formalities the Bill was considered by a House of Commons Select Committee on 17th April 1896. The proposed route was similar to those considered in 1879 and 1884, the Bill requiring approval for four interlinked railways. At Watford, as in all the earlier Bills, a triangular junction was proposed with the Watford and Rickmansworth line, by then part of the LNWR. The transmission of through traffic to the area served by the proposed railway continued to be a positive element in the minds of the promoters of the line. From the fork of the junction at Watford the railway would progress through stations at Old Bushey, Heath Bourne Road and Elstree to Edgware, all areas determined as particularly eligible for suburban development.

Some 284 yards before the line reached Edgware station, a junction would be constructed, powers being sought to project a short length of railway from this point to make an end-on connection with the Great Northern. According to the plans laid before Parliament only one platform at Edgware would be required to provide through facilities to Watford, the design of the station considered capable of such adaptation Yet the GNR remained detached from the proceedings, matching the stance it took in 1864 and even going so far as to object to the new railway having access to its Edgware station. Retaining the scheme put forward in previous proposals, the Bill contained provision for a connection with the Midland Railway. Accordingly, the junction established on the approach to Edgware from Watford would also provide access to a new length of line that would parallel the Edgware and Highgate for approximately 1½ miles connecting with the up line of the Midland Railway at Mill Hill. However, such was the opposition of the Midland to this particular proposal that it was withdrawn from the Bill before it reached the Select Committee. The cost for constructing the line was placed at £157,000.

Although the distances from Watford to Kings Cross and Euston using the Great Northern and the LNWR respectively were similar, there was some variation in their routes to the City. The LNWR route from Watford to Broad Street was achieved via the North London Railway and covered 22½ miles. The distance from Watford to Moorgate via the GNR and City Widened Lines was given as 19 miles.

The Bill was promoted by a group of people associated with Watford and its neighbourhood who had formed themselves into a syndicate. Supporting witnesses were drawn from local tradesmen, local farmers and even a representative of the Cannon Brewery whose company had indicated that it would use the line. Objections from the local authorities and the Colne Valley Water Company were quickly settled; other objections caused a lengthy debate.

The LNWR expressed concern about damage that might befall the embankment carrying its main line under which the Watford and Edgware would run. The Company also contested the compulsory powers sought in the Bill to connect with the metals of the former Rickmansworth and Watford Company.

Professor Hubert Herkomer, who owned and resided in a mansion that doubled as an art school on the outskirts of the village of Bushey, considered that the new line would pass too close to his property. Describing himself as an 'artist of world wide repute' and his art school as perhaps the most important of its kind in the Country, Herkomer had selected Bushey for its tranquillity and rural character. The Professor therefore felt that he would be compelled to move owing to the noise of trains passing within 110 yards of his land. His view that the railway would carve a route through his estate for a considerable distance had been countered by the promoters of the line who had offered to move it a further seventy yards away. Apparently the Professor's house had cost him £50,000 to purchase and convert but the promoters were quick to demonstrate that the passage of trains would not be visible at the front of the property but from the tradesmen's entrance. Herkomer would not be appeased, believing that the value of his estate would be greatly damaged should it be subdivided by a railway.

The 1896 Bill was lost, the Select Committee being of the opinion that it should not proceed further. One of the deciding factors, in addition to Herkomer's protestations, was the line being seen as one that presented very little chance of securing remunerative traffic. The full case prepared by the LNWR to oppose the line was not heard.

In 1897 a new Watford, Edgware and London Railway Bill appeared before a Select Committee on Railway Bills, bearing a number of similarities to its predecessor of a year earlier. However, the formation of a triangular junction at Watford was abandoned, the connection with the LNWR now only facing the High Street station. Included among the construction projects for the new line was the excavation of a 250-yard tunnel beneath Caldecott Hill. Professor Herkomer had been placated by a northward diversion of the line away from his property but formal negotiation was still necessary with the GNR. The company stated that it would oppose the Bill unless its promoters deleted all reference to running powers further than Finsbury Park and withdrew its plan for establishing a connection with the Midland Railway. During the ensuing period of parliamentary debate both issues were removed. In noting the Bill's subsequent success, the GNR intimated an intention to work the new railway subject to a favourable outcome of discussions with the directors of the Watford and Edgware.

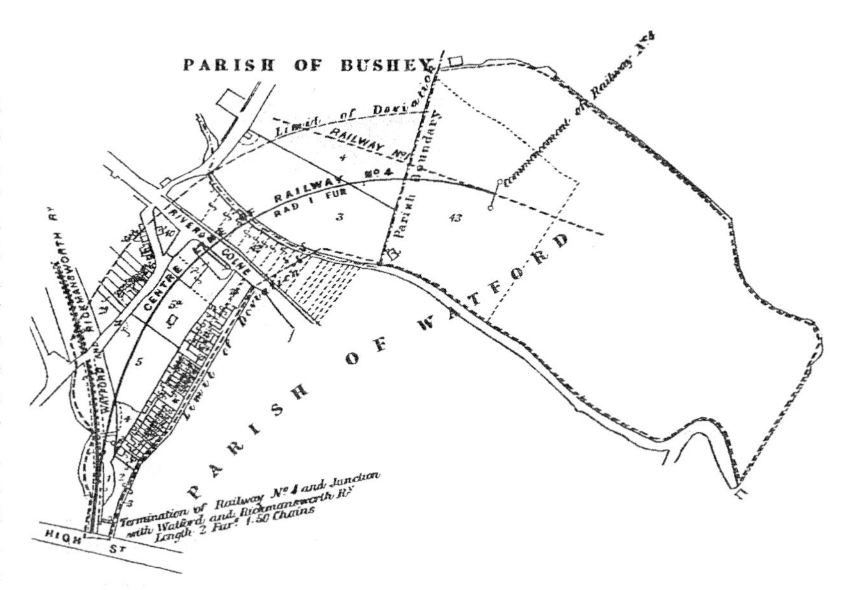

The map showing the line of the route submitted in support of the 1896 Watford, Edgware and London Railway Bill illustrates the divergence of a spur (Railway No. 4) to Watford High Street station. The second objective of the line was Watford Junction where Railway No. 1 was to terminate. However, this link was subsequently deleted from the plan accompanying the 1897 Bill, deposited following the failure of the 1896 Bill at the Select Committee stage without the opposition of the LNWR even being heard.

After the Bill's successful passage through the Commons, it was heard by a Select Committee in the House of Lords during July 1897, the main evidence being that of the London & North Western Railway. From the transcript of the proceedings, it can be determined that the LNWR was still set against the projection of the line from Edgware into its territory. The company considered that the line would be unable to provide a comparable service to that which it offered, commenting that there was little significance to which London terminus passengers might wish to travel.

Counsel for the LNWR described Edgware as the most decaying little country village that could be found in the neighbourhood of London. He went on to record that the area remained unequalled in terms of being so near to the metropolis yet undeveloped for so long since the coming of the railway. As a final broadside, serious concerns were expressed that there would be no profit for shareholders, the scheme being described as nothing more than speculation by a group of investors.

Despite such a strong argument against the construction of the line, the Bill was allowed to proceed following the settling of clauses designed for the protection of the LNWR. By August 1902 the powers secured by the Watford, Edgware and London Railway Company lapsed, financial difficulties and a lack of support from the Great Northern contributing greatly to its demise.

CHAPTER TWO

The Watford and Edgware Railway Company

Despite its character being seriously maligned by the LNWR in its petition against the 1897 Bill of the Watford and Edgware Railway Company, Edgware soon attracted the interest of another transport undertaking. In 1898, the Metropolitan Tramways and Omnibus Company submitted a plan that would bring trams to the town. The plan failed and it was not until December 1904 that trams began operating to Edgware from Cricklewood on a new route operated by Metropolitan Electric Tramways.

The proposal to improve public transport facilities at Edgware by the construction of a tramway was soon followed by another that would link the town to the capital's Underground system. But first we must consider the influence of other developments made in this direction. A significant plan to link the centre of London with the northern suburbs was initially put forward in 1893 when a scheme known as the Charing Cross, Euston and Hampstead Railway (CCEHR) emerged. Dogged by years of indecisiveness, whilst the question of finance was settled, it took the intervention of an American company under the control of Charles Tyson Yerkes to raise the necessary capital to allow construction work to proceed.

Yerkes, who was to play a major role in the building of London's tube railways, took over the CCEHR in October 1900. The subsequent Bill, promoting the construction of the line, was deposited and agreed in Parliament during the 1901 session. In 1902, a Bill passed through Parliament allowing the construction of the Edgware and Hampstead Railway that would connect with the proposed tube line of the Charing Cross, Euston and Hampstead at Golders Green. On 25th March 1903, powers were obtained by the CCEHR to take over the Edgware and Hampstead and consequently the entire construction project to Edgware.

The announcement of an extension of the tube to Edgware sparked a revival of interest in the construction of a railway between Edgware and Watford. However on this occasion the line was to be projected from the Edgware terminus of the CCEHR and not that of the GNR. The line was sponsored by a group of landowners with property in the area through which a railway linking Watford and Edgware might pass. They were supported by John Conacher, a former general manager of the Cambrian Railways, the North British Railway and now manager of the London Metropolitan Electric Supply Company.

The day following the successful passage through Parliament of the Bill allowing the CCEHR to assume responsibility for the Edgware and Hampstead, the Watford and Edgware Railway Bill was considered by a Select Committee of the House of Commons. Information provided for the Committee determined the line as being 6 miles and one furlong (220 yards) with a double track configuration being used throughout its entire length. Upon leaving Edgware the line would progress in a north westerly direction, paralleling Watling Street which it would cross at Brockley Hill. A station would be provided at Elstree to serve the village, the station of the same name on the Midland Railway being considered of little use to the area, having been built some distance away. Running to the south of Aldenham Reservoir, the line would turn through Caldecott Hill and the northern edge of Bushey. Here it paralleled and ran south of The Avenue and Bushey Hall Road, terminating on the east side of Watford High Street after passing beneath a wrought iron or steel girder bridge carrying the main line of the London and North Western Railway.

The line attracted some opposition but on this occasion none came from the LNWR. Both Middlesex and Hertfordshire County Councils did raise individual objections (although that from Hertfordshire was later withdrawn) on the ground of competition. In 1902, Middlesex County Council had sought, for the third time, permission to connect with an authorised tramway at the County Boundary near Bushey Heath yet to be built by Hertfordshire County Council. From this point Middlesex County Council intended extending the tramway to Edgware. Permission failed to be granted but if the opposite had applied, a tram route from Cricklewood along the Edgware Road to Edgware and Watford would have been built. Objections to the tramway came from local people and included the owner of Bentley Park and Professor Herkomer, who described it as 'monstrous' because of its proposed use of public roads. Opposition to the Watford and Edgware Railway was promoted by the distribution of a circular that decried the promotion of the line by persons who were not connected with the district. In recording that the construction of the railway was entirely dependent on the completion of the Charing Cross, Euston and Hampstead line to Edgware, the circular sought support for another line more suitable to the requirements of the district. The alternative scheme was supported by the Metropolitan Railway and would be the subject of a Bill to be laid before Parliament the following November. In the outcome only two persons were sufficiently agitated by the circular to append their signatures to its petition, one being the Rector of Edgware, the other a local farmer with a 300 acre holding.

Plans were formulated for the pacification of the Rector, requiring the company to enter a dialogue with the Charing Cross, Euston and Hampstead company in order to straighten the point where the two lines would join. As a result the route of the railway would be moved to a point considerably further from the rectory, its proximity having given rise to the objection. The objection raised by the farmer centred on the alteration of local roads to accommodate the railway and was purely based on a question of compensation for damage sustained by his estate.

The petitions against the Bill that caused the most concern were those of the Charing Cross, Euston and Hampstead Railway. The company was concerned about a clause in the Bill that would instigate a through working agreement which it had no intention of entering. The offending clause was removed and arrangements put in hand for joint facilities to be provided at Edgware station. Over and above this settlement was a submission from the Charing Cross, Euston and Hampstead that the proposed railway was totally unnecessary and would 'not serve any public need sufficient to justify the expenditure of capital (£400,000) which its construction would entail'. The CCEHR also alleged that the Watford and Edgware Company had no intention of working the line citing as evidence its request for through running and the lack of powers seeking the construction of a generating station. This allegation was countered by the company which stated that it would be prepared to purchase its power from any one of a number of sources. These, of course, included the London Metropolitan Electric Supply Company of which John Conacher was manager.

When Conacher was interviewed, he attested that he saw the projection of tube lines into the country as an initiative to relieve the pressure on the more densely populated parts of London. He considered the line to be well laid out and should be worked as an extension of the line from Charing Cross to Edgware. The great advantage of the line, above that sanctioned in 1897, was that it would be of double track configuration from Watford to Charing Cross. By joining the GNR line, the anticipated increase in traffic would require the doubling of the track between Edgware and Finchley.

The amended Bill reached the House of Lords on 30th June 1903, by which time all opposition had been removed and it was subsequently referred on as unopposed, receiving Royal Assent on 11th August.

The construction of the Watford and Edgware Railway was now held in abeyance until the completion of the line to Edgware. However in 1906 the company obtained powers to assume responsibility for the line originally proposed by the Edgware and Hampstead and

Overleaf **Powers obtained to build the Watford, Edgware and London Railway expired in August 1902, financial difficulties and withdrawal of support of the Great Northern Railway contributing, in no small measure, to its demise. The next plan to link the towns of Edgware and Watford by railway involved an extension of the Charing Cross, Euston and Hampstead Railway. In contrast to earlier proposals, the line would be extended from a new station to be constructed for the CCEHR at Edgware that would herald the coming of the tube. The Watford and Edgware Railway Bill received Royal Assent on 11th August 1903. The map shows the route to Edgware via the Edgware and Hampstead Railway. This was no doubt correct at the time of the parliamentary deposit, the E&H having been taken over by the CCEHR in March.**

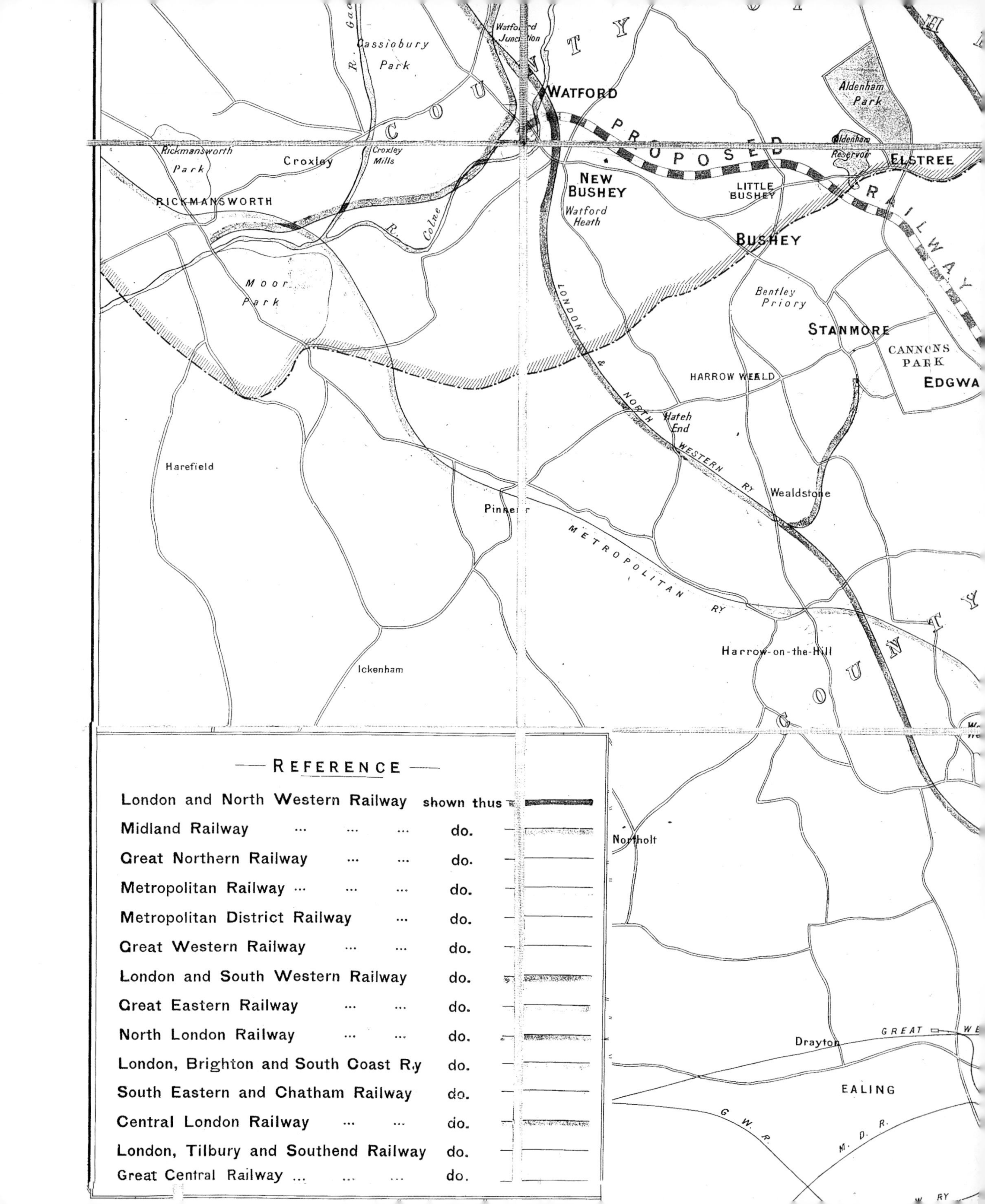
REFERENCE
London and North Western Railway shown thus
Midland Railway ... ... do.
Great Northern Railway ... ... do.
Metropolitan Railway ... ... do.
Metropolitan District Railway ... do.
Great Western Railway ... ... do.
London and South Western Railway do.
Great Eastern Railway ... ... do.
North London Railway ... ... do.
London, Brighton and South Coast R.y do.
South Eastern and Chatham Railway do.
Central London Railway ... ... do.
London, Tilbury and Southend Railway do.
Great Central Railway ... ... do.
Cassiobury Park
R. Gade
Watford Junction
WATFORD
COUNTY
Aldenham Park
Aldenham Reservoir
ELSTREE
PROPOSED RAILWAY
Rickmansworth Park
Croxley
Croxley Mills
RICKMANSWORTH
R. Colne
NEW BUSHEY
Watford Heath
LITTLE BUSHEY
BUSHEY
Moor Park
LONDON & NORTH WESTERN RY
Bentley Priory
STANMORE
CANNONS PARK
EDGWA
HARROW WEALD
Hatch End
Harefield
Wealdstone
Pinner
METROPOLITAN RY
Harrow-on-the-Hill
COUNTY
Ickenham
Northolt
Drayton
GREAT WE
EALING
G. W. R.
M. D. R.

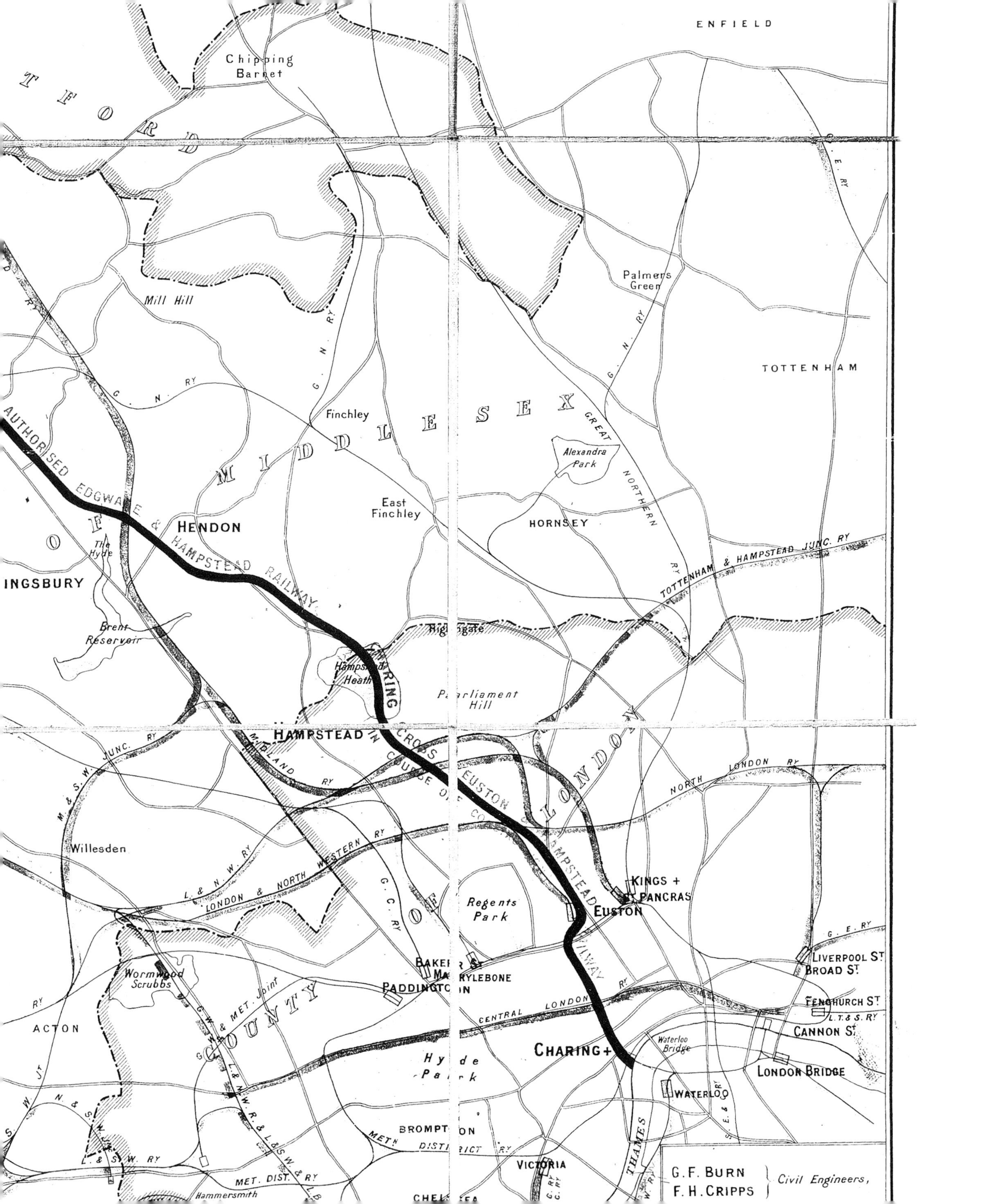

ENFIELD
Chipping Barnet
Mill Hill
Palmers Green
TOTTENHAM
Finchley
East Finchley
MIDDLESEX
Alexandra Park
HORNSEY
HENDON
AUTHORISED EDGWARE & HAMPSTEAD RAILWAY
INGSBURY
The Hyde
Brent Reservoir
Hampstead Heath
Parliament Hill
HAMPSTEAD
TOTTENHAM & HAMPSTEAD JUNC. RY
GREAT NORTHERN RY
G. N. RY
G. E. RY
NORTH LONDON RY
MIDLAND RY
M. & S. W. JUNC. RY
Willesden
L. & N. W. RY
LONDON & NORTH WESTERN RY
G. C. RY
Regents Park
KINGS + PANCRAS
EUSTON
LIVERPOOL ST
BROAD ST
PADDINGTON
FENCHURCH ST
L. T. & S. RY
CANNON ST
Wormwood Scrubbs
ACTON
CENTRAL LONDON RY
G. W. & MET. Joint
COUNTY OF LONDON
Hyde Park
CHARING +
Waterloo Bridge
LONDON BRIDGE
WATERLOO
S. E. & C. RY
BROMPTON
METN DISTRICT RY
VICTORIA
THAMES
L. & S. W. RY
MET. DIST. RY
Hammersmith
N. & S. W. JT
G. F. BURN
F. H. CRIPPS
Civil Engineers,

in consequence construction of the entire length of line between Golders Green and Watford. The same year saw an agreement reached between the CCEHR, Watford and Edgware and Underground Electric Railway (UERL) companies. From this, it was determined that line to the north of Golders Green would be operated as a separate venture worked by American style interurban cars drawing current from an overhead line. Alternatively, railcars powered by batteries or petrol would be permitted should the Watford and Edgware have cash flow problems.

Following his appointment in 1906 to the Board of the Watford and Edgware, Charles Steel soon became its Chairman. Almost immediately, the company began to suffer under the weight of expiring powers for compulsory land purchases. A Bill was deposited in 1907 to secure extensions of time for land acquisition along the whole of the Golders Green to Watford route, to amalgamate capital with the EHR, and provide for the line from Golders Green to Watford to be built and worked as a light railway, but this failed at the Committee stage.

The powers transferred to the Watford and Edgware in 1906 allowing construction of the Golders Green to Edgware section consequently returned to the Underground. In a Bill deposited in 1909 the UERL laid down its own plans by projecting a line from Golders Green. However, there was to be some delay in its construction following the merger in 1912 of the Edgware and Hampstead with the London Electric Railway Company, an organisation established two years before by amalgamation of the UERL's tube lines. In the same year, a further Bill confirmed the LER's intention to build an extension to Edgware, but the estimated 1914 start was deferred by the onset of war.

Statutory powers secured by the Watford and Edgware expired in 1911 yet the company stubbornly remained in existence, convening an annual shareholder's meeting to fulfil legal requirements. On 21st July 1922, a meeting of the Directors was held for the purpose of receiving a special report. This reflected upon some long and arduous negotiations which had taken place with Frank Pick, then Joint Assistant Managing Director of the Underground Group, and had resulted in his offer of £4,250 for the company. The Directors resolved that the offer should be submitted to the shareholders with a strong recommendation for acceptance. Once obtained, the Watford and Edgware came under the administration of the Underground Group of companies. The UERL held 80.3% of the issued WER shares and a considerable area of land was also passed to it. In 1934 the WER was registered under the Companies Act, 1929, prior to its being wound up.

Contemporary accounts suggest that there was no immediate action after acquisition of the Watford and Edgware by the UERL. However, Frank Pick would have been aware that the population of the suburbs was showing significant increases. By purchasing the outstanding shares of the company, he had effectively removed all opposition from the original promoters to any UERL Bill that sought powers for the construction of a line to Watford. The improvement of the transport services provided was deemed essential and within a few months, a preliminary report was drawn up listing proposals for extensions to lines operated by the London Electric Railway. The document, produced in late January 1923, was intended as groundwork for a Bill to be promoted during the next parliamentary session. The nine schemes in order of precedence were:

1. New north and south deep level tube, Elephant to Baker Street with extensions south via Peckham and SECR to Orpington and north via St John's Wood to Cricklewood. or junction with Metropolitan Railway.
2. Abolishment of Circle working and through running over Midland Railway to Upminster. Remodelling of Aldgate and Aldgate East stations.
3. Extension from Highgate to High Barnet via Finchley (GNR).
4. Extension from Finsbury Park to Enfield and Hertford via Wood Green and Winchmore Hill.
5. Extension from Kennington to Streatham via Brixton and Clapham Park.
6. Junction with Midland Railway at Hendon and through running to St Albans and Luton.
7. Reconstruction of Oxford Circus stations to provide better interchange facilities.
8. Completion of Edgware and Watford Railway.
9. Alternative working on southern end of C&SLR to Sutton and Epsom.

Of the items under consideration, those numbered six and eight are relevant to our story. The LER had previously attempted negotiations regarding an extension to St Albans and Luton via Hendon (the extension commencing at a point beyond Hendon Central), as it was aware of the benefits to be obtained by the through connection to town instead of the existing change at St Pancras. Since the Great War, the area served had begun to develop and although an initial proposal was for the line to terminate at Harpenden, there was a preference for the extension to continue to Luton. Both Luton and St Albans had sizeable populations, which travelled to London daily.

The completion of the Edgware and Watford Railway was listed as being a doubtful proposition. Nevertheless, the Underground company was of the opinion that certain rights had been secured with the acquisition of the Watford and Edgware Railway and intended to exercise any powers it had obtained. Watford was considered to offer scope for an additional line with some residents having to rely on road transport for a considerable distance in order to reach existing railways. The actual areas of population listed where stations could be built were Stanmore (1,843), Bushey Heath (6,500) and Bushey (8,088). Watford was credited with a population of 40,939, the proposed site for the new station being within the Cassio area. However, the company had yet to analyse an agreement with the London Midland and Scottish Railway (formerly LNWR) apropos any other railways being built in the area. In the outcome, a Bill was not submitted to Parliament to pursue any of the aforementioned proposals.

Around the time of the opening of the London Electric Railway's line to Hendon, in November 1923, some investigative work was being undertaken by a Mr Zac E Knapp and a number of officers from the company. Knapp, who had arrived in this country with colleagues from the United States in 1901, took up the appointment of Assistant Engineer for the Underground Group. His lengthy remit had been to oversee the electrification and modernisation of the District Railway, equipping of the London Electric Railway, the erection of the power station at Lots Road and the introduction of new rolling stock. In February 1921, he assumed the position of Director of Construction for the London Electric Railway.

The extension of the Hampstead Line to Hendon included the temporary provision of stabling facilities at Golders Green. The LER, having decided against initial proposals, made a far-reaching decision whereby the line would be projected beyond Edgware to Bushey with a depot at Elstree. Knapp's visit was therefore prompted by the necessity to determine the actual site.

Amongst the records of the LER's New Works and Improvements Committee, established in June 1924, is a minute dated 18th August 1924 reviewing proposals for inclusion in a Bill to be placed before Parliament for the forthcoming 1925 session. This is the first appearance of a tangible scheme to build a line between Edgware and Bushey since transfer of the WER to the Underground Group, approval to proceed being given by the Committee on 13th October.

By 27th October, plans were submitted which determined the site of Bushey station as being on the east side of Aldenham Road. The application of some forward thinking determined that land on both sides of this thoroughfare should be scheduled in the Bill to allow the line to be projected to Watford at a later date. Bushey station would be constructed on property owned by the Royal Masonic School; this establishment having moved to the area in 1903 from a site in Lordship Lane, Wood Green. The School had its main entrance situated in the Avenue with a subsidiary entrance in Finch Lane.

On 6th November, a memorandum was submitted to the New Works and Improvements Committee, which reported that difficulty was being experienced in acquiring a strip of land opposite the Edgware station required for the projection of the railway northwards. The owner was apparently asking a very substantial sum for its use which, on completion of the railway, would be reconveyed to him. In addition, the company would cover the cost of installing supporting girders to a depth of 20ft or 30ft along the frontage used. It was decided to try to acquire the property and other land in the same ownership on the best possible terms. However, eleven days later all proposals regarding the extension were put on hold, the company having decided not to seek parliamentary approval.

In February 1925, the UERL received notification from W R Davidge of Victoria Street, SW1 stating that he had been instructed by the Bushey Urban District Council to submit proposals for a town-planning scheme. The company acceded to his request for plans and sections of its proposals for the extension of the railway from Edgware to Bushey in order that he might provide a scheme for a route. Davidge was set to become involved again with the railway in 1937 under different circumstances, as will be explained in Chapter 5.

1926 and Station Road, Edgware has achieved its maximum width dictated by the erection of shops with flatted accommodation above on both sides of the thoroughfare. Of interest are the original Edgware bus garage opened in April 1925 at the rear of the station buildings, the four-road Underground Depot and sidings built adjacent to the terminus and preparatory work on the Elstree Extension. In readiness for the continuance of the row of shops along Station Road, a concrete raft has been constructed behind which is a bridge built to carry a service road above the new line.

To ascertain the next turn of events consideration must be given to the responsibility of the Union Surplus Lands Company (USLC). With 'Union' in its title, there can be little doubt that there was American influence behind the company's conception in 1914. Zac Knapp was its first Manager for Maintenance and Construction, his employer's remit being to hold real estate purchased for future developments for which powers had yet to be secured.

The difficulties experienced in acquiring land had some influence on the decision to defer an extension north of Edgware, it falling to the USLC to complete the necessary deals. On 26th September 1926, purchases were made from Mr Edward Streather (£1,732) and Mr Leslie Raymond (£3,210) for land at Edgware and north of Church Lane, Edgware. With one problem overcome, the USLC was then faced with another. This involved a number of sites along the line of route near the proposed terminus at Bushey.

By 1927, acquisition of the estate of the late artist and film director Professor Herkomer was proving to be a problem. In February 1927 the Assistant Secretary of the Union Surplus Lands Company, J. L. B. Lindsay, was asked to report on the procurement of land at Bushey. He responded that no progress had been made with the purchase of Lady Herkomer's land or a freehold house and associated property in Chiltern Avenue. Negotiations were finally concluded some two years later when 2,405 acres were acquired from the Herkomer estate for £11,057 and the whole Chiltern Avenue site for £11,753.

The Watford and Edgware Company continued in existence, meeting once a year in order to fulfil statutory obligation. But the scheme for which it had been brought into existence was now pigeonholed; improvements to the Piccadilly Line moving to the forefront when extensions to the capital's tube network were being planned.

The plan to forge a rail link between Edgware and Watford was eventually to end in failure. However, any of the plans that occurred over the next twelve years could so easily have brought about its revival instead of an exasperating series of false starts; the first of which occurred in 1931.

The reverse angle, taken at the same time, shows the service road bridge (later Rectory Lane) and the concrete raft in greater detail. Work has commenced on the construction of retail premises at the end of the depot building.

CHAPTER THREE

A Period of False Starts

In June 1930, Mr J P Thomas, Operating Manager for the Underground Group, wrote to Frank Pick on the subject of train service improvements for the Hampstead and City Line. His memorandum contained a recommendation that the company should expend £23,600 on the provision of additional terminal accommodation at Edgware (£15,000) and supplementary signalling at several points along the line amounting to £8,600. At that time, siding accommodation at Edgware comprised eight roads, four within the depot which adjoined the east wall of the station, paralleled by a further four roads in the open. Thomas's plan was to provide a third platform at Edgware and two additional sidings for 7-car trains; such a move enabling trains then terminating at Golders Green and Colindale to be projected the whole length of the line. As a result, there would be no idle mileage between Golders Green and Edgware, estimated as being 120,000 miles per annum, which at 4d per mile represented a saving of £2,000 per annum.

The New Works and Improvements Committee considered the proposal the following month but deemed it unsatisfactory. The main contention was that if the line were extended towards Elstree, a considerable amount of expenditure would have been incurred at Edgware to no purpose. It was therefore decided that plans should be submitted for an alternative proposal to extend the line beyond Edgware station for approximately 500 yards in order to provide similar facilities as outlined in Thomas's original submission.

Revision was a short time coming. On 25th July, A R Cooper submitted a rough sketch to the Committee showing an extension of the line 850 feet beyond Edgware station and Church Lane bridge in order to provide stabling for eight or ten 7-car trains. The cost of the project was estimated at £25,000 and, upon the subsequent extension of the line, only £2,600 would be lost. The Committee therefore decided that the work should be completed as soon as possible if agreement with the Local Authorities could be secured for constructing the line beneath the road at Edgware station. Thomas concurred with the decision, reasoned that the matter had become urgent and suggested that the necessary consents should be sought during August.

Towards the end of September 1930, difficulties had arisen. Cooper wrote to Pick to inform him that the company had no statutory powers to burrow under the highway, although retaining walls had been constructed on land opposite the station entrance. Despite this setback, he believed that it might still be possible to obtain the necessary approval.

Another problem had also surfaced regarding the public footpath that crossed the proposed trackbed acquired by the Union Surplus Lands Company at Purcell's Farm. On either side of the strip, a 30-foot road had been laid down as part of the development of the adjoining estate. Hendon Urban District Council now proposed widening the footpath in order to join both sections of the road and, accordingly, notice had been served on the company. With a summons in the offing, a meeting with the Hendon and

Middlesex Councils was considered necessary in order to bring about a swift conclusion to the situation.

Complications still persisted. The company realised that the only method by which it could obtain authorisation to proceed was to seek parliamentary approval, although Middlesex County Council had intimated that works beneath Church Lane could be freely undertaken. A decision was therefore taken that powers should be sought in the 1931 Railways Bill for the extension of tracks at least as far as the Watford By-Pass. Provision would also be made for property to be scheduled in the Bill not already acquired by the Union Surplus Lands Company for the remainder of the extension to Elstree. This additional step was proposed in view of the rapidly rising property values.

The New Works and Improvements Committee gave further consideration to the scheme on 16th February 1931. On this occasion an alternative plan was put forward for the construction of additional accommodation for rolling stock on the west side of Edgware station which comprised five new sidings together with a third platform. Having given careful thought to both submissions, the Committee agreed to withdraw that which provided for the construction of sidings beyond the station. Powers would then be sought in a late Bill for the acquisition of land to allow the most recent proposal to proceed.

The ensuing late Bill sought powers to divert the course of a footpath which crossed the Underground line beyond the station by means of a footbridge; the public right of way being stopped up in the process. The footpath, which impeded the new track plan, connected Deans Lane and Church Lane and was to be reinstated upon completion of the project. The third platform at Edgware came into use on 20th November 1932.

During early 1931, town-planning schemes were drawn up for the area through which the proposed northward extension of the Edgware line would pass. To protect the interests of the Underground Group it was decided to disclose to each local authority the proposed route of the Edgware and Bushey railway. Later in the year, J R Chambers, who had served with Pick on the Royal Commission on Cross River Traffic, wrote to him on the same topic. Chambers had acquired land on the Watford By-Pass, which had been set down in the Watford Town Planning Scheme as being for dwelling houses. His concern was that should a station be planned for the site it might be necessary to erect shops, but Pick replied that no specific plans for a railway existed due to financial restrictions.

One of the first issues considered by the London Passenger Transport Board's (LPTB) Engineering Committee upon inception in July 1933 was the site for the terminus at Bushey. On 7th July this was determined as being at the junction of the proposed station approach road from Bushey High Street with a proposed 60ft town-planned road designed to connect Sparrows Hill with the Watford By-Pass. A further stipulation was that the station approach road should also be 60ft in width, with Bushey Urban District Council undertaking to secure any necessary consents for this purpose from the adjoining owners.

On 24th October 1933 a Chartered Surveyor by the name of Alan Daly saw Pick with a proposal for the extension of the Edgware line to Bullbaiters Farm in Borehamwood. Diverging from the proposed line of route at Elstree station, Daly's motive was to seek transport facilities to the new centre of the British film industry. The property between Borehamwood and Edgware was then considered ripe for redevelopment and Daly was acting as a representative for the owners of property on the suggested line of route from the Moat Mount Estate to Borehamwood. He intimated that he and his colleagues would be prepared to assist in the construction of the line (assumed to cost about half a million) possibly by guaranteeing the interest on capital for the first five years.

Pick explained the major difficulties in the way of adopting this proposal, particularly the problem of handling the traffic at Golders Green if more traffic had to be carried from points further north. Nevertheless, he undertook to have the proposal studied and referred to the Special Preparatory Committee of the Standing Joint Committee for consideration.

The LPTB began to refer to the terminus of the proposed line as Borehamwood East. In a letter sent to Pick in December 1933 Daly commented, 'You do appreciate, I know, the need for the extension to this district as a means of access not only for the local inhabitants but particularly for those who are engaged in the British film industry, which is more and more becoming of national character'.

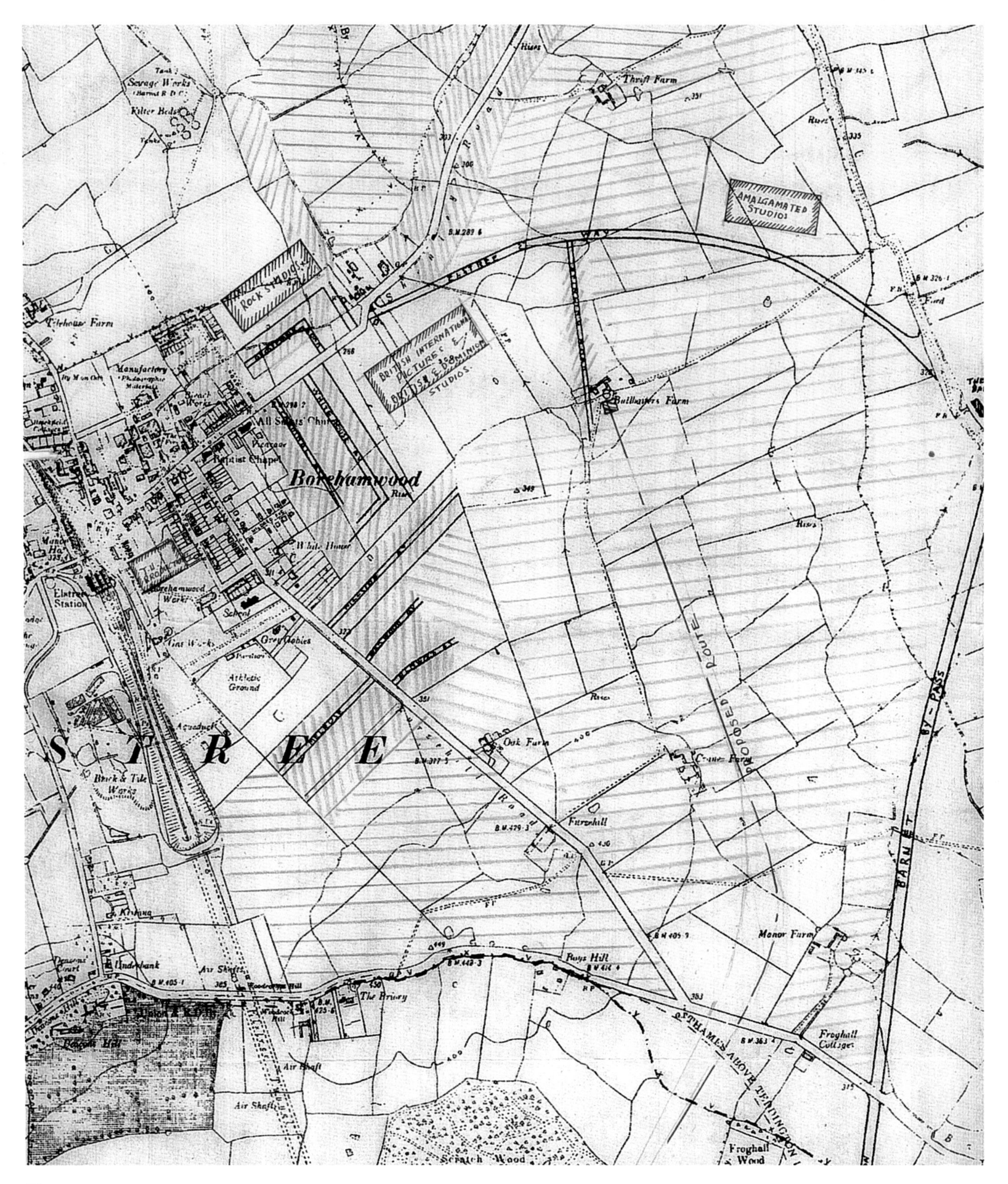

Sewage Works
Filter Beds
Thrift Farm
AMALGAMATED STUDIOS
ROCK STUDIOS
BRITISH INTERNATIONAL PICTURES & BRITISH & DOMINION STUDIOS
Tilehouse Farm
Manufactory
Bullhaiters Farm
All Saints' Church
Baptist Chapel
Borehamwood
White House
Elstree Station
Borehamwood Works
School
Gas Works
Athletic Ground
Aqueduct
S T R E E
Brick & Tile Works
Oak Farm
Crane Farm
PROPOSED ROUTE
Furzehill
BARNET BY-PASS
Manor Farm
Underbank
Air Shafts
Woodcock Hill
The Priory
Rays Hill
Froghall Cottage
Air Shaft
Scratch Wood
Froghall Wood

As if to emphasise the situation, Daly's note of 29th June 1934 contained the information that he had recently arranged to erect a further four film studios and wanted the best possible travel facilities. Pick was also reminded of his own suggestion in sending all City bound traffic along the LNER route to link up with the tube at Highgate. The assumption here was that this diversion to the City might relieve congestion at Golders Green, which would remain unaffected by the extension. Schemes to electrify LNER tracks, including the line from Finchley to Edgware for use by the tube railways, would be submitted to Parliament for the 1936 session.

Pick responded stating that it was impossible for any decision to be reached regarding railway developments in this area. The Ministry of Transport required the Board and Main Line companies to consider the development of facilities on the east side of London, the financial position that this represented being so serious that no immediate solution appeared likely.

Pick sought mediation from the Standing Joint Committee, a body comprising representatives from the Board and the four main line railway companies, in order to consider issues of common material interest and to settle any disputes arising therefrom. On 2nd August 1934, the Joint Committee sent a memorandum containing details of Daly's proposal, for comment to the London and Home Counties Traffic Advisory Committee, established under the London Traffic Act ten years earlier to provide the Minister of Transport with advice and assistance. Under a later remit the Advisory Committee was asked to consider transport problems to the north and east of London, which made it ideally suited to consider an extension to Borehamwood.

However, it was not until 8th December 1936 that the Advisory Committee announced that an extension to Borehamwood should be deferred until experience had been gained of the extension to Elstree. This statement proved somewhat overdue in the light of events some five months earlier, as we shall observe.

On 5th June 1935, following the press announcement of the New Works Programme, Daly (now with offices at Bush House in the Aldwych) wrote to Pick asking that serious consideration be given to extending the line to Borehamwood, instigating a further lengthy exchange of correspondence.

Another year was to pass before Pick finally responded that, although he would ask the Board to give Daly's proposal further consideration, he thought it unlikely it would proceed, listing his reasons in a letter dated 7th July 1936 as follows:

1. The existence of the former Midland Railway mainline and the proposals for its electrification.
2. The necessity to limit the volume of traffic arriving at Edgware for conveyance upon the Morden–Edgware Line due to the margin of capacity being small.
3. The pressure the Board was under to find a rolling stock depot on the north side of London as near as possible to Edgware.
4. The very large demands then being made upon the expansion of the population of London by the considered scheme of extension into undeveloped country, and the question whether London could continue to expand as it had been doing in recent years.

In sending a copy of his reply to his Chairman, Pick commented that he did not think that the Board could entertain this proposal, which it formally rejected on 16th July 1936. At the same meeting, the Elstree extension proposal was approved. In realising that his plans were unlikely to influence the Board, Daly wrote to Pick thanking him his kindness and consideration regarding the transport needs of the Borehamwood area and hoped that in the near future there would be an extension to the area as a natural child to the parent branch.

During 1934, a proposal to project the Metropolitan Line from Stanmore to Elstree was discussed by the Board's Engineering Committee. The idea behind this move was to allow an extension of the Metropolitan Railway to Bushey or its termination at the proposed Aldenham depot. The project required a double tunnel of 1.2 miles built to take surface stock that would join the planned route to Aldenham just south of Elstree station and Aldenham Reservoir. The line of the extension was ruled by the possibility of getting under or over the Watford By-Pass, and reports confirmed that all the necessary land acquisitions had been made.

On the strength of this proposal, some senior officers at 55 Broadway began to have serious doubts regarding the proposed line to Bushey. There was even a suggestion that the Board should intimate to the local authorities that the land in question was no longer reserved for a railway except for an extension of the

Facing page **On 24th October 1933, an entrepreneurial estate agent by the name of Alan Daly met with Frank Pick with a proposal to extend the line from Edgware to Borehamwood (Bullbaiters Farm). The purpose of the extension was twofold, the first providing a link to the new centre being created for the British film industry, the second to afford traffic facilities to an area between Edgware and Borehamwood, then considered ripe for development. Daly even stated that he would be prepared to help finance the venture but such generosity failed to sway Pick, although he did arrange for the proposal to be offered to the Board as an alternative to the Elstree Extension. Of note are the Rock Studios, now the BBC's Elstree Centre and TH Productions, latterly the Gate Studios and currently home of Aerofilms, some of whose work is illustrated in this book.**

Stanmore line. The voice of reason came from Frank Pick who contended that it would be impossible to abandon the route of the projected Edgware to Bushey railway. This was in view of the possibility that the LNER line to Edgware might be electrified and extended instead of that operated by the LPTB. Pick's argument won the day and it was decided that the reservation of land for the railway should not be abandoned.

A variation of this scheme materialised in May 1935 in a letter written by the Deputy Chairman of the London Midland and Scottish Railway, Sir Josiah Stamp, to the Secretary of the Standing Joint Committee. Stamp requested that consideration be given to producing a scheme for developing suburban traffic in the area served by the LMS Midland Section to St Albans and Harpenden. He felt that this could be achieved by linking the LMS lines with the Board's existing or intended tube railways. The Standing Joint Committee referred all discussion to the Traffic Advisory Committee but stated that the matter was not to be treated as one of urgency.

J P Thomas became involved and in January 1936 compiled a memorandum on the subject for the LPTB's Engineering Committee. Apparently, several meetings had taken place between Thomas and the Chief Commercial Manager for the LMS to establish the various schemes by which the proposals could be accomplished.

Thomas produced two plans showing the construction of new lines connecting the Board's railway at Edgware or Stanmore, or both, with the LMS line at Elstree where interchange platforms with the local train services would be provided. That proposed from Edgware would follow the first two miles of the authorised route of the Edgware and Bushey Railway and would not preclude the construction of the remainder of the railway at a later date. The line from Stanmore would involve about a mile less of new construction but the distance from Elstree to Charing Cross would be about 1¾ miles longer by this route than that via Edgware. Both schemes would open up new areas awaiting development.

Thomas preferred the Stanmore proposal for the reason that the Metropolitan Line would achieve a good margin of capacity following the construction of the new line between Finchley Road and Baker Street. On the other hand, the Edgware line was already working near to capacity, which was set to rise even further following completion of other projects involving lines in the area.

In receiving the report, the Engineering Committee agreed that the proposals it contained should be kept under wraps. A request was made of the LPTB's Chief Engineer A R Cooper, that any powers sought from Parliament for the extension of the Edgware line should have the limits of deviation drawn sufficiently wide at the appropriate point. This would allow for the provision of an interchange station with a possible extension of the Stanmore line.

The Traffic Advisory Committee's report was published in December 1936. Under the chairmanship of J P Thomas, it considered that an area of considerable size and character suitable of suburban development existed in the London Passenger Transport Area east of the LMS Railway extending from Mill Hill to St Albans. The area situated between the LMS and LNER railways had been largely withheld from residential development with the exception of satellite communities converging upon existing stations such as Radlett, Elstree, Potters Bar and Barnet.

The Committee reasoned that should London continue to expand, then this territory of approximately 36 square miles, with its centre some fourteen miles from Charing Cross, offered another opening for suburban expansion. However, in view of the absence of a through train service to the West End there was a strong possibility that the land would continue to stay sterile. It was therefore considered that a physical connection between the Finchley to Edgware line and the LMS near Mill Hill station provided some potential. With the electrification between Mill Hill and St Albans, a through service could be operated from the LMS over the Finchley and Highgate line to the West End. Nevertheless there remained the question of capacity and the Traffic Committee suggested that a widening of the Morden–Edgware line from Finchley to Camden Town and the West End and from Mill Hill to St Albans would be inevitable, at a cost of some £7.5 million. The Board's planned Elstree Extension was also taken into consideration, which would automatically provide a through West End service and parallel the LMS route to Elstree, with local bus services filling the gap between the two stations. In consequence, the Committee recommended that:

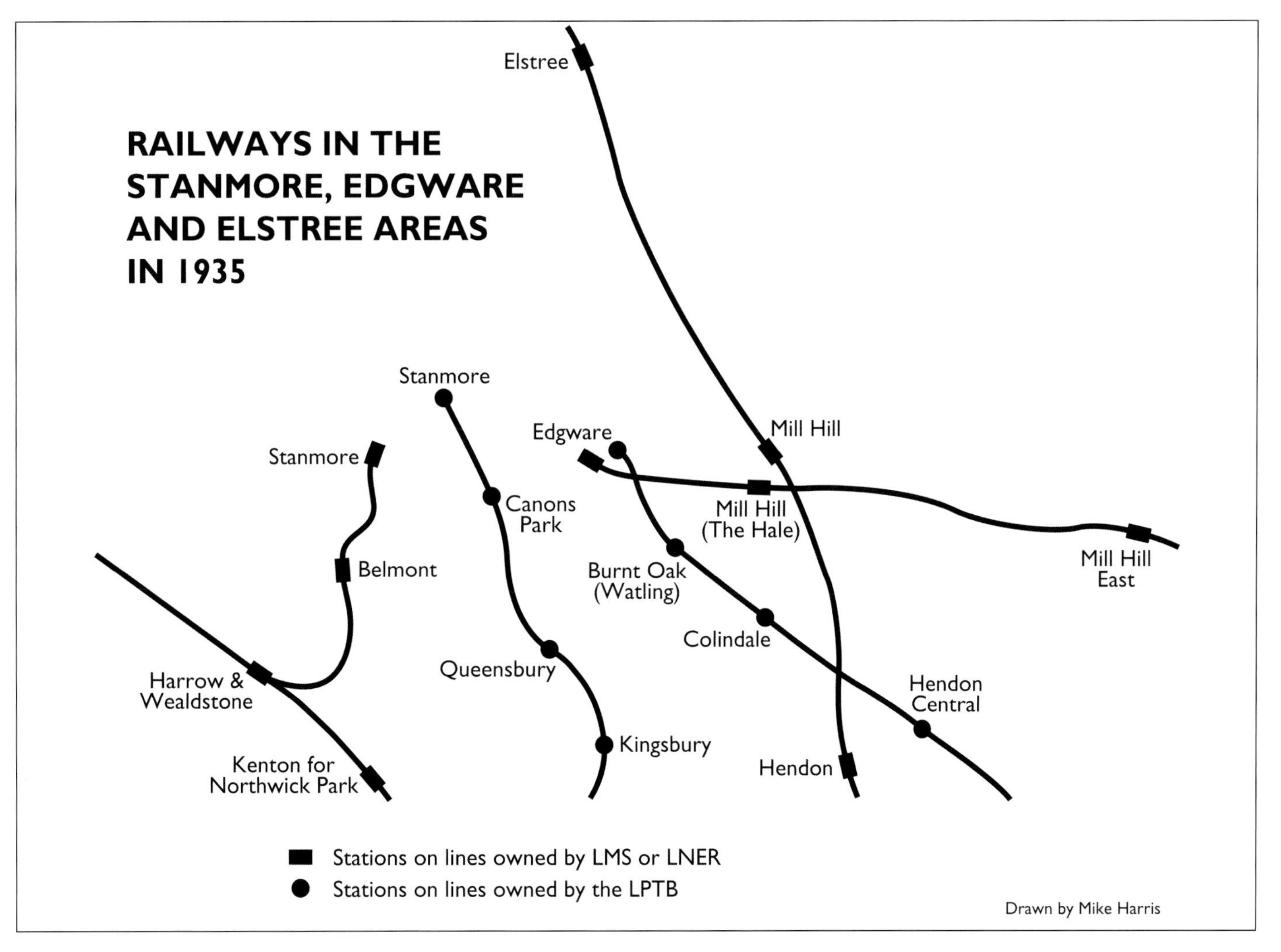

1. Further action regarding the electrification of the LMS to St Albans should be deferred until experience was obtained of the Board's extension to Elstree and the spare capacity of the Highgate line.
2. As part of the engineering works involved in the doubling of the single line between Finchley and Edgware, consideration should be given to the layout of the line at the point where it crossed over the LMS at Mill Hill to facilitate a physical connection with the LMS electrified lines, provided that no great expense was incurred in doing so.
3. That consideration be given to the interchange of traffic between the two lines mentioned in (2) using the two Mill Hill stations.

The first formal move to seek parliamentary approval of the extension of the line from Edgware to Elstree came from the LPTB's Estate Committee at its meeting held on 28th November 1935. The Committee also recommended the surrender of powers for the further development of the line beyond Elstree to Bushey, the latter having been the projected terminus since the acquisition of the Watford and Edgware Railway in 1922. Although popularly known as the Elstree Extension, it is possible for some confusion to arise regarding the actual areas served by the new railway. For the sake of clarity, the line now being pursued by the Board would actually terminate at site just beyond the proposed depot at Aldenham, Elstree being the penultimate station. There were to be a number of names suggested for stations on the branch during the planning stages, as we shall see.

CHAPTER FOUR

The Search for a New Depot

Since the end of the First World War, the population of the suburbs to the north and east of London had increased by one third without any significant changes in the transport services provided in those areas. Improvements to the capital's railway networks had been the subject of debate for a considerable period, a debate that culminated in a number of proposals under the New Works Programme 1935–40. These included expansion of the Morden–Edgware, Northern City and Central London Railway lines, and were contained in the 1936 London Passenger Transport and London and North Eastern Railway (London Transport) Bills. Little opposition was received and the Bills completed their journeys through Parliament, receiving Royal Assent on 31st July. The actual powers granted allowed new construction to be undertaken, and the doubling and electrification of former LNER metals where steam haulage was then the order of the day.

During February 1936, the LPTB's Engineering Committee was giving urgent attention to the need for additional siding accommodation for the whole of the Northern City and the Morden–Edgware lines. Mr J P Thomas, now General Manager (Railways), was consequently requested to submit a report indicating the most satisfactory provision for depot and siding accommodation after completion of the New Works Programme. The report would also be based on the alternative assumptions that there would and would not be an extension from Edgware to Elstree, and the further assumption that if extended, the maximum service north of Edgware would be twelve trains per hour. As previously recorded, and no doubt due to the consideration of other proposals, the extension had not formed part of the initial submissions in the 1936 Bill.

On 21st February 1936, J P Thomas produced his report, which concluded that the initial services on the Morden–Edgware and Northern City lines, after completion of the programme, would call for the operation of thirty additional trains including engineer's spares. Traffic sidings for these units would be required, together with a further six then currently stabled at Highgate (Archway) in the dead-end tunnels. The report also contended that provision could be made for stabling 21 of the trains at Wellington sidings (later Highgate Depot), on the Highgate–Finchley branch, eight at High Barnet and seven at Edgware, where the existing number of trains stabled would increase from thirteen to twenty.

As far as the requirements of the Operating Department were concerned, there appeared no difficulty in meeting additional needs by using existing accommodation. But with the development of the north London area which was expected to follow quickly upon the operation of extensions to the Board's lines and the consequent expansion of train services, further siding provision would become necessary. Thomas suggested that the number of additional trains could reach 45 within a period of four to five years.

The Board decided that, in order to provide some margin of spare accommodation, space should be reserved on the west side of Edgware station for the construction of a further four or five sidings over and above the twenty proposed in Thomas's report. In the interim, the owners of 25 and 26 Fairfield Crescent, Edgware were informed that part of their property might be required, later revised to No.25 only.

In pursuing a location for a new maintenance depot that would also provide accommodation for additional rolling stock as traffic on the line developed, some thought was given to using a site adjacent to a proposed station to be called Finchley Manor. This would be sited between East Finchley and Finchley Central (formerly Finchley Church End) next to which was a parcel of land that provided space for allotments and a football ground. As the size and shape of the plot and its orientation to the railway did not lend itself to the convenient formation of carriage sidings, the plan was rejected.

On 26th February 1936, W. S. Graff-Baker, wrote to Pick regarding the storage and maintenance of rolling stock. At that time, the cars employed on the Morden–Edgware line numbered 790 and maintenance work, apart from general overhaul, was divided between the depots at Morden and Golders Green. Space at these depots was already taxed to the utmost limit; Golders Green was described as badly designed and inefficient in operation.

The author is indebted to the late J Graeme Bruce OBE who was employed at Golders Green Depot during the New Works Programme. His description of the existing facilities at Golders Green is of interest:

'There was no doubt in all our minds at the time that a multiple unit train depot should be double-ended. Golders Green was a nightmare with trains entering or leaving having to pass over a double crossover under the control of a shunter using hand control levers for the points. Standard safety instructions for all depots decreed that all train movements had to be completed through the shunting neck, and at Golders Green the shunting neck was beyond the throat. This situation was asking for derailments that locked up not only the depot itself but also the train service. With a double-ended depot this problem was at least halved, a simultaneous derailment at both ends being considered highly unlikely'.

The depot also suffered a number of additional disadvantages, the brevity of some of its sidings a prime example. In order to use this shorter accommodation, trains had to be uncoupled and the subsequent movements, including those of a daily recurrence, only added to the continual congestion of the site. Matters were worsened by the introduction of nine-car trains where little siding capacity existed for trains of more than seven cars. A short reception road installed for trains entering the depot from the north served only to aggravate the situation; trains of nine-car length being obliged to use the tracks running to and from Hampstead.

Sixty-four cars, then in use on the Northern City Line, were currently maintained at Drayton Park depot. Here accommodation was cramped, of a primitive nature and totally unsuitable for work to be carried out on the new stock required for the proposed extensions. Neither Golders Green nor Drayton Park depots were capable of expansion or improvement to any material extent, especially as the number of cars for operating the extended train services would number around 1,100, a figure based on the initial presumption that new cars of the earlier standard stock design would be used.

A new depot was therefore proposed which could supplement either those at Morden and Golders Green or totally replace Golders Green and Drayton Park. It was already appreciated that using several smaller depots was much more costly than one large installation to deal with the equivalent amount of stock. Current estimates then put the expense of continuing Golders Green depot and additional smaller depots at more than £10,000 per annum over and above the cost of running one large depot.

Following recommendations received from Thomas and Graff-Baker, Pick reported to the Board that on the existing railways the only possible site for such a depot was located between Page Street and Dole Street, Mill Hill, adjacent to the single line which ran from Finchley (Church End) to Edgware. Regeneration of this section of railway had formed part of the LNER (London Transport) Bill of 1936, in which provision had been made for the track to be doubled and electrified. Graff-Baker also suggested that the new depot should be built on similar lines to that adopted for Cockfosters. Specialised shops would be built in order to undertake such work carried out by Golders Green and Drayton Park depots and normal shop production required for the Morden–Edgware and Great Northern and City Lines.

If the scheme for a depot at Mill Hill were to proceed, the approximate allocation of cars of standard stock design would be as follows:

Depot or Station	*Number of Cars to be Allocated*
Edgware	150
High Barnet	50
Mill Hill	300
Golders Green	175
Morden	300
Drayton Park	40
Wellington Sidings	80
Total	1095

The first suggested location for Mill Hill depot was a 19½-acre site south of the line. This was an area owned by Hendon Borough Council and formed part of Copthall Park, a recognised scheduled open space of approximately 100 acres in the town-planning scheme for the area. As the Ministry of Health had sealed this particular scheme, it was binding on all parties, although the Board still made an initial approach regarding its acquisition. The Council refused the sale but the Board did not accept immediate defeat and requested that its Estate Agent pursue the possibility of acquiring land on the opposite side of the line. Simultaneously, Thomas was asked to submit comparative estimated operating and maintenance costs for a depot at Mill Hill (and minimum siding accommodation at Golders Green and Edgware) with those for a depot at Elstree combined with the retention of Golders Green depot and the maximum number of sidings at Edgware. Until all reports were available, consideration of the extension from Edgware to Elstree was deferred.

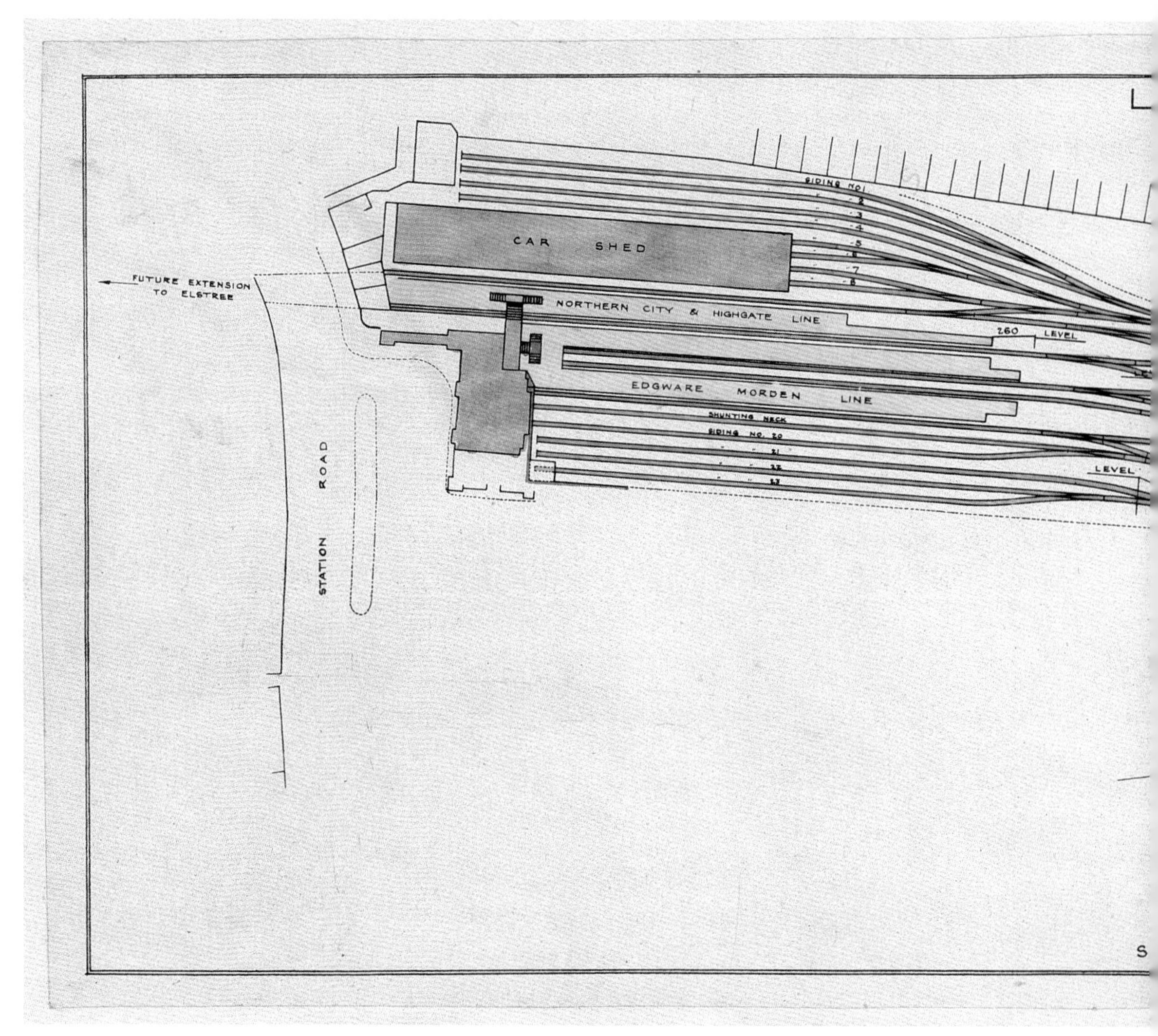

Amongst the provisions contained in the LNER (London Transport) Act of 1936 was the electrification of the line from Finsbury Park to Finchley (Church End) and thence to Edgware; the latter section being double tracked in the process. However, the construction of the spur between the LPTB station at Edgware and the LNER line was to be the responsibility of the Board, using powers obtained within the London Passenger Transport Act of 1936. At the time this plan was produced, Royal Assent for the 1936 Bills was still some four months away. So too was the decision by the Board for submission of a Bill to Parliament to promote the construction of the Elstree Branch, although its inclusion will be noted, the project having already attracted considerable correspondence and discussion. Although approved, the track layout for Edgware was revised a number of times in view of the accommodation to be provided at the new Aldenham depot, the sidings in the fork of the lines to Morden and the LNER being an early victim. Some consideration was also given to the layout when objections regarding the operation of the existing Northern Line were raised. This was finally resolved in December 1937 when a scheme was adopted involving the construction of a flyover for the connecting line with the LNER Edgware branch.

Hendon Borough Council responded by stating that the area immediately north of the railway had been town-planned with a density of eight houses to the acre and the LPTB's attentions were again drawn to the area previously considered on the south side of the railway. For the purpose of negotiation, the Estate Agent was instructed to investigate the possibility of purchasing a site of similar size elsewhere, which could then be exchanged for the original location suggested for the depot. The proposal to effect a land deal with Hendon Council had arisen at a meeting of the Board's Engineering Committee in early March when it was agreed that either Burnt Oak Sports Ground, which the Board owned, or an acquired area of Green Belt be used for the purpose. In early June, the Board learned of the failure of its latest plan. In meeting with the Engineer to Hendon Council, the Estate Agent broached the subject of a land exchange, which had been declined. Although the loss of 19½ acres from an area of 100 acres was deemed insignificant, it was only by reason of the town planning proposals that the Council was unable to entertain those of the Board. The only avenue open by which the land at Mill Hill could be acquired by the Board was for the site to be scheduled in its next Bill to Parliament and this would automatically attract a petition from Hendon Council. Strong resistance was also expected from the owners of surrounding houses who had bought them on the understanding that the Park would remain an open space into perpetuity. The Ministry of Health adopted a detached stance, stating that the matter only concerned the two interested parties.

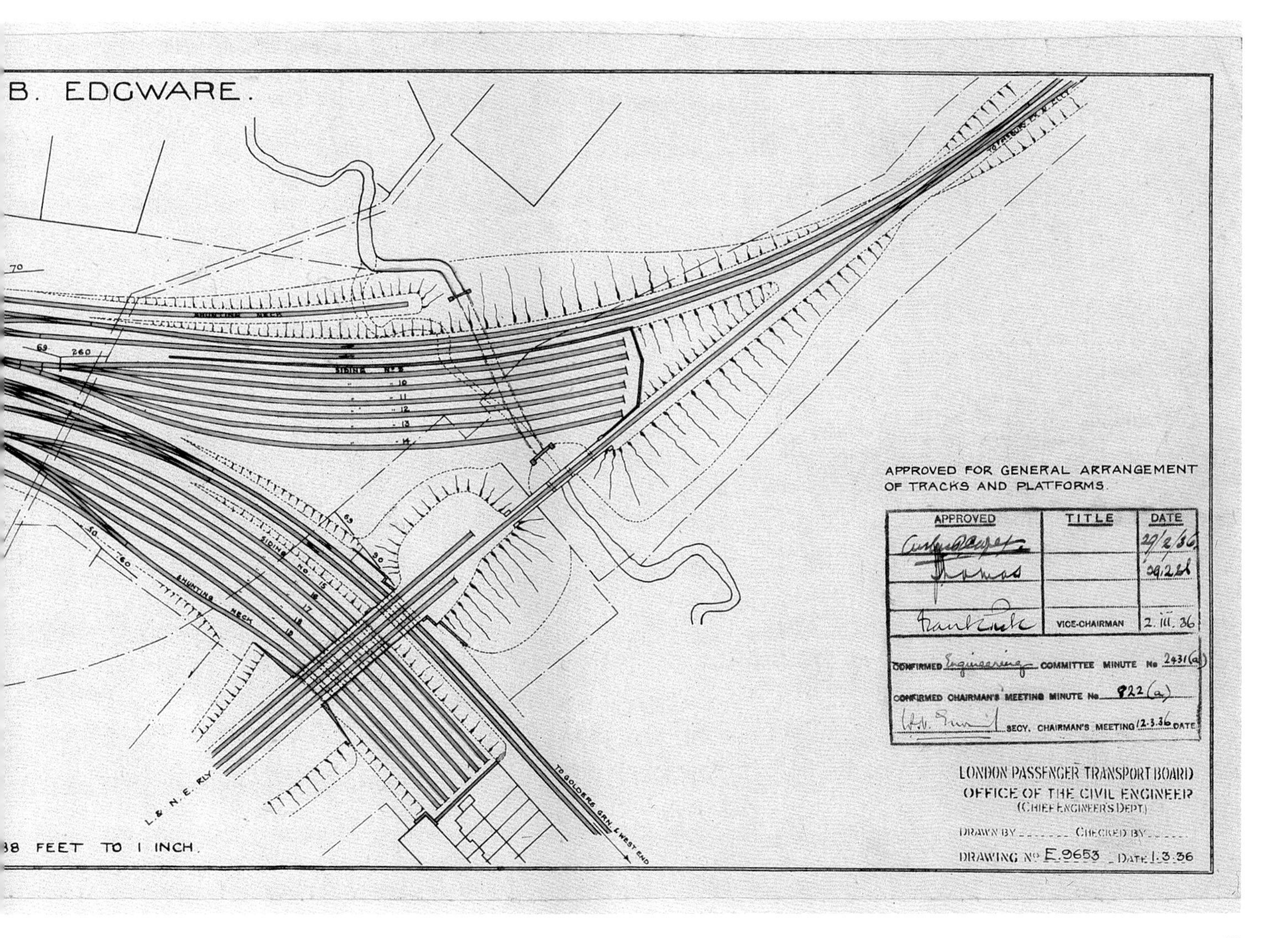

The Board formed an opinion that should a Bill fail to secure the acquisition of land, then it would be too late to apply for powers for an alternative depot site during the 1936–1937 Parliamentary session. Ideally the new rolling stock for the line would be delivered to the new depot, but delays in finding a suitable location had already placed the prospect of this in doubt. The centre of focus subsequently shifted from Mill Hill to a scheme that would involve the construction of a 2¾-mile railway from Edgware to Elstree, with a double-ended, progressive depot in sight of its terminus at Aldenham.

Graff-Baker picked up on the request made of J P Thomas for the comparison of maintenance and operating costs of building a new depot at Mill Hill with that of a similar installation adjacent to Aldenham Reservoir. He reported that his original estimated saving of £10,000 per annum after the construction of a depot at Mill Hill and the subsequent closing of Drayton Park and Golders Green depots equated with the scheme for a depot on the Elstree branch and retention of that at Golders Green. A further saving could be made over the Mill Hill estimate by the provision of sidings only at Golders Green.

Arrangements were quickly put in hand for the necessary statistical information to be made available. Plans were also formulated for the acquisition of a triangular field at the junction of Elstree Road and the Watford By-Pass, although much of the land required for the Elstree Extension had already been secured. This had been made possible by amalgamating the lands secured from the Watford and Edgware Railway Company with those acquired by the Board in connection with the proposed extension, resulting in a total of 295 acres, of which 159 were subsequently deemed surplus to requirements and put up for sale. Some of the land had been given without charge and this placed the Board under some obligation to provide the railway. Indeed, as development of the neighbourhood had proceeded, a strip of land reserved for the railway had become conspicuous, as had the planning of adjacent streets; all such action having been taken in advance of parliamentary approval. The value of the land then still to be acquired for the extension was placed at just £10,000.

From an operating viewpoint, the new scheme involved some additional car mileage whereby Morden–Edgware trains, now maintained at Golders Green would, under altered conditions, be required to run to and from Elstree for maintenance. Correspondingly, trains then stabled at Edgware would be berthed at Golders Green.

The site for the new depot was considered satisfactory for the new Morden–Edgware services via Highgate but not so ideally placed for the new Northern City services operating to Alexandra Palace and High Barnet. The nearest point to the depot for the latter routes was Church End, Finchley some 6½ miles distant. Nevertheless, both Thomas and Graff-Baker remained confident that provided the new rolling stock for both lines was interchangeable it should be possible to avoid any superfluous mileage.

Since the initial planning of the New Works Programme, serious consideration had been given to the rolling stock required to operate each of the schemes it embraced for improvements to the tube network. Not only were new cars required for the additional traffic derived from the extensions to existing lines, but also for the replacement of old and inefficient stock then in service on the Great Northern and City and Central London lines. At the time, rolling stock on the Morden–Edgware Line was based upon a standard design produced by the Underground Group and introduced on the Hampstead Line in 1923 for the Edgware extension and subsequent replacement of the clangorous gate stock.

Some considerable thought had also been given to overcrowding, a problem which had already become of serious dimension on the Morden–Edgware, the lengthening of trains appearing the most likely solution. The trial late night running of non-service trains consisting of nine cars in the autumn of 1937 resulted in a train of identical length entering passenger service in early November; a further three entering the schedules in February 1938. Apart from necessary adaptations to signalling and track circuits, no platforms were extended at stations located in the West End that would benefit most from the longer trains initiative. Nevertheless, a programme was put in hand to extend the platforms of the surface stations from Golders Green northwards to accept nine car trains and revise plans for stations on the Elstree branch to meet this requirement.

Edgware station presented a problem as the platforms were incapable of being enlarged, as trains of extended length just fitted between the buffer stops at the end of No.1 platform and the points leading to the depot layout. It was proposed that some consideration be given to projecting one of the tracks that would serve the Elstree Extension under Station Road for a distance of 100 feet (imitating to a smaller degree the 1931 proposals), and temporarily extend the opposite platform. By the following month, a new platform to accept nine-car trains on the site of the existing bay road was included in the first of many schemes for rebuilding the station. A report subsequently issued noted that it would be more economical to proceed with that adaptation than to commence any work upon the Elstree Extension. Plans for Aldenham Depot were also redrawn in order that nine-car trains could be accommodated.

But there was an alternative, which came from the inventive mind of Graff-Baker. In 1935, the same year that he succeeded W A Agnew as Chief Mechanical Engineer (Railways), Graff-Baker began the pursuit of funding for an experimental train with underfloor control equipment. By such innovation, it was estimated that an increase in capacity of 20% could be achieved.

In February 1936, faced with a costly plan that entailed extending some 90 platform faces on the Morden–Edgware line, J P Thomas took up Graff-Baker's proposals regarding rolling stock. Thomas proposed that the whole of the Morden–Edgware and its future branches be operated by the new trains. The displaced standard stock would be dispatched for use on the Central London Line once a programme had been completed to increase tunnel diameter, update the traction current supply system from three to four-rail and lengthen some station platforms.

In response to Graff-Baker's plans, the LPTB approved expenditure for the construction of a six-car experimental train, soon increased to four trains as other traction equipment manufacturers became involved in the project. When Thomas made his submission, delivery of the prototype stock was still some months away, and the Board's approval was based upon its acceptance of the new design. The first of the experimental trains, classified 1935 stock, began a series of test runs at the end of November 1936 and, based on its success, an order was placed for 1,050 cars in March 1937, increased to 1,121 the following October.

From 28th August 1937 the Morden–Edgware Line and its proposed new branches became known as the Northern Line. However, the line would not be the only recipient of the new 1938 Tube Stock, but would receive the major part of an order for 1,121 cars, with the Bakerloo Line receiving 238 augmented by 52 out of 58 refurbished 1927 trailer cars, the remaining six allocated to the Northern. In one of the initial attempts to ascertain new stock requirements, sixteen cars were added to the order for the Elstree Extension. Thereafter this addition was not shown separately as the total number of cars required for the new Northern Line services was upwardly revised. Provision was also made for some cars to be supplied with special equipment in order that nine-car trains could be operated during peak hours, reflecting the earlier decision to run trains of nine-car length using the existing Standard Stock.

By March 1938, an ambitiously proposed seven-car peak service for the Northern Line had been drawn up, some sixteen through trains per hour venturing on to the Elstree Extension, eight from the West End via Finchley Central and eight from the City via Golders Green. Two months later the projected through service was dramatically reduced to seven trains per hour in the peak, six during the day and three on Sundays all operating via the West End and Finchley Central.

The standardisation of rolling stock on both the Northern and the Northern City lines was considered a perfect solution permitting examination, inspection and washing to be carried out at the new depot and Morden. Before the decision to replace all existing rolling stock had been reached the only way by which this could be achieved was to place a further order for cars of Standard Stock design. There also remained the problem of being unable to work the former Great Northern and City cars back to either depot more frequently than every six days but this could be resolved by the installation of a car washing machine at Wellington sidings between visits to the main depot.

Some thought should be given at this point to the concept of the 'progressive depot' which had been the subject of a report by the Chief Mechanical Engineer of the Underground Group, W A Agnew, in March 1931. The system took into account a number of procedures as each train came out of service before stabling and by its adoption, reduced time in the sheds to 71 minutes. The four basic operations comprised examination, sweeping, washing and interior dusting followed by the preparation of the train for service.

A variation of the scheme and that upon which the layout of Aldenham Depot was based offered a speedier completion in 64 minutes. In Agnew's original submission, the suggested depot layout required a shed with ten roads, eight equipped with pits. At Aldenham twelve pit-equipped roads were planned, where trains entering the shed would be examined. Whilst this operation was being conducted, the floors of the cars would be swept and interiors dusted. All twelve roads provided direct access to a four-road car-cleaning shed, equipped with staging for operatives. Here a cleaning material would be applied to the windows of the cars in preparation for their excursion through the external depot washing machine. Significant savings were anticipated when compared with existing practices, as most of the work would be completed during the day.

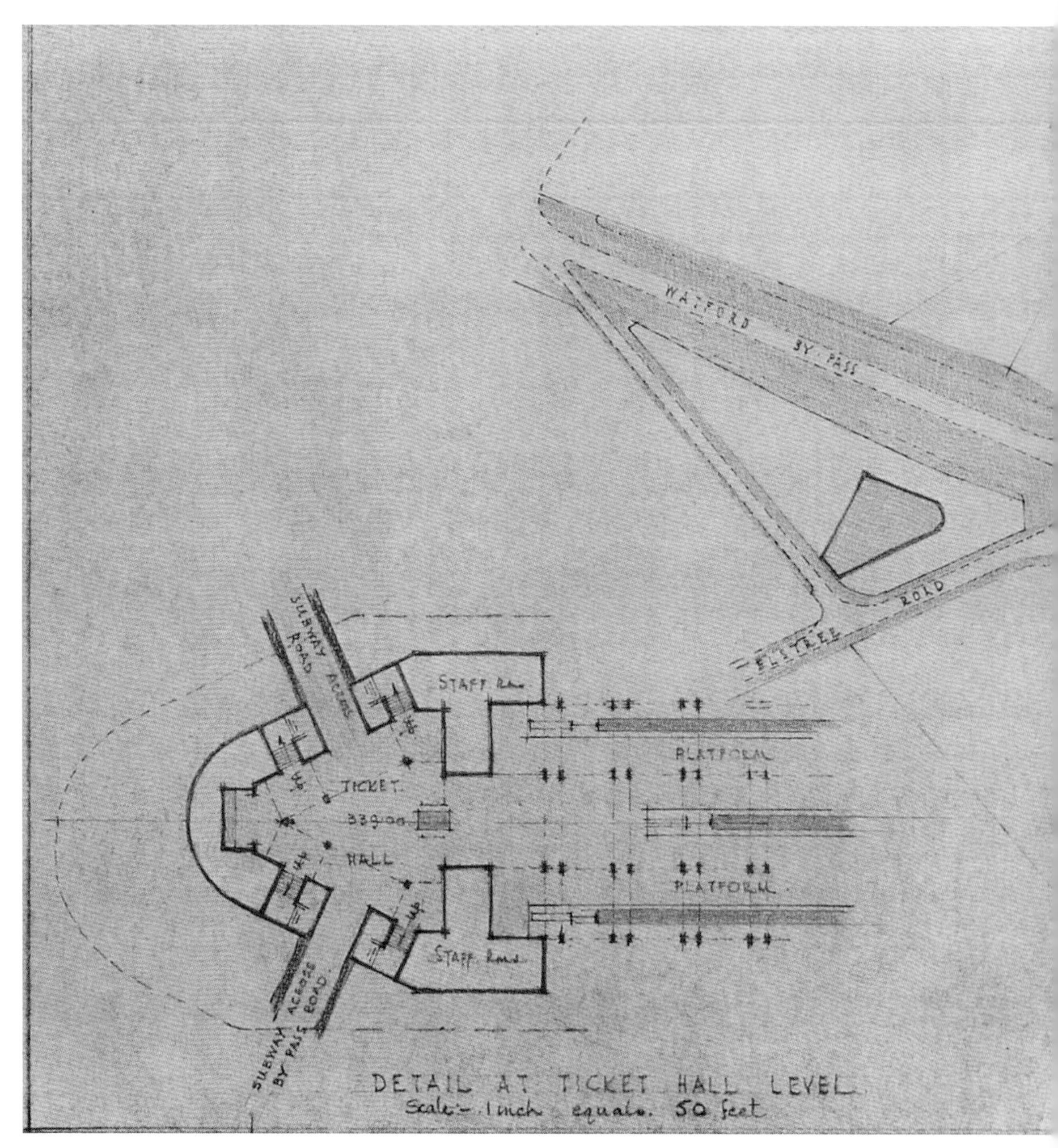

This coloured plan of the terminal station was provided to accompany the plans submitted with the 1937 Bill. The Board was anxious to provide easy interchange with the local bus services, so subways beneath the roads converging at the roundabout were provided for that purpose. The design for the station was later vested with Charles Holden who confirmed his acceptance of the commission on 24th March 1938.

Adaptations were also made to the plans for depot facilities at Aldenham Depot in preparation for the arrival of 1938 Tube Stock. The formation of the new trains comprised semi-permanently coupled units in which each car had a specific place. This was made necessary by on-board equipment required for the operation of the passenger air doors, improved lighting and ventilation and, not least, an increase in the motor cars required for improved acceleration. The new depot was therefore planned with a central traverser in order that intermediate cars of a unit could be removed without excessive shunting. Aldenham would have become the first depot so equipped but in the event this honour went to Ruislip.

On 16th July 1936, the London Passenger Transport Board agreed that the extension of the Morden–Edgware line to Elstree should be submitted to Parliament as part of its 1937 Bill. However, the road ahead was to prove difficult and fraught with many problems, the first of which would become apparent as the formal procedures began.

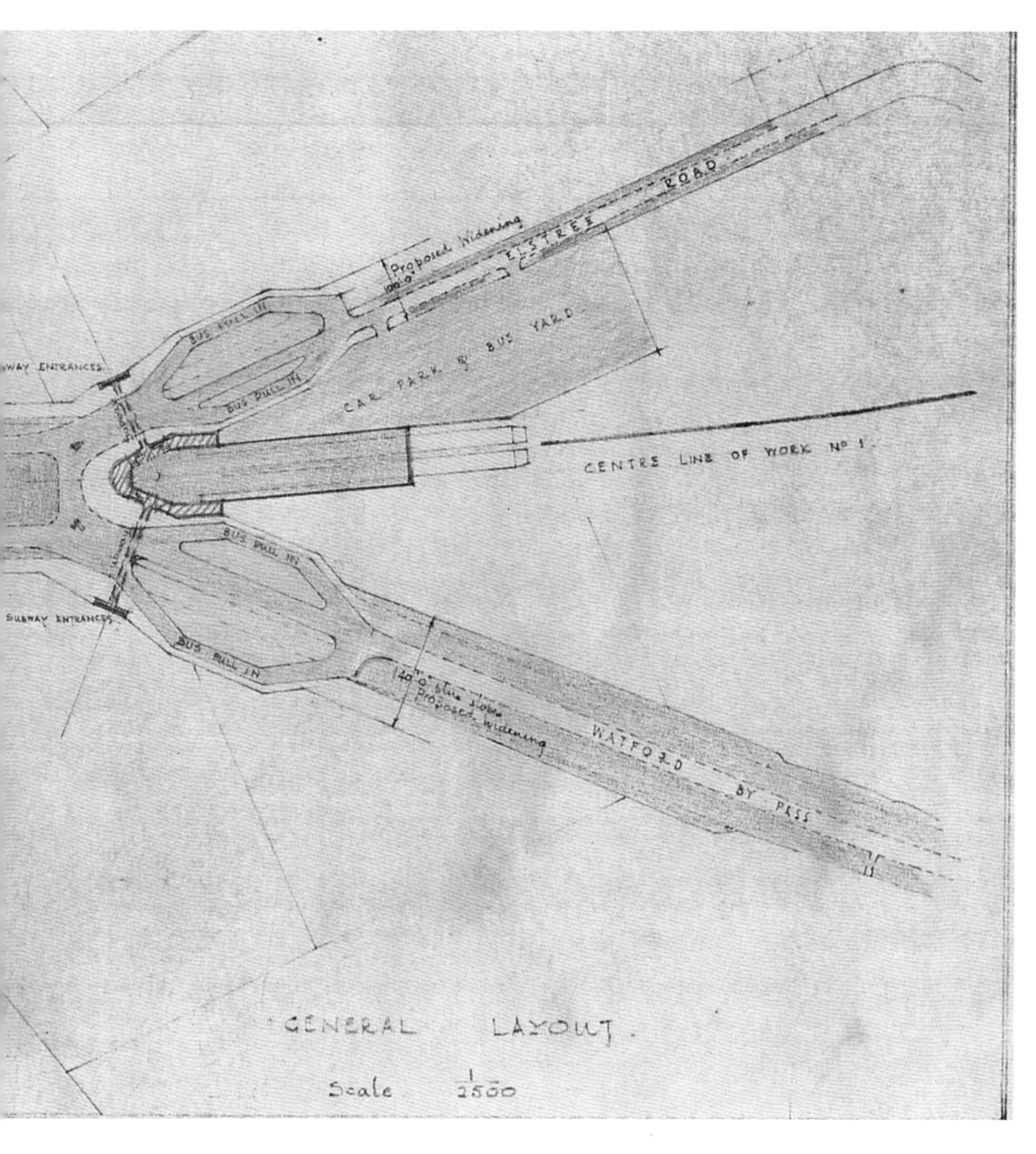

CHAPTER FIVE

The 1937 Bill

Drawn up to accompany the 1937 Bill, the route taken by the Elstree Extension closely followed that of the Watford and Edgware Railway promoted some 34 years earlier. One significant change to the area was the Watford By-Pass, opened in 1927. The numbers on the plan refer to a list of the landowners through whose property the line had been directed.

The route of the extension, as submitted to Parliament in the London Passenger Transport Board's 1937 Bill, closely followed that proposed by the Watford and Edgware Railway.

Once Edgware station had been rebuilt, trains entering the Elstree branch would depart the station in a north westerly direction immediately passing beneath Station Road where a height of 12ft 6ins above the running rail surface would be maintained. It will be recalled that shops and flats directly opposite the station had been built on a concrete raft in anticipation of the extension during 1926, which year also saw the partial completion of a length of trackbed in this area. By 1937 the route of the railway near to Edgware station could still be defined as a green path between the houses, partly in use as tennis courts. The projected line closely followed that authorised in 1903 although plans had been redrawn by the Board's engineers in order to obtain better alignments and improved gradients.

The service road at the rear of the shops in Station Road bridged the proposed extension and marked the start of a 500ft section of line bounded by retaining walls on a rising gradient of 1 in 59. The course the railway would follow continued to remain apparent as it entered a cutting and later an embankment constructed on land left untouched by housing developers. Arrangements had been made with the local council for the erection of a footbridge at the point where the line bisected Purcells Avenue. The rising embankment, bordered by Hillside Gardens and Glendale Avenue, would provide access to a brick and plate girder viaduct of 22

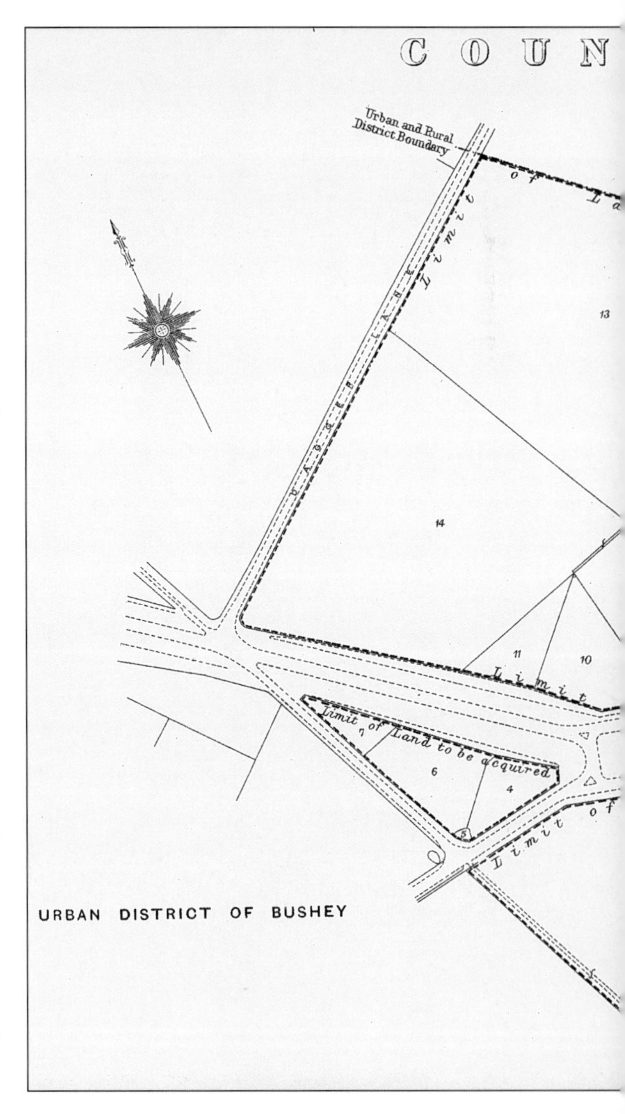

arches, which in turn led to a four span girder bridge above the Watford By-Pass, and thence to the first station 0.78 miles from Edgware. The first station would be built on a viaduct of twelve arches with an extension of the existing Spur Road acting as a service road at its north end spanned by a 55ft girder bridge. Designed on the lines of South Harrow station on the Piccadilly Line, the entrance to the ticket office would be under Spur Road bridge.

Leaving the station the line would initially run along an embankment and above a pedestrian subway that would preserve an existing bridleway linking a local farm to the Watford By-Pass. With a ruling gradient of 1 in 53, the line would continue north west, entering a cutting, which preceded the entrance to twin shield-driven tunnels 1,575 feet in length beneath Elstree Hill. The tunnels were to be lined using segments made surplus by the extension of station tunnels on the Central and Bakerloo lines, the diameter deficiency of 3¾ inches being addressed by the insertion of iron and creosoted deal packings. A storage facility for the iron segments would be established above the portal at the southern end of the tunnels.

Emerging from the descending slope, the twin bore tunnels would give access to a deep cutting containing the second station, 1.95 miles from Edgware. Elstree Hill would be carried above the station with the street-level building erected on its north east side. Running the length of the station, but behind its south wall at a slightly lower level, would be two reversing roads from the depot complex.

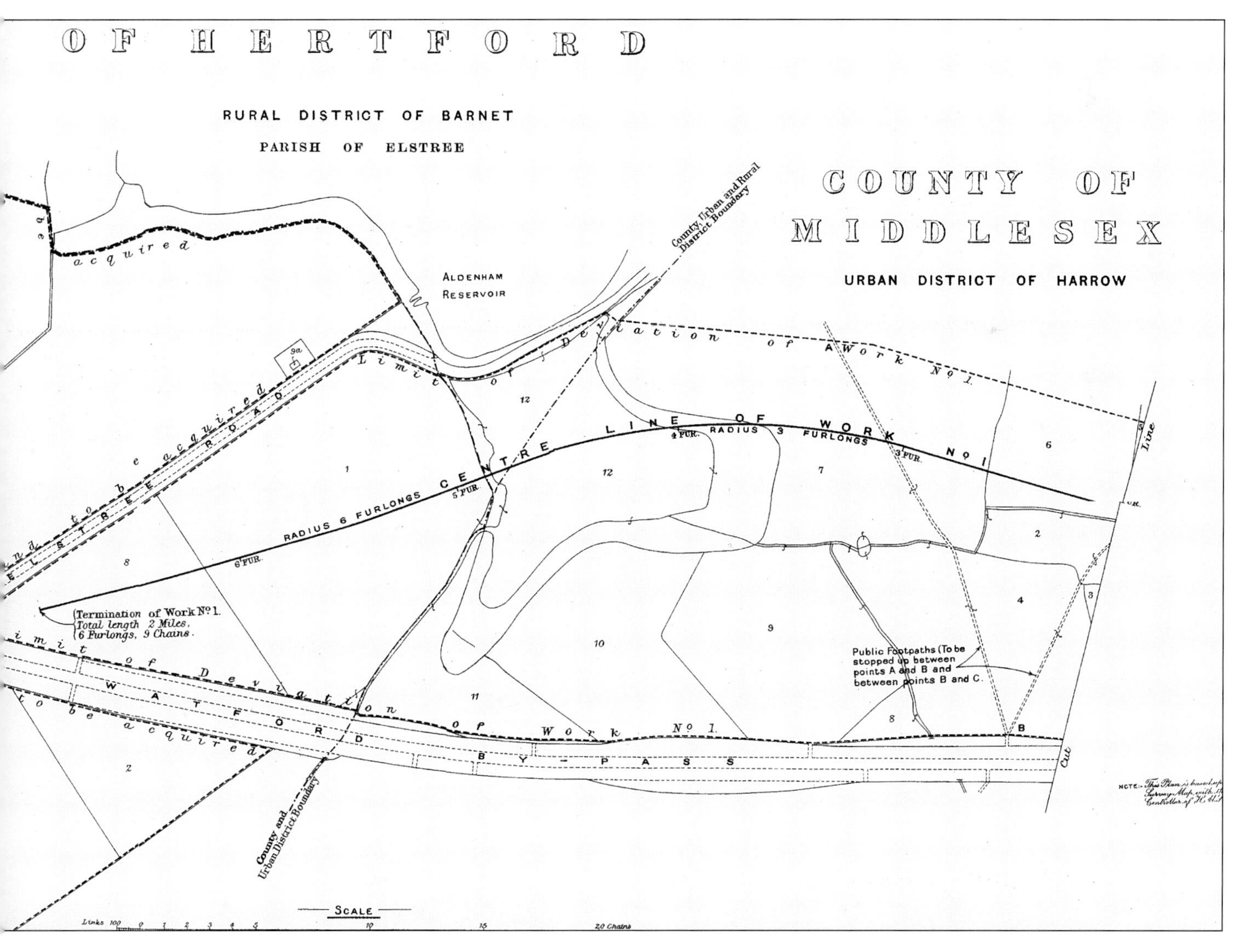

Leaving the second station the line would describe a gentle curve to the north west of the new Aldenham Underground depot and terminate at a three-road, two platform station situated at the junction of the Watford By-Pass and the Elstree–Watford Road, 2.86 miles from Edgware and some 13 miles from Tottenham Court Road.

According to Pick's 10th July 1936 report to the Board, the estimate for the Elstree Extension, fully equipped, was £1,110,000 including £270,000 for construction of the depot. Constructional works, excluding power supply, equipment and signalling, was placed at £512,000 resulting in an outlay of under £200,000 per mile. A further £80,000 was required for the provision of sixteen cars, considered sufficient for the operation of the line, for which working expenses of £24,287 had been calculated. This evaluation had been based upon the full cost of car mileage to work

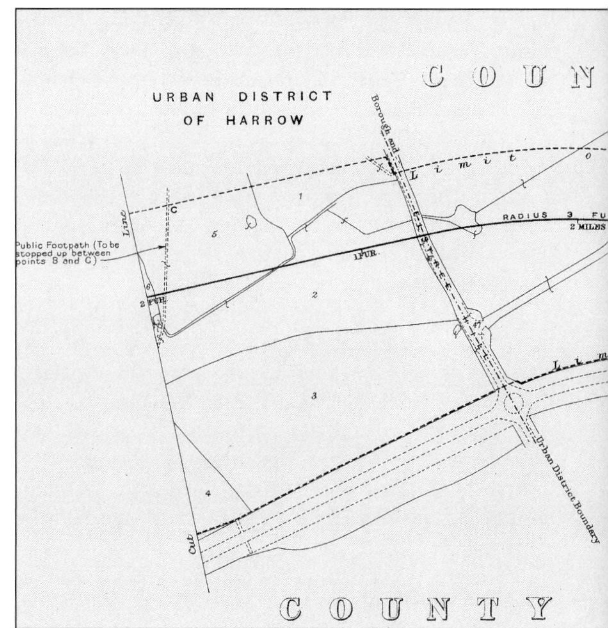

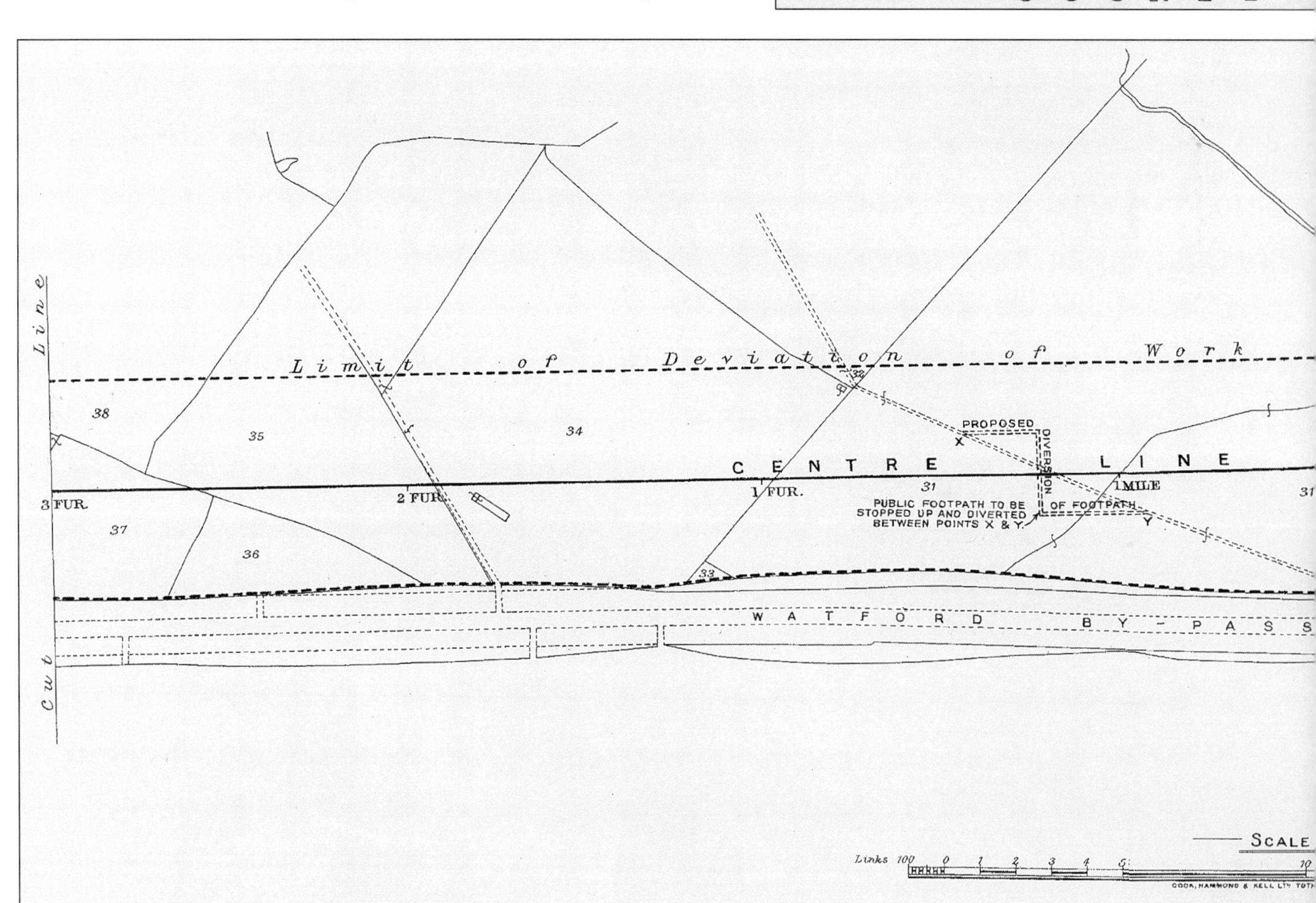

Further plans from the 1937 Bill presented to Parliament in November 1936. These sections include Elstree South and Brockley Hill station sites.

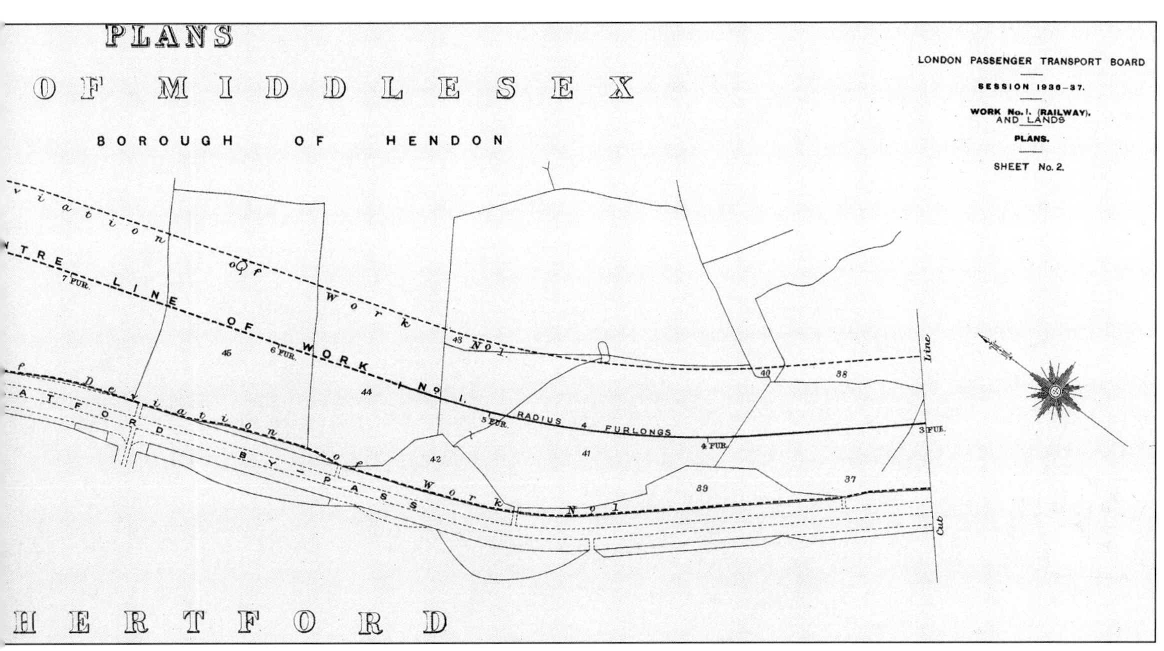

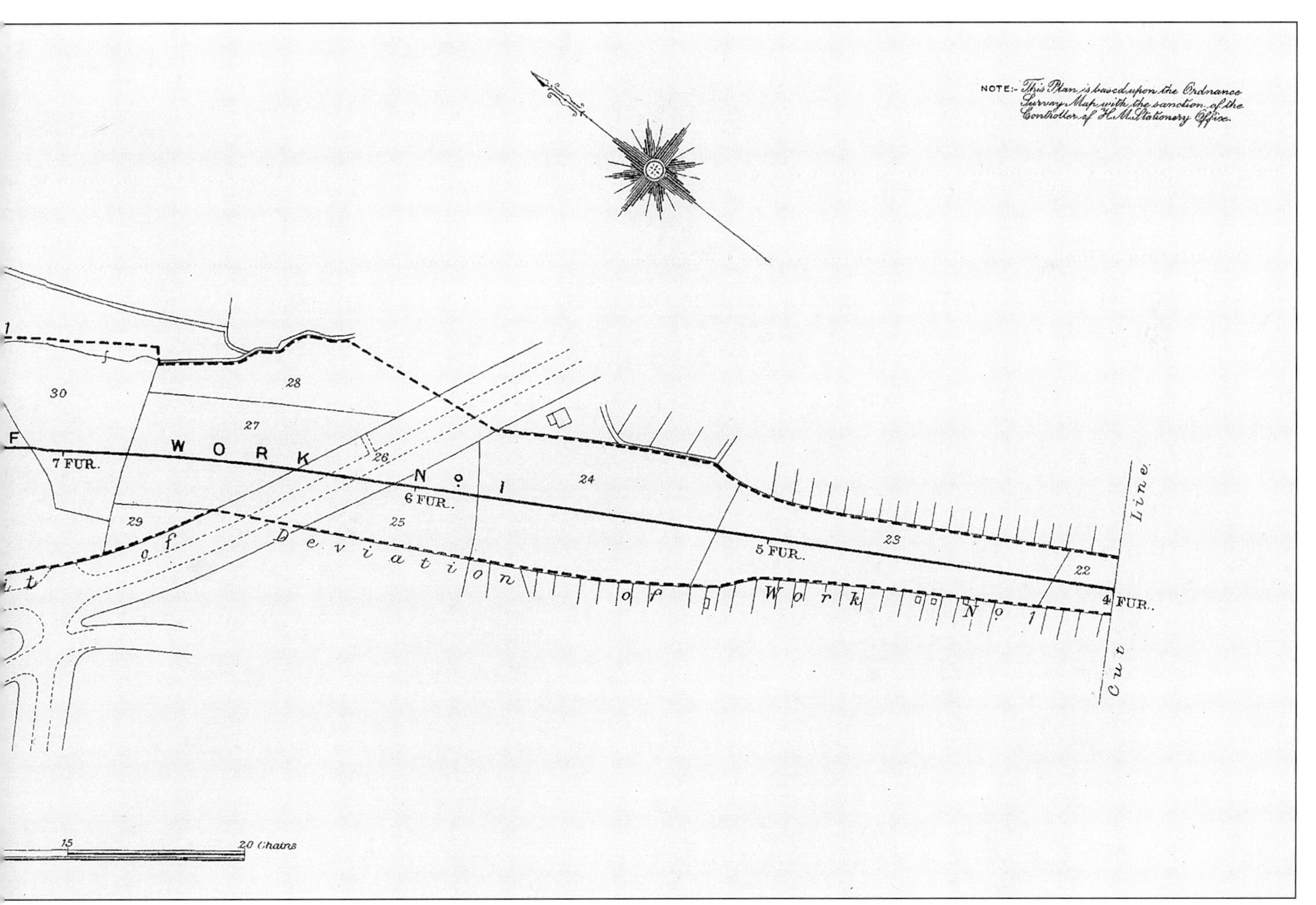

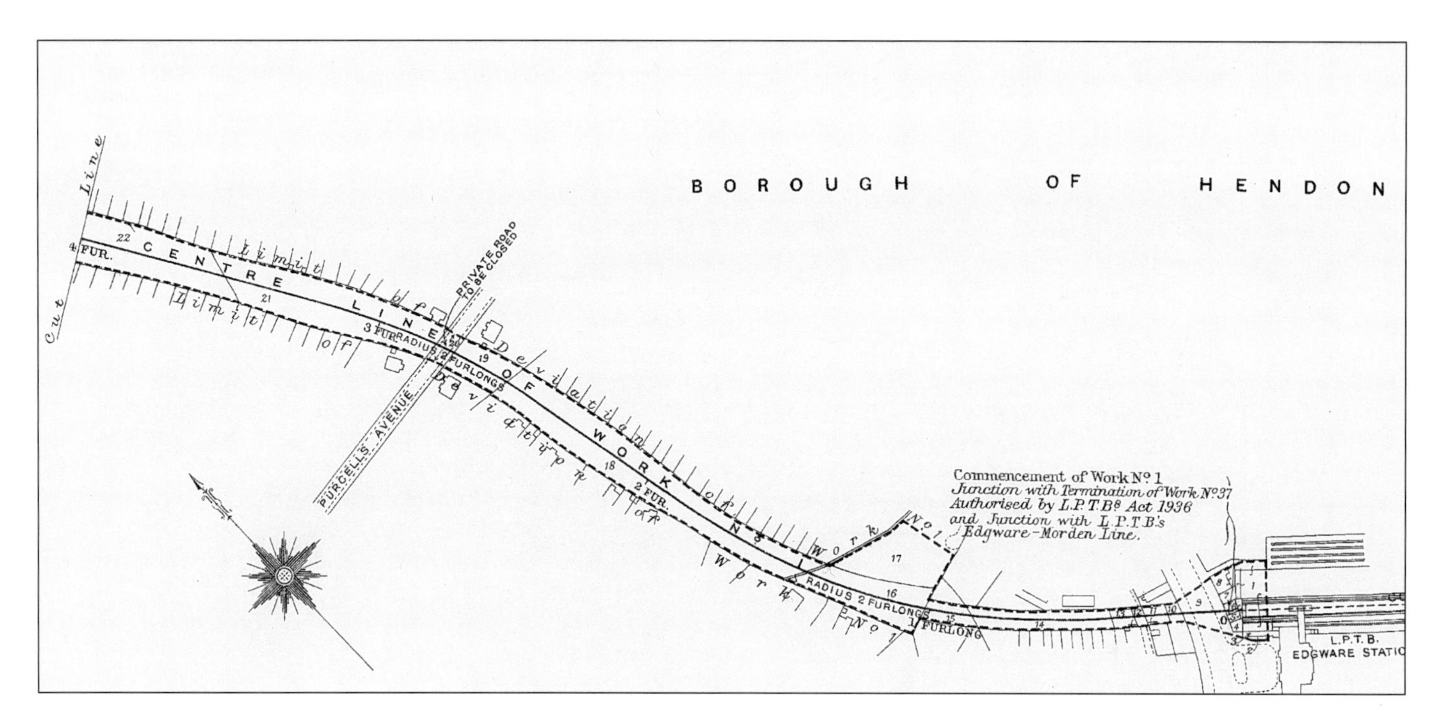

Extract from the 1937 Bill showing alignment of first part of extension beyond Edgware.

seven 7-car trains per hour in the rush hours and six 3-car trains per hour during off peak times although the pattern of service had yet to be decided. The proposed timetable was considered ample for a traffic potential of 4,290,000 passenger journeys per annum.

For the purposes of estimating passenger numbers, the population of the area served by the extension was set at 33,000, an increase of 23,000 over the population existing in 1934, requiring an addition of roundly 6,000 new homes. Of this figure, the greatest number of inhabitants was to be found in the area immediately to the north of Edgware. Although conjectured, this figure was considered conservative, it having been assumed that the area would continue to be developed as a fairly good class residential district. Conversely, the density of population in the area surrounding the terminal station had been placed at four persons per acre, which only rose to a miserable 4½ if the acreage of the private parks at Hilfield and Aldenham House were discounted.

The prospective return on capital was placed at 7.7%. This figure had been calculated after three important assumptions had been made; the first presupposing that the number of passenger journeys on the extension would represent an average of 130 rides per head of population served. Such a figure was deemed justifiable when the following comparable figures of rides per head of estimated population was taken into consideration:

Section of Line	Rides Per Head (1934)
Brent – Edgware	253
North Ealing – South Harrow	306
Rayners Lane – Uxbridge	125
Wembley Park – Harrow	246
North Harrow – Rickmansworth	174
Manor House – Cockfosters	119

The second assumption was that the average fare paid per passenger would be 5d in deference to the 4.47d average fare at Edgware. The final assumption was that the working expenses for the line would be £24,287.

In the 1936 Bill, the financial projections laid before the Parliamentary Committee had presumed an average of 115 rides per head of population on the several extensions to which the Bill related. This was later considered a cautious estimate, and having regard for the more desirable character of the area to be served by the extension and the better class of development expected, there appeared to be every justification for raising the rides per head to the aforementioned 130. If the figure contained in the 1936 Bill was adopted, this would have the effect of reducing the estimated return on capital from 7.7% to 6.5%.

No deduction from the estimated revenue had been made in respect of any additional mileage required to carry the traffic south of Edgware. It had been considered that, after completion of the Highgate branch extensions and the electrification of the LNER branch lines, the peak hour services on congested sections of the Morden–Edgware system would be brought up to the maximum capacity of the line, without any consideration being given to the construction of the extension. On the less congested sections, excess traffic created by the extension was anticipated too trivial in relation to the whole traffic on the system to warrant the operation of additional mileage.

However, one crucial question remained: would there be sufficient capacity on the Morden–Edgware line to carry additional traffic created by the extension? In contemplating such an eventuality, some thought had been given to this problem once all the improvements had been finished. Calculations on the future density of traffic for 1943–46, assuming the completion of all new works, foresaw a 31% increase in traffic passing through Warren Street during the winter morning peak.

If the Elstree Extension yielded an increase in traffic higher than that anticipated (e. g. 180 rides per head of population instead of 130), then it was estimated that the density of the most congested part of the line would show a 36% rise. Proposals were therefore being considered to enable passenger capacity of the maximum future service to be 41% above that which then existed.

The task of compiling the estimates had fallen to the Board's recently-appointed Fares Officer, A B B Valentine, using information provided by the General Manager (Railways), the Chief Engineer and the Actuary. In a memorandum to Pick, he considered that the calculation of future traffic on the Elstree Extension could be regarded as conservative and the estimated return on capital of 7.7% more likely to be understated than exaggerated. Yet, Valentine held an opinion that further factors were in need of being taken into account before a decision to proceed was reached. The Vice Chairman's attention was therefore drawn to the additional population of the area served (23,000) – considered trivial when compared with other schemes already included in the New Works Programme that required an aggregate of some 600,000 people for their support.

Although the extension was most likely to attract an additional population sufficient to yield a return of above 7%, it would only do so at the cost of delaying a similar level of growth required to maintain the other schemes in the Programme.

Valentine also contended that the future capacity of the Morden–Edgware line would be sufficient to carry the additional traffic originating from the current North London electrification scheme and the Elstree Extension. His opinion was based on the practicability of operating over the City and West End sections of the system a peak hour service of 43 seven-car trains of the new type stock. The General Manager (Railways) had reservations and had stated that until the future capacity of the line could be more confidently assessed, it could be argued that there was a case for the deferment of the Elstree branch.

Valentine's final point concentrated on the benefits of the Edgware–Elstree Extension compared with those of the proposed extension between Ruislip and Denham. This appraisal had been undertaken in case the Board be required to choose between the two proposals due to financial restrictions. He noted that the Denham proposal did not represent a similar risk to the Elstree Extension, the proposed extension of the Central Line being only an improvement on facilities in an area already served by the GWR. A larger proportion of the territory adjoining the Denham Extension was unsuitable for development on account of the Colne Valley and Canal; the area was also further away from the centre of London. The Elstree Proposal, Valentine concluded, appeared more attractive and would open up new country currently without any convenient railway facilities.

Pick's Personal Assistant, Anthony Bull, considered the report clouded the issue, observing that Valentine had made no attempt to compare the advantages of the Elstree and Denham extensions. He also contended that his colleague had failed to give serious thought to works that might be omitted from the programme in order to provide scope for the Elstree Extension. Finally, Bull resurrected the question regarding the extension of the Stanmore line to a junction south of Elstree Station, expressing a view that Valentine's report should have included a reference to its possible construction.

Facing page **A set of photographs was especially produced for the Select Committee of the House of Lords convened in June 1937 to consider the 1937 LPTB Bill. These aerial views were commissioned by Hertfordshire County Council in support of its petition against the construction of the line. Counsel engaged by the Authority made great play of the fact that housing development practically ceased around the Watford By-Pass, north of Edgware.**

The Bill was deposited in Parliament on 27th November 1936, the Elstree Extension being the only section of new railway for which powers were being sought.

The parliamentary newspaper notice was published in *The Times* on 4th December 1936, and extracts were published in relevant local newspapers. The deadline for depositing petitions against the Bill was set at 30th January 1937 and by that date, 29 had been received. Of these, three were petitioners against the construction of the Elstree Extension, being Harrow Urban District Council, Hertfordshire County Council and Middlesex County Council; their deliberations were made available for perusal by the Board at its meeting held on 4th February.

IN THE ADMINISTRATIVE COUNTIES OF MIDDLESEX AND HERTFORD:—
Work No. 1—A railway 2 miles 6 furlongs 9 chains or thereabouts in length situate in the Borough of Hendon, the Urban District of Harrow, the Parish of Elstree in the Rural District of Barnet and the Urban District of Bushey.

The parliamentary notice as published in *The Times* 4th December 1936.

Within its list of eight objections, Harrow Urban District Council observed that Aldenham Reservoir was now classified as a public open space. 'It is of great public importance', the statement continued, 'that the area should be available as part of the Green Belt. Construction of the railway at a level of 20 feet above the surface would seriously interfere with proposals'. Here was the first of many occasions when conditions contained in the LCC's Town Planning Scheme No.19 would be used as the basis for objection regarding any planned development in the vicinity of Aldenham Reservoir. Of the little that was achieved from the Scheme introduced as an adjunct to the Town and Country Planning Act of 1932, only the creation of the Green Belt was of significance. Mainly comprising a broad band of farmland, parkland and recreation ground encompassing the capital, the Green Belt was intended to ensure the careful control of any building development. The City dweller would therefore have easy access to the Green Belt, unrestricted development of the outer suburbs having been restrained.

Hertfordshire County Council had two objections on a similar theme amongst the eleven it submitted. The first recorded 'Terminal site open to strong criticism, pre-eminently suited for Green Belt scheme. Building and development will militate against expansion of the Belt'. The second damningly declared that the 'Proposal would change the character of the district. Little Aldenham Reservoir is a quiet beauty spot, bird sanctuary and unspoilt pleasure resort. Spoilation by railway would be irreparable, caused by sidings and depot and completed by urbanisation'. The County Council continued, 'Proposal should not be authorised. Other sites available particularly further south between Watford By-Pass and Edgwarebury Lane where ample land abutting Watford By Pass. Additional cost of acquisition could be offset by shortening of line'.

Prompted by the County Council's opposition, plans were drawn up showing a depot north of the first station. Immediately a request was made for a submission of comparison costs for levelling both sites and their resulting capacity. But on 29th May 1937, before any statistics were produced, J P Thomas laid the scheme to rest when he declared the plan only permitted a single-ended depot to be built. Any derailment or obstruction at the exit would effectively impound all the rolling stock in the depot, the layout of which also involved excessive shunting for the cleaning and overhaul of the stock.

Finally Middlesex County Council objected to the Board's acquisition of the site at Aldenham but added that if powers were granted, the Board must provide the Council with other land in the neighbourhood 'not less suitable'.

These, however, were just the formal objections. Publication in *The Times* of the Board's intention to seek powers to build the extension provoked some hostile correspondence within its columns. The first attack was launched on 5th April 1937, by the publication of a memorandum written by a rear admiral, no less, as figurehead of ten associations of residents and ratepayers living in the area to be served by the Elstree Extension. Far from entering into constructive criticism, the commuting naval officer subjected the Board to a barrage of sustained fire concerning the 'insanitary' conditions caused by overcrowding on the Morden–Edgware Line. Loosing off a further broadside, he denounced the Board's proposal for staggering working times as too drastic concluding with a stern view of the high level of fares currently charged. A letter from Frank Pick, published in response on 12th April, failed to pour oil on troubled waters.

ALDENHAM RESERVOIR

Showing Rural Character of Surroundings

Looking at the site of the proposed terminus, Counsel claimed that if it were impossible to prevent the construction of the line, then indiscriminate development similar to that at Morden would occur.

Hill Tree Farm
Elstree Hill
Edgware Bury
North Western Avenue
Watford By-pass)
Stanmore - Elstree
Road Roundabout
Watling Street

Elstree Village

As the hapless lawyer tried vainly to use photographic evidence in furtherance of his clients' opposition to the railway, Pick pointed out that on the edge of this view was Elstree Village where more housing was being built.

The projected line entered Harrow's area of responsibility west of Elstree Hill, having left the Borough of Hendon whose objections were somewhat stymied when its local MP gave support to the Board's proposals.

Elstree Village

Watling Street

North Western Avenue (Watford Way)

Pick was able to point out that the Canons Park Estate had been broken up for housing, Spur Road connecting the development and the planned Brockley Hill station. He clearly must have felt there was scope for further development in this area.

The fully built-up area between Edgware station and Brockley Hill showing the strip of land reserved for the extension.

Correspondence in *The Times* regarding the Elstree Extension during April 1937.

THE EDGWARE TUBE

TO THE EDITOR OF THE TIMES

Sir,—The proposal to extend the Edgware Tube Railway to Elstree has aroused considerable indignation among the dwellers in the north-west suburban area served by this railway.

As chairman of the Hampstead Garden Suburb Residents' Association, whose 1,500 members are vitally interested in this matter, and with the concurrence of nine other associations dependent upon this Tube railway, I ask for your powerful support.

To-day the Edgware Tube is one of the most overloaded of all the Tubes, and the L.P.T.B. in their annual report, 1936, admit that facilities are inadequate, that the number of trains has reached the limit, and that they have no remedy to offer except new trains of 14 per cent. larger capacity in the dim future, and a suggestion to alter the working times of half the population so as to spread out the rush hours and thus reduce the maximum loads.

The L.P.T. Bill, 1937, now before Parliament, seeks powers to extend the Tube, and in the light of what has happened in the successive extensions to Golders Green and then to Hendon and Edgware it is certain that a large community will be established at Elstree to overload the Tube still more.

Suggestions have emanated from the L.P.T.B. that the L.N.E.R. Edgware line, when electrified, together with the existing L.M.S. line to Elstree, and the Metropolitan line to Stanmore may provide some relief to the Edgware tube in 1941, but this relief is not likely to be realized unless the present high fares and rates be reduced to tube level, and, as yet, there is no promise to reduce. The L.N.E.R. route *via* Finsbury Park provides an avenue of approach to the City independent of the tubes, but the efficacy of the new link with the tube *via* Highgate appears to be limited by Camden Town junction, already working to full capacity, and presumably unable to accommodate more trains from either Edgware or Highgate.

An immediate reduction of fares on the L.N.E.R. and L.M.S., and the Metropolitan would tend to attract passengers away from the Edgware Tube, and would provide a useful indication of the relief likely to be realized when the schemes are completed in 1941. This has already been suggested by the Hendon Borough Council to the Middlesex County Council for transmission to the L.P.T.B., and apparently the Railway Rates Tribunal has power to authorize this reduction.

The present overcrowding and atmospheric pollution are excessive, and it is surprising that the House of Commons and its Ministry of Health have not taken steps to remove the peril to health in the very insanitary conditions on the tube trains at the rush hours.

It will be a real calamity if this Bill be enacted without any protection for travellers. Hendon Borough Council have reserved the right to appear before the House of Lords committee, but it is hoped that some M.P.s may yet be found with the necessary courage to take drastic action on or before the third reading so as to persuade the L.P.T.B. to take immediate steps to remedy the very objectionable conditions now existing on the Edgware Tube.

Yours, etc.,

E. O. HEFFORD, Engineer Rear-Admiral.

2, Bigwood Road, N.W.11.

THE EDGWARE TUBE

TO THE EDITOR OF THE TIMES

Sir,—I was interested to read the letter from Engineer Rear-Admiral Hefford on Monday, as my federation, which represents the non-political ratepayers' associations in the county of Middlesex, has had this question under consideration.

My federation feels that it would be useless endeavouring to stop entirely the extension of the Edgware tube beyond its present terminus. However, it is in agreement with the Hampstead Garden Suburb Residents' Association in its feeling that before the extension takes place something should be done to alleviate the serious overcrowding which at present occurs on the line, and to prevent the increase of overcrowding which will occur if the line is extended without safeguards. At the last meeting of the council of the federation the following resolution was passed unanimously, and a copy has been sent to every member of Parliament representing a Middlesex constituency:—

While F.O.R.A.M. in principle does not desire to oppose the L.P.T.B. Bill (Elstree tube extension), which, we understand, enters the Committee stage on the 16th inst., this county federation is unanimously agreed that before the desired powers are granted there should be definite undertakings and guarantees that:—

(*a*) Adequate arrangements shall be made to obviate any further congestion at points on the existing line. At present there is great difficulty in getting to and from town morning and evening, especially from intermediate stations such as Hendon and Golders Green; and it is felt that with the extension to Elstree these conditions will be much worsened unless additional facilities are devised for their relief.

(*b*) Comparative fares shall be arranged among the various companies concerned in the solution of this problem of consequential increased overcrowding of trains.

Sympathetic replies have been received from several of the members of Parliament.

Yours faithfully,

H. BUENO DE MESQUITA, Hon. General Secretary, the Federation of Ratepayers' and Kindred Associations of Middlesex.

April 6.

RAILWAYS IN NORTH LONDON

THE EDGWARE-MORDEN LINE

POLICY OF THE L.P.T.B.

TO THE EDITOR OF THE TIMES

Sir,—It is somewhat unfortunate that a matter which is before Parliament and will be considered judicially by a Parliamentary Committee should have become the subject of outside controversy. The Board feel that as there is so much misunderstanding of their intentions some reply from them should be given at this time. They therefore ask the courtesy of your columns.

The Board are aware of the congestion of traffic at and beyond Golders Green upon the Edgware-Morden line in the peak hours. It was the fact of this congestion which directed the Board's attention to securing some means of relief. It is proposed, under the programme of works now in execution, to extend the Highgate branch of the Edgware-Morden line northwards to make a junction with the London and North Eastern Railway at East Finchley, so as to allow of through services of trains from this line to be run to Barnet and to Edgware over the London and North Eastern Railway's tracks, and in order to ensure that as full a service as possible shall be given to Edgware it is proposed to double the tracks upon this line. The effect of providing this additional through service of trains northwards will be that at Church End, Finchley, probably a quarter of the traffic which now converges at Golders Green will be diverted to the new service of trains, thus affording immediate relief. At Edgware there will be available two services of trains, one *via* Golders Green, the other *via* Highgate, both serving the West End and the City.

At the same time the Board propose to replace the rolling stock on the existing Edgware-Morden line with trains of a new type which will afford 14 per cent. more seating capacity than is now available. The combined effect of this programme will be to provide 40 per cent. additional seating accommodation in the services for the area in question.

The extension of the railway from Edgware to Aldenham is necessary primarily to provide a new rolling-stock depôt. Provision must be made for approximately 550 new cars. The existing provision at Golders Green, Edgware, and Wellington sidings is wholly inadequate for the purpose. Without a new depôt it will be impossible to work the northern railways efficiently.

The built-up area has now extended much beyond Edgware, and the provision of the extension to Aldenham will deal with an existing traffic more conveniently. The extent to which the territory beyond Aldenham is to be developed is in the hands of the local and town-planning authorities. The Board would be glad if the Green Belt were completed across the Aldenham station, as it would afford to the Board another type of traffic which would not demand facilities in the peak hours, and the Board are prepared in their works at or near Aldenham to give careful regard to the amenities of the district.

The Board are also aware of the disparity in more branch of the late Metropolitan Railway and the fares charged at Edgware on the Edgware-Morden line. The fares on the late Metropolitan Railway are governed by the Railways Act of 1921 and are dealt with in the same way as the main line railway companies' fares. The fares on the Edgware-Morden line are governed by the several Acts establishing the Underground Railways. There are difficulties in the way of equating these fares. The Board are in negotiation with the main line railway companies interested and hope that some adjustment will be possible which will result in making more effective the railway at Stanmore, especially as works are already being executed which will enable a through service of trains from the Bakerloo line to be run to Stanmore, giving from this point yet another direct service to and from the City and West End as at Edgware.

It is idle to take a part of the Board's programme and discuss it in isolation. If the whole of the works which the Board has in contemplation in the northern sector of London are considered in their relationship to one another there is not any question at all that a quite considerable improvement in the travelling facilities of the area will be provided. Altogether the Board are spending in this connexion a sum of no less than £13,000,000.

Yours faithfully,

FRANK PICK.

London Passenger Transport Board, 55, Broadway, S.W.1, April 9.

RAILWAYS IN NORTH LONDON

TO THE EDITOR OF THE TIMES

Sir,—Mr. Frank Pick in his letter to you has missed the crux of the problem. Granted that a proportion of passengers now joining the Edgware line at Edgware and Golders Green will be diverted to the Highgate line, that does not reduce the total number of pasengers travelling to the West End along the Camden Town-Charing Cross bottle-neck. On the contrary they will be reinforced by the full body of passengers from Barnet to the West End; and while many of these probably now travel by train, omnibus, and Tube *via* Highgate or Golders Green, others now come up by L.N.E.R. to King's Cross and then by the Piccadilly Tube. The electrification of the L.N.E.R. lines will probably lead to new development around Mill Hill and Totteridge, as well as at Aldenham, with a further addition to the number of passengers.

To-day Highgate gets 14 Charing Cross trains an hour to 24 for Golders Green. The electrification of the Barnet and Edgware lines will shift the whole centre of gravity, and it may prove that the Highgate line will need the majority of trains. Therefore while there will be less pressure at Golders Green the remaining travellers there will have to reconcile themselves to fewer trains. The real crux is the Camden Town-Charing Cross bottle-neck, which is already working at capacity, and the only remedy is to build four tracks in place of the existing two. Unless this is done I fail to see how by using new rolling-stock with 14 per cent. more "seating capacity" London Transport can provide 40 per cent. "additional seating accommodation" through the bottle-neck.

These points are not merely a matter of "outside controversy." They are vital evidence for the Parliamentary Committee considering the new Bill. London Transport's new projects should have been combined with the construction of four tracks through the bottle-neck and also a coordination of the Tube and surface line fares, both of which contribute to the London "pool." Also a "flying" junction is essential at Church End, but there is no intimation that this is being built. The problem has unfortunately been tackled piecemeal, and so seems likely to add to the congestion on the inner sections of this line.

It would be helpful if Mr. Frank Pick could discuss these points. To get down to brass tacks, I invite him to publish (*a*) the rush-hour schedule to-day over the sections Edgware-Golders Green-Charing Cross and Highgate-Charing Cross; and (*b*) the proposed rush-hour schedule for the sections Edgware-Golders Green-Charing Cross, Edgware-Highgate-Charing Cross, and High Barnet-Highgate-Charing Cross. Then we would know where we stood.

Yours faithfully,

NORMAN CRUMP.

Leafland, Wood Vale, N.10.

THE EDGWARE TUBE

TO THE EDITOR OF THE TIMES

Sir,—May I be permitted to comment on certain aspects of this controversy to which Mr. Frank Pick refers in his letter published in your columns on April 12?

In the first place, I cannot agree with Mr. Pick that public discussion of a question of public—or even national—importance is a matter for regret. The L.P.T.B. are in a position to bring their whole weight to bear during the judicial consideration by the Parliamentary Committee. It is certainly unfortunate that an enormous bulk of public opinion is opposed to the Board's proposals, but I can see no reason why the Committee should be kept ignorant of this fact during their deliberations.

Mr. Pick states in effect that the extension of the Highgate line to join the electrified L.N.E.R. at East Finchley will allow through services to Barnet and to Edgware, and will provide 26 per cent. more seating accommodation for the services for the area in question.

Admiral Hefford states in his letter in your issue of April 5 that Camden Town Station, through which all traffic on the Edgware and Highgate branches, existing or projected, must pass, is already working to full capacity during the rush hours.

The trains on both Edgware and Highgate lines are at present confessedly very seriously overcrowded.

Will the linking up of these lines through the L.N.E.R. allow the passage of more traffic through the Camden Town bottleneck or will it merely allow the same amount of traffic to be drawn from different stations, giving perhaps a 26 per cent. increased quota to the Edgware district at the expense of nearer-in stations?

Further, there are at present 12 tube stations north of Camden Town. There are eight stations, in populous districts, on the unelectrified L.N.E.R. lines from Barnet and Edgware to Highgate, and it is proposed to erect a new tube station at Aldenham. When all these new districts are serviced with electric trains will the traffic conditions be better or worse?

Mr. Pick writes: "The built-up area has now extended much beyond Edgware, and the provision of the extension to Aldenham will deal with an existing traffic more conveniently."

In making the above statement Mr. Pick is completely misinformed. "Greater Edgware" has extended along the Watford By-pass almost to its junction with the Stanmore spur road and the ultimate house stands more than two miles from the proposed Aldenham site and less than one mile from Edgware Station, which itself is centrally placed in Edgware. Beyond this extension one house, and one only, has been built since the War on the line of the proposed railway, which after leaving Edgware runs for two miles through open country.

Mr. Pick says: " The Board would be glad if the Green Belt were completed across the Aldenham Station." If this is indeed so it is surprising that the Board's plans for the development of their own land immediately adjacent to the proposed station include the erection of shops. Further, it hardly appears practicable for public bodies to acquire, for sterilization, land round the proposed station at the greatly enhanced prices obtaining since the publication of the Board's plans.

Mr. Pick writes: " The extension of the railway from Edgware to Aldenham is necessary primarily to provide a new rolling stock depôt." This necessity is apparent, but, if it is indeed the prime object of the extension, it is difficult to understand why the Board rejected the alternative site for the sidings which was proposed to them and which lies just outside Edgware and on the line of their proposed extension. Their reasons must indeed be cogent, since—at a time when other projected works are being postponed on the score of economy—they prefer to extend their line a mile and three-quarters farther, to cut through a 100ft. contour, to fill in a lake, and to erect a station and shops in open country where they do not desire the creation of a new community.

Mr. Pick quite rightly points out that the Board's projects for North London must be considered as a whole and not in isolated parts. It is recognized that the rolling stock depôt is a necessary part of these projects, but Mr. Pick would surely not suggest that the abandonment of the proposed station at Aldenham would disorganize in any way any other part whatsoever of the Board's £13,000,000 programme.

Yours faithfully,

A. J. CHILD.

Heathbourne Cottage, Bushey Heath, Herts.

Other correspondents wrote directly to the Board, the contents of their letters ranging from mild anxiety to deep resentment. Some local residents expressed concern that the Board was projecting an already overburdened element of its system without due regard for improvements to the service provided. One Golders Green resident called for details of the Board's proposals in its attempts to reduce extreme travelling discomfort and suggested the lengthening of trains or quadrupling of tracks between Golders Green and Charing Cross as a possible solution. In threatening to take the issue to the Ministry of Transport, the correspondent described the Elstree Extension as a megalomaniacal project and was hopeful of its failure. A similar enquiry was received from a retired Royal Artillery Captain living in Glendale Avenue, Edgware. The Board's response to both gentlemen was to advise them of the alternative routes to the City and West End following electrification of the LNER route that would establish greatly augmented services from Edgware. New stock for the Morden–Edgware line was now becoming a distinct possibility and this too was offered as a future improvement.

The Captain's letter also contained a similar enquiry to others received regarding the division of Purcells Avenue by the extension. Two out of the four Avenue residents adjacent to the proposed railway engaged solicitors to pursue the question of the depreciation their properties might suffer. A similar approach was adopted by the owner of a house next to one of the complainants, but without the benefit of legal representation. The Board considered the properties affected as having been conveyed to the original developers by the Union Surplus Lands Company in 1928 on the understanding that the route of the railway had been known for some time. Yet there were some misgivings from the Board's Legal Officer who privately noted that the properties had been omitted from the Book of Reference drawn up to accompany the Bill through Parliament.

Inexplicably it was a resident of Glendale Avenue, Edgware who received a detailed response from the Board following his suggestion that the line should continue in cutting under Purcells Avenue. This issue had also been raised by two of the aforementioned residents living in the thoroughfare, who considered that the need for a footbridge would be obviated if the line were below road level and bridged to allow the continued passage of vehicular traffic. A member of the Chief Engineer's office staff reported that upon reaching the Watford By-Pass, the railway must either be 15 feet beneath the road or 20 feet above it. In elevating the railway, Purcells Avenue would be bisected approximately 4ft above the existing surface. Tunnelling beneath the By-Pass would result in the station being 35 feet lower than detailed in the parliamentary deposit. By lowering the elevation of the first station the planned 1 in 53 gradient encountered at its country end would increase to 1 in 38, considered prohibitive for inclines of more than a mile in length. This was a questionable statement when consideration is given to the improved specification of the new tube stock.

"We are here to-day to consider a matter of very vital interest to Edgware and other parts of Hendon," remarked the Chairman at the outset of his introductory remarks.

Mr. Jones expressed himself as being delighted with the great audience present, since it made clear that they on the platform had interpreted the wishes of a large section of the public in their attitude towards London Transport's proposals.

He explained that the meeting was organised by the Edgware Ratepayers' Association in conjunction with the Mill Hill Ratepayers' and Residents' Association and it was representative of churches, political bodies, the Chamber of Commerce, Rotary and the Townswomen's Guild among others. They all had one purpose: to lodge their protest against London Transport's proposed scheme.

The meeting would first consider the proposals contained in the Bill; then the ground of the objections would be stated; and finally suggestions would be made as to how the situation could be remedied.

Mr. Jones stressed that they did not object to the extension purely as an extension but because in their estimation it would have the effect of further congesting the Tube by creating a new centre of population.

The Chairman concluded by enumerating the proposals contained in the Transport Bill.

Mr. Taylor said they objected to the proposed extension of the Edgware Tube to Elstree because the line was already unable satisfactorily to carry the people seeking to use it.

The L.P.T.B. claimed that they needed the extension for the accommodation of rolling stock involved in the L.N.E.R. electrification.

He was informed that approximately £750,000 would be the cost of providing the extension.

A Disgrace

"Stables costing three-quarters of a million are a disgrace," said Mr. Taylor.

The objectors to the Bill were, he thought, in a strong position, because of the small population of Aldenham, which would become, were the extension allowed, "literally festooned with sidings."

Matter of Principle

Mr. Taylor said he looked upon it as a matter of principle.

The L.P.T.B. should not be allowed to extend continually outwards until they improved travelling conditions in London.

Another correspondent, residing in Warwick Avenue, Edgware urged the Board to build a station near the Broadfields Estate, having found only details of the terminus at Aldenham in his local paper. J P Thomas was at this time quite reluctant to supply additional information to the public regarding the siting of stations on the extension, although in reply he stated that the first would be roughly the same distance from Warwick Avenue as the Edgware terminus.

Writing to the Managing Director of London Transport, the Rector of Elstree Catholic Church sought information regarding the Board's intentions for future projections of the line beyond its Aldenham terminus. The opaque response he received initiated another letter recording a sighting of surveyors and engineers at work within a few hundred yards of his property in Shenley Road, Borehamwood which he thought might be affected by the coming of a railway. The Parliamentary Officer confirmed that the Board's engineers were not undertaking surveys in the area, which the confused clergyman found hard to accept.

'One out of 600 Approves Tube Extension' ran a headline in the Hendon, Cricklewood, Golders Green and Mill Hill edition of the *Hampstead and Burnt Oak Gazette* for Friday 12th March 1937'. 'Huge Protest Meeting at Edgware Passes Two Resolutions.' The report of the meeting, which was described as being one of the largest and most representative ever held in Edgware, listed considerable opposition to the Elstree Extension. The gathering had been organised by the Edgware Ratepayers'

Association in conjunction with similar bodies from the surrounding district. Such was the resistance that only one hand was raised in dissent when a resolution was moved to approve the action by Hendon Borough Council to oppose the extension. The objectors then endorsed a condition whereby the Board would be impelled to introduce a satisfactory scheme for improving travelling conditions between Hendon and the West End of London. A second motion called for the electrification of the LMS line from Elstree to St Pancras and its extension by a new tube from St Pancras to the West End. Added to this was a request for two new stations and unification of fares.

During the course of discussions at the meeting, it was mentioned that there was no real centre of population at Aldenham, a situation that was likely to be reversed following the coming of the 'tube'. Those assembled therefore recorded their determination not to allow the Board to create such a nucleus without first providing proper facilities for current commuters.

Described as a 'Voice from Aldenham' by the newspaper, Mr G A Riding, Headmaster of Aldenham School spoke of his displeasure at the proposal to fill in Little Aldenham Reservoir in order for the depot to be built. This would, he felt, have the effect of denying the beauty of the area to its many visitors. He then informed those present that there was very little chance of the Bill being blocked unless Counsel was briefed to contest it during the Committee stages.

One hand only was raised in dissent when the first resolution was put to the meeting. It was worded thus:

This Meeting fully endorses the action of the Hendon Borough Council in their decision to oppose the clause in the London Passenger Transport Board's Bill now before Parliament (which seeks power to extend the Tube Railway from Edgware to Aldenham, near Elstree) until such time as the London Passenger Transport Board puts into practice a satisfactory scheme for improving the utterly inadequate travelling facilities that now exist between the Borough of Hendon and the West End of London.

In a study of the carrying capacity of the Tube they had to look to such stations as Euston, Tottenham Court Road, Leicester Square and Goodge Street.

"The situation at Tottenham Court Road is almost beyond words.

"We used to laugh at Parisians in their Metro. I don't think our Tube is a bit better."

At present there was no real centre of population at Aldenham, but with a Tube serving that area there soon would be. They were determined not to allow London Transport to create a new centre of population without first providing proper facilities for present travellers to town.

Concluding, Mr. Taylor said he looked for their unanimous support when the resolutions were put to the meeting.

Moving the first resolution, Mr. Arnot said he considered Hendon travellers even less fortunate than their Edgware fellows. At Edgware, there was at least some chance of obtaining a seat, but by the time trains reached Hendon Central via Burnt Oak, a densely populated area, and Colindale there was standing room only!

"If you've got a grouse in Edgware, then we've got a greater grouse. I see there is a representative of the Hampstead Ratepayers' Association present here to-night. Well, God help them!

"Are we going to tolerate this any more?" Mr. Arnot asked the huge audience.

"No," was the unanimous answer.

The L.P.T.B., said Mr. Arnot, was a monopoly.

"Are they doing their duty by the travelling public of this district?"

"No," answered the audience once more.

Mr. Arnot urged them to use all possible influence to block the Transport Bill. If any of them had friends who were Members of Parliament they should persuade them to oppose London Transport's scheme.

Extracts from the *Hampstead and Burnt Oak Gazette* dated 12th March 1937.

The London and Home Counties Traffic Advisory Committee noted the Board's proposals at its meeting held on 17th March. During the proceedings, its Secretary read a letter from the National Citizen's Union detailing its members' protest against the Elstree Extension. This was made on the ground that this would bring more traffic to the Hampstead tube and aggravate the position at Golders Green station.

Objections to the extension continued through the consultation process and beyond. On 7th January 1937, the Board rolled out its big guns in order to meet a deputation comprising all local councils and the seemingly omnipresent G A Riding, Headmaster of Aldenham School. Their concerns ranged mainly over the issues previously recorded, although the Board received a mild rebuke for failing to consult with local authorities before proceeding with its Bill. Suggestions that the railway should stop short of Aldenham Reservoir or continue to Bushey with no intermediate stations at Elstree or Bushey Heath provided a new topic for debate. However Pick stated that the Board did not possess the financial resources for further projection of the railway but should this become possible, the line would only ever be extended as far as Bushey.

With continued resistance regarding the extension, it was surprising that any supporting evidence from an individual would ever be submitted. Nevertheless, Mr J P C Done of Done Hunter and Company, issued a masterly report, his firm having a pecuniary interest as agent for Major Nichol and All Souls College, the two major landowners in the area. Done stated that his clients had experienced many opportunities for selling portions of their estates during the past few years but had declined as they wished to reserve their lands for a better class of development. Done reasoned that if no railway had been contemplated then approximately half of the lands would have already been sold. However the anticipated construction of the Elstree Extension had restrained all such notion pending the possibility of his clients maintaining control of their property by establishing leasehold arrangements.

All Souls College and Colonel Nichol also owned most of the land beyond the sites of the first and second stations and here both parties were anxious to preserve the neighbourhood from indiscriminate building. Land situated between the Watford By-Pass and Watling Street had therefore been reserved for houses to the value of £2,000 upwards, speculative builders being unsuccessful in purchasing any part of the square mile site. Plans for the area ranged from three to four houses per acre in the privately owned plots, to eight houses per acre in a town-planned situation on land owned by the College and the Colonel.

In response to the concerns of Hendon Council that the proposed extension would force up the price of land for the Green Belt scheme, the College agreed that current market prices would apply at the time of sale. The co-operation between the Board and the two landowners was considered paramount if proper development control was to be maintained and in consequence the Board had been provided with land for the railway at a nominal amount.

Done also touched upon the criticism levelled at the Board whereby its proposals for the Elstree Extension would interfere with the amentities of the district. This presumed that those living in established residences were entitled to prevent expansion in order that they might enjoy rural exclusion. He contended the area would be eventually developed with or without the new line, those currently not dependent on its construction presumably having use of a motor car.

Done's report noted that Harrow UDC had objected to the stopping up of two local footpaths in the vicinity of Aldenham Reservoir on the site reserved for the new depot. However, he considered this unfounded as the paths had been established for farm labourers but now had become exclusively trodden by the feet of weekend ramblers who would suffer no hardship by their curtailment.

The Bill came before a Select Committee of the House of Commons on 16th March 1937, under the chairmanship of Sir David Reid and, after a hearing that lasted six days, was passed without amendment. The Elstree Extension went unopposed, local council objections being reserved for the Lords pending negotiations.

On 26th April, the House of Commons met to debate a motion to reject the Bill in the report stage. The main points raised in support of the motion were:

a. Overcrowding on the Morden–Edgware Line, which, it was maintained, would not be relieved to any appreciable extent by the Board's proposals.
b. The disparity of fares on the Edgware and Stanmore lines.
c. The despoiling of amenities at Aldenham.

But the Board was fortunate in that the Bill was supported by the Member for Hendon, Sir Reginald Blair, who gave details of the proposals for relieving congestion on the Morden–Edgware Line. He also supplied valid reasons for Aldenham being selected as the site for the new depot.

Blair had been well briefed by the Board after he had forwarded a newspaper cutting of the meeting held in Edgware on 9th March. He stated that whilst prepared to hear representations from local authorities, he did not favour a press campaign and requested relevant information that would enable him deal with questions at meetings.

Armed with sufficient facts, Blair attended the Commons debate in which he was supported by the Member for Hampstead and a member from the original Select Committee. The Permanent Secretary to the Ministry of Transport concluded the proceedings with further details of the Board's Scheme of New Works and suggested that objections to the Elstree Extension be dealt with before a Committee of the House of Lords. Pressed to a division, a motion to defeat the Bill was lost by 134 votes to 55.

The Bill reached the House of Lords for its first reading on 29th April 1937 and came before a Select Committee on Tuesday 8th June. Discussion on the Elstree Extension continued into the third day of the four-day hearing and produced fierce but enlightening debate. Now was the critical moment for the protestations of Hertfordshire County Council and Harrow Urban District Council to be aired, both having briefed Counsel to support their petitions. During his opening remarks, Counsel engaged by the Board, stated that there would be a requirement of 515 cars of new stock to operate services on the two routes from Edgware to the City and West End together with the electrified branches to Alexandra Palace and Barnet. Of this number, 175 would be accommodated at Aldenham, the remainder stabled at Golders Green (175), Drayton Park (40) and Edgware (125), all transferring to the new depot at regular intervals for three-weekly inspections. Major overhauls, however, would still be undertaken at Acton Works.

In promoting the construction of Aldenham Depot, Counsel stated that the old depots at Golders Green and 'Greatham Park' were old fashioned and quite inadequate to deal with the rolling stock required for the extended system. There can be no doubt that Greatham Park was a slip of the tongue for Drayton Park.

Frank Pick was called to give evidence on the first day of the proceedings and was soon providing statistical information about the Elstree Extension. He considered the site of the Aldenham terminus, at approximately 13½ miles from Charing Cross, equated with the extremity of other lines recently electrified and constructed; Cockfosters being 12½, Hounslow 13½ and South Harrow 14. Despite having these figures at his fingertips, Pick's geography failed him when he placed Cockfosters on the Bakerloo Line, but nobody noticed. To further emphasise his point, Pick maintained that terminals set at these distances were capable of being reached in an approximate but effective journey time of thirty minutes from the City and West End.

This aerial view of Cockfosters was included in the LPTB's 1937 Bill for the Aldenham extension. The track layout and design of the terminal station have many similarities with those planned for the Northern Line extension.

Pick considered the construction of the Elstree Extension to be one of extreme urgency estimating that the number of cars required to operate the northern services might soon increase from 515 to 550. With a requirement of a site for the new depot of approximately three-quarters of a mile in length and an area of 40 acres, there was none more suitable than that adjacent to Aldenham Reservoir. A further prerequisite dictated an entirely level location. The new trains included a specification for axle roller bearings and Pick suggested that even a slight gradient of 1 in 300, might be responsible for instances of unsupervised stock movements, a surprising comment on a new design. As previously recorded, the cost of the depot would be £270,000, the figure being separately calculated as it could not be exclusively charged to the construction of the extension.

To stress the importance of the Board's double-ended, progressive depot policy, Pick provided details of the service failures which had occurred on the Piccadilly Line in the years 1930–1932 ostensibly due to single-ended depot operation. During the period, there were three failures and delays per 100,000 service car miles. However with the introduction of double-ended depots and the daytime servicing of cars under the progressive system, the years 1934–36 showed a failure rate per 100,000 car miles of 1⅓ representing a reduction of over 50%.

During exchanges, information emerged regarding the agreement reached with Bushey Urban District Council in connection with its town-planning proposals. These had been drawn up in anticipation of the railway being built, and provision made for the terminus at the junction of Elstree Road with the Watford By-Pass. Similar negotiations had also been conducted with All Souls College, Oxford regarding the siting of the first station in the proximity of a new housing estate.

When questioned about the site of the first station, Pick pointed out that it was located in the Borough of Hendon, from which no objections had been received. Nevertheless he asserted the station would provide a convenient road/rail interchange facility and that it would be foolish not to build a station at such an important intersection. Indeed Pick was quite open about the problems experienced by the Board in erecting stations in side roads, where resiting had been the only satisfactory response. He cited Uxbridge as one example, where the station was then currently being moved 600 yards to the High Street following the demolition of a large block of property. A similar situation had existed at Osterley where the original station had been abandoned in favour of a new site on the Great West Road. Quick to promote the Board's contribution to a reduction in the amount of traffic from roads leading to the capital, Pick mentioned that the new Osterley and Uxbridge stations had been designed with parking provision for a sizeable number of cars. Similar facilities were planned for all three stations on the new extension.

With gentle examination from the Board's Counsel, Pick tried to allay fears regarding the despoiling of the area surrounding Aldenham Reservoir which apparently was one of the few nesting sites of the great crested grebe. The beauty spot, favoured by bathers according to his personal observations, would be left untouched; only part of the smaller reservoir would be dammed and partially filled in. To prevent the depot from becoming an eyesore, it was the intention of the Board to plant poplar trees along the margins of the site. This action emulated that taken at Morden, where the depot had been built on parkland, and Cockfosters, where the depot had been erected along the boundary of the Trent Park home of Sir Philip Sassoon. When questioned about the Green Belt proposals, Pick confirmed the Board would be pleased if the area around the depot and terminal station were so established. However, he adjudged as ridiculous a suggestion by Harrow Council that there should be no stations on the extension.

Counsel acting for Hertfordshire County and Harrow Urban District Councils then undertook cross-examination of the Vice-Chairman. In the opening round of questions, he was asked to comment upon the accepted hypothesis that when railway stations were built, a population is immediately created. Pick responded that earlier extensions had been constructed before purposeful town planning had been introduced. He added that the undesirable effect of indiscriminate building on the local authorities and the Board had been eradicated in this instance due to the existence of a scheme that would control any development taking place in the vicinity of the terminus. Pick stated that the Board was often urged by people to build new railways and it was a most unusual circumstance that here the opposite applied.

At the time of the initial promotion of the Bill, a decision was taken at Board level not to continue the line to Bushey. This had resulted in the terminal station being designed to provide good road/rail interchange facilities with subways giving direct access to the station in addition to providing a safe crossing of all converging roads. Similar interchange facilities were envisaged for the penultimate station, which would serve the film studios at Borehamwood. Rising to Counsel's challenge that film stars did not travel by tube, Pick retorted that their countless supernumeraries did.

It will be recalled that the Board had investigated three alternative sites where its new depot might be situated; that between East Finchley and Finchley Central deemed unsuitable, the Mill Hill sites (presumably counted as one) unavailable, and that at Edgwarebury claimed to be too small to allow the construction of a double-ended depot. However, Counsel thought he had three alternative sites to suggest to Pick. The first was the LNER station site at Edgware, which Pick immediately dismissed. He informed his inquisitor that an arrangement had been entered into with the LNER whereby it would combine its station facilities on one site and allow the Board use of the former goods yard for siding accommodation. The second suggested site encompassed the area reserved for the first station which was immediately deemed unsuitable as the railway would be following a high level course at this point. The third site was at Edgwarebury and had been surveyed by the Board in April 1937 as third in the trio of locations previously mentioned. Pick's deposition invalidated the site as it comprised just a quarter-mile of level land where that at Aldenham could provide the required length of approximately three quarters of a mile. However, there is room for some argument here. In responding to a letter from an objector regarding the severing of Purcells Avenue, stress was placed on the need for the railway to traverse the thoroughfare about four feet above the road surface in order to reach the height required to cross the Watford By-Pass. If the line had continued in cutting, as correspondents suggested, it would run beneath the By-Pass, a point that could easily have strengthened the hand of W R Davidge when called as a witness.

William Robert Davidge appeared during the enquiry to support objections raised in the petition of Hertfordshire County Council, in his capacity as a Town Planning Consultant. The main thrust of his evidence reflected upon his opinion that there were several suitable sites in the vicinity of Edgware where a new depot could be constructed. However, any furtherance of this theme would have rendered his evidence inadmissible, alternative schemes requiring, at the very least, the attendance of the landowners whose property was affected. Nevertheless questioning was allowed to continue in respect of the Edgwarebury site as this had been rejected as unsatisfactory by Frank Pick earlier in the proceedings. Davidge concluded that should the extension to Aldenham be abandoned, the line could be curtailed and a station built adjacent to Spur Road at a much lower level, where there also appeared to be an abundance of available land for the depot. This would obviate the need for further projection of the line and with it the cost of boring an expensive tunnel beneath Elstree Hill. He maintained that the line could be taken under the Watford By-Pass, the gradients beyond Edgware station being slightly reduced to compensate. This proposal became the subject of great debate when the Board's Counsel contended the railway must be at a height of twenty feet above the By-Pass. Davidge, more experienced in the field of surveying, maintained height was unnecessary if his plans were adopted for a ground level depot at Edgwarebury. As he had only walked the site and had yet to conduct an inspection using professional equipment, Counsel immediately discounted any promotion of an unsurveyed area.

The interrogation of Henry Hemley, Vice-Chairman of Bushey Urban District Council, furnished a number of interesting disclosures. At the time, the population of Bushey was placed at 14,000 and housing development was reported as continuing in the direction of the projected terminal station at Aldenham. Town planning of the area had been undertaken in 1925 and 1934 by the Urban District Council, its members being led to believe that Hertfordshire County Council had been expecting the construction of the railway along the route of the Watford and Edgware. In its 1934 town plan, Bushey had allowed for the railway to terminate at its centre but there appears to have been a lack of any campaigning for it. Land at Clay Hill, Bushey, where the north end of Ashfield Avenue has since been built, was among that inherited by the LPTB.

The evidence of J H Done, as agent for the All Souls Estate reiterated much of his earlier deposition in support of the new railway. He remained of the opinion that development of the area surrounding the first station had been delayed due entirely to anticipation of the railway, this practice being demonstrated for almost a decade by some landowners. Indeed their investments had paid off; land worth £500 per acre eight years previously was now valued at between £800 and £900. This could easily have influenced the decision of the Board not to build its new depot within the area, having presumably instructed Counsel to oppose most strongly Davidge's similar proposal. Reference was made to a sign installed by a speculative builder which read: '92 acres for sale on the Edgwarebury House Estate adjoining station on proposed tube railway with space for 550 to 600 houses with 18,000 feet of frontage.'

The Select Committee approved the Elstree Extension subject to receiving an undertaking that offers made during the negotiation stage would be implemented namely:

1. To construct passenger subways beneath Watford By-Pass.
2. To provide a bus lay-by and car park at the terminal station.
3. To provide a screen of trees for Aldenham depot.

Nine witnesses had been called during the hearing, among them Sir Theodore Chambers, who appeared in his capacity as Vice Chairman of the Hertfordshire Society, and who deeply opposed the construction of the railway as it was likely to establish a new centre of population. Presumably having recently entered the language, the phrase 'dormitory town' was used extensively by Counsel throughout the proceedings to describe this type of development.

There can be no doubt that much activity took place in both camps in the intervening period between the Bill receiving approval of the Select Committee on 11th June and its third and final reading in the House of Lords. Deep discussion took place between W R Davidge and Lord Brocket, Chairman of the Hertfordshire Society, in a final attempt to prevent the Elstree Extension penetrating the County. Davidge, presumably anxious to redeem some of his reputation, provided additional information for his Lordship, which could have easily brought about the demise of the Bill as it reached the final hurdle.

Lord Ashfield, Chairman of the LPTB, was present during the final debate on 14th July and was able to respond to a myriad of questions and comments put forward by Members. Lord Brockett proved his most prolific opponent stating that the second reading (Select Committee) must have slipped through while he was away.

Brocket followed with an accusation that the Board must have employed sleight of hand to acquire land for the extension by taking over another Company (the Watford and Edgware). Ashfield's response was that the Board had agreed to sell any surplus lands for the purposes of Green Belt at the original asking price. He also added cynically that green belts would be useless unless they could be easily accessed.

Lord Brocket then stated that he knew of another site for the depot, outside the restriction imposed by the Green Belt. Drawn up by W R Davidge, Brocket's alternative deviated beyond the site of the first station (the location of which would remain) and curve up the valley towards Edgwarebury, terminating on site adjacent to the LMS main line. This line was one mile shorter than that proposed in the Bill with easier gradients and curves of the same minimum radius. At the Brocket/Davidge terminus, a large tract of level land would be available for the construction of a depot. In promoting this new site, the antagonists knew that they would be invalidating the Board's main objection for a depot at Edgwarebury, where the unevenness of the terrain helped bring about its swift demise during the Select Committee proceedings.

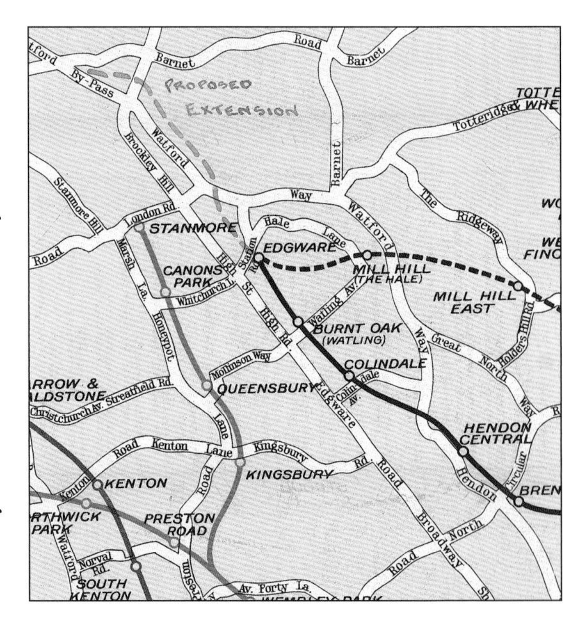

The No.1 1937 geographical Underground map included the authorised extensions of the Northern Line to Alexandra Palace, Barnet and Edgware via Mill Hill but not the planned extension north of Edgware, not yet authorised. Some copies of this map were altered by hand to accompany submissions to Parliament.

Ashfield had already had his own survey of the area carried out and deemed the Brocket/Davidge proposal totally inadequate. His comment was no doubt prompted by the Board having made significant land purchases to correspond with the planned route of the railway and the possibility of further extension towards Watford. Lord Erne supported the original proposal stating that the Government's view was that the necessity for the proposed extension and depot had already been established. To refuse the necessary powers would delay and might jeopardise the whole scheme of urgently needed improvements.

Nevertheless, Brocket pursued his route revision during the debate in the Upper House even going so far as to request a fourteen-day adjournment to allow time for a joint LPTB/Davidge survey to be conducted. With this appeal denied, Lord Brocket carried his amendment to a division but saw it defeated by 53 votes to 24. Read for a third time, the Bill received Royal Assent on 20th July 1937.

Magnanimous in defeat, Brocket agreed with the statement made by Ashfield that railways should be provided at locations convenient to the public. He then sarcastically added that he was aware that only one house had been built within a mile and a half of the proposed terminus since the Great War.

A 1937 Underground poster map showing the proposed extension to Elstree. No publicity was given initially to the planned intermediate stations.

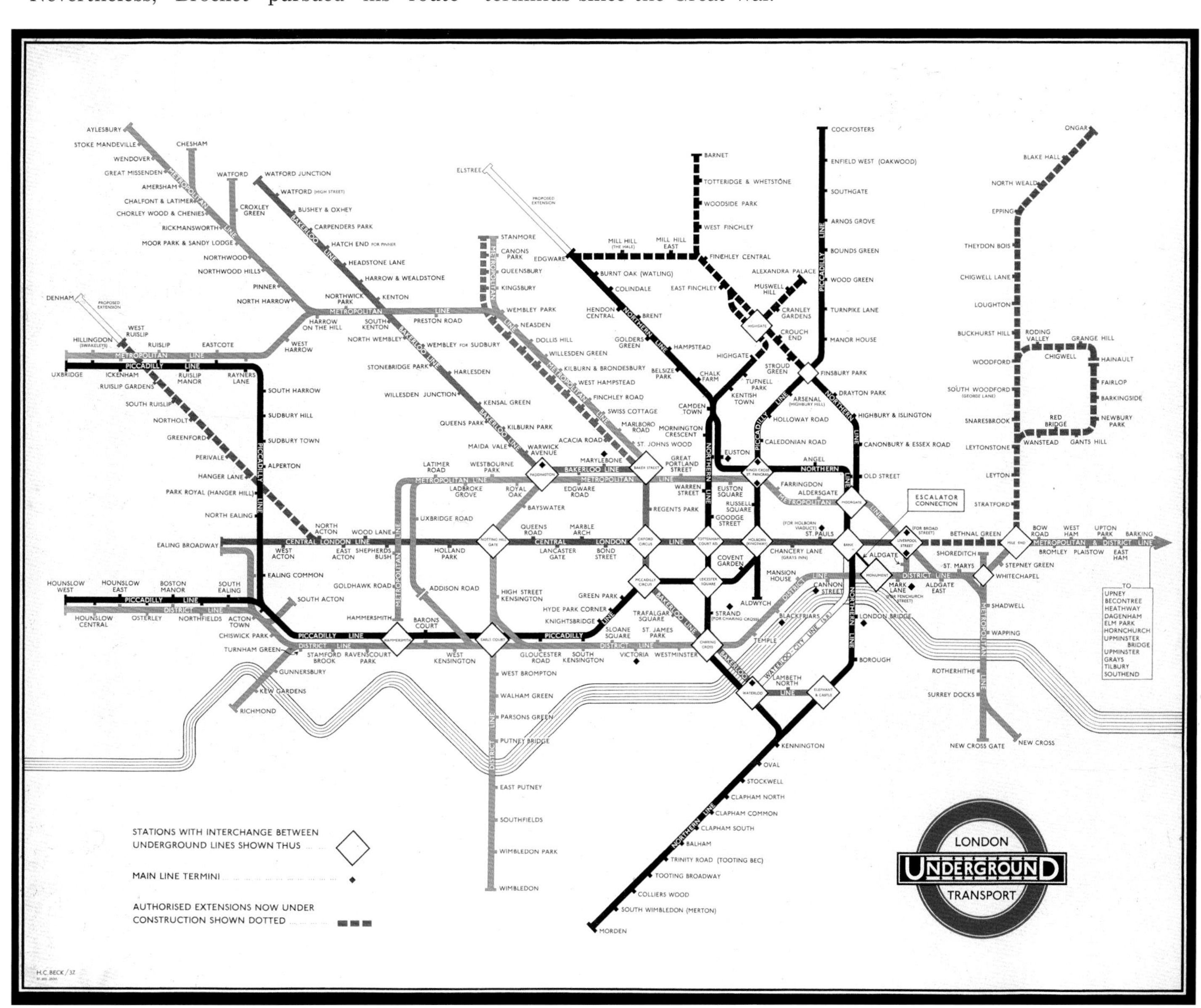

CHAPTER SIX

Elstree Extension Developments

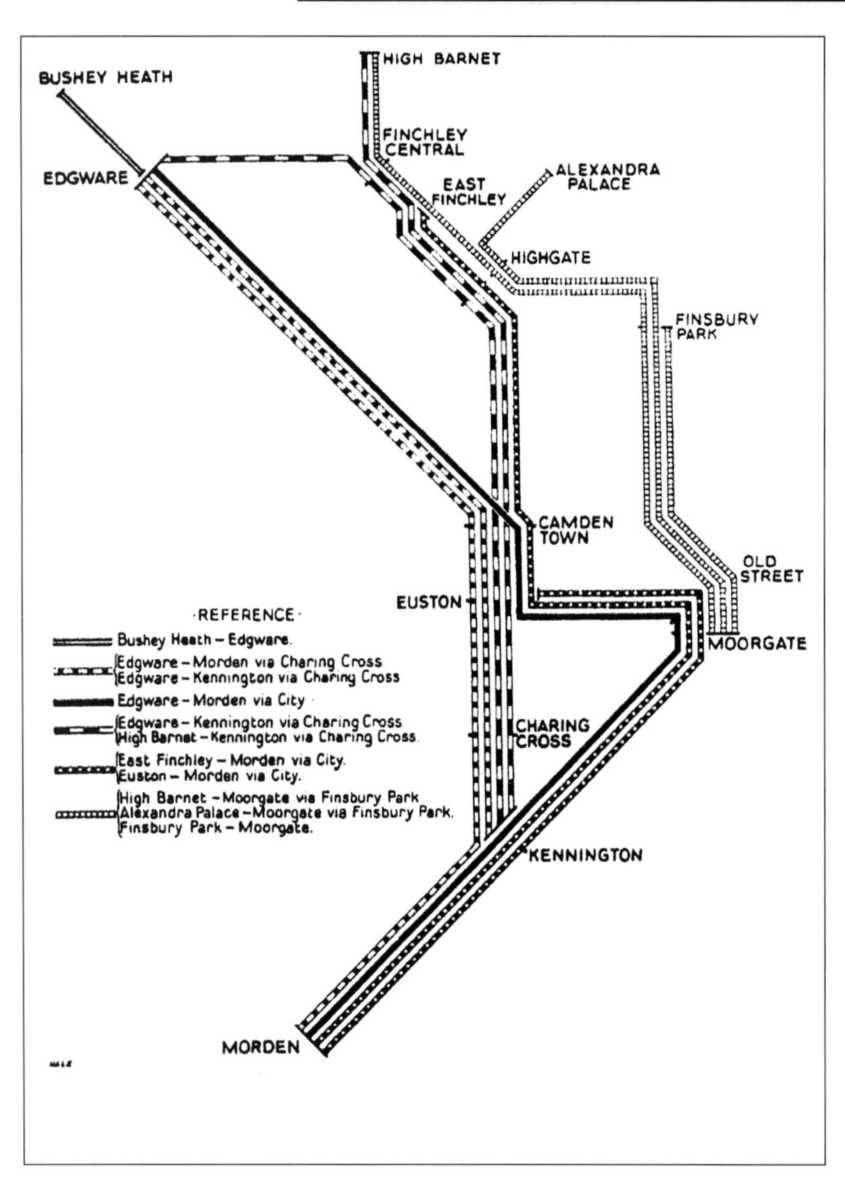

Once the London Passenger Transport Board had secured powers to build the Elstree Extension, it was required to submit a scheme of work to the Ministry of Transport to be appended to the 1935–40 New Works Programme. A document was subsequently compiled which corresponded mainly with the formal statement made at the time of the deposit of the 1937 Bill in Parliament, although access to Aldenham Depot was now given as the primary reason for construction. Nevertheless, the report suggested that the new length of line should bring in a satisfactory return on capital expenditure, which would help balance less remunerative works included in the programme.

For some time, it has been popularly held that the Elstree Extension would initially operate as a shuttle service. Yet, during the author's researches no document has come to light to substantiate this presupposition. The shuttle operation theory probably arises from an article in *Modern Transport* for 9th April 1938 describing close headway operation and illustrated with a diagram (reproduced left) showing the projected train services for the Northern Line. From such evidence, it could easily be assumed that the Elstree Extension would function independently. However, when the diagram made a second appearance in the same journal dated 23rd July 1938, the accompanying article included a statement that 'services to Bushey Heath remain to be decided'. In fact, operation of the Extension was the subject of indecision for some time. During 1934, it will be recalled, Frank Pick had implied that all City-bound traffic from Edgware would be routed via Highgate.

The layout of the southern approaches to Edgware station therefore became pivotal to the pattern of service eventually adopted. In October 1935, the Engineering Committee received details of the track plan produced for submission in the Board's extensive 1936 Bill, which sought approval for the majority of the work within the 1935–40 New Works Programme. Conversely, the electrification and doubling of the route between Finchley Central and Edgware were amongst the proposals contained in the 1936 London and North Eastern Railway (London Transport) Bill. The twice-hourly steam hauled service on this length of line would be replaced by tube trains of increased frequency diverted into the LPTB station at Edgware via a new linking curve. This connection, powers for which were sought in the Board's 1936 Bill, would allow introduction of a passenger service on the extension originating from the Highgate branch. January 1936 brought the first proposed amendment, giving passenger trains travelling via Golders Green access to the extension, necessary to meet the requirement for the through running of empty stock from both branches. The following July, with the Board's approval to build the extension just days away, Pick was able to annotate a document '*Elstree Extension. If and when, trains to depart (Edgware) from Highgate side only*'

In September 1936, further revision to the track layout at Edgware was issued to provide a new connection that would allow trains working through to Aldenham depot from the Hampstead line direct access to the Elstree Extension. No doubt influencing the path of the new link was the ease in overcoming the obstacle caused by the existence of the LNER line to Edgware. When the track formation of this route had been laid some seventy years earlier, it had been necessary to span a watercourse known as Dean's Brook and the depression in which it flowed, as the line neared its terminus. With careful adaptation, which involved boxing in the river, the Board's engineers could project the new length of line beyond the LNER branch using the existing bridge. The revision resulted in a loss of sidings in the fork created within the divergence of the connecting curve, the remaining accommodation considered sufficient in view of that to be provided by the new depot at Aldenham.

Schemes for the development of Edgware station were not confined to track alterations. In February 1937, Theodore Thomas, newly appointed General Manager (Road Transport), submitted a memorandum advocating a doubling of the forecourt area to allow satisfactory bus operation. The Board's Estate Agent was therefore asked to pursue the purchase of properties situated between the existing forecourt and the LNER station yard. The second part of this ambitious proposal suggested consideration be given to moving the station further east above the running lines. In so doing the depth of the existing forecourt could be increased with an exit established through the site of the existing bus garage into Station Road, via a new road built in conjunction with the LNER.

Facing page **This plan was probably responsible in promoting the notion that the extension would be operated as a shuttle service. In fact, at the time this diagram made its appearance in *Modern Transport*, 9th April 1938, plans had already been formulated for the layout at Edgware in order to cope with traffic entering or leaving the branch. Later revelations in the same periodical asserted that no firm decision had been made regarding the pattern of train service to Bushey Heath.**

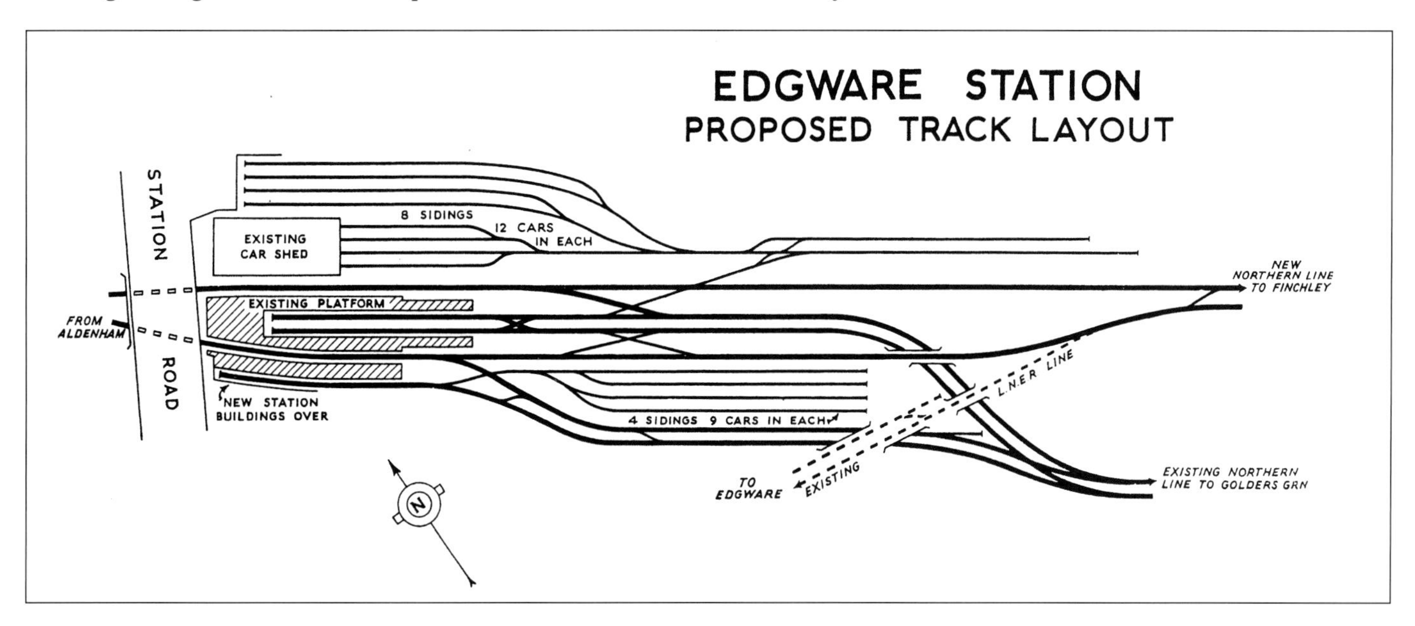

Facing page **On 16th July 1936, the London Passenger Transport Board formally approved the Elstree Extension, following an abortive attempt to secure land to build a new depot in the Mill Hill area. This plan produced within five weeks of that decision shows the original scheme applied to the station layout at Edgware. Here direct access to the extension would be from a new connection to the electrified LNER line from Finchley, passengers arriving at the erstwhile terminus via Golders Green being obliged to change trains. A garage for commuters, perhaps similar to the one at Morden, appears on the plan.**

There was now a lull in the proceedings whilst the 1937 Bill was debated in Parliament but within a few weeks of it entering the statute books, the track layout at Edgware was once more back on the agenda. Now was the time to consider operation of nine-car trains and in consequence the track configuration at Edgware was again reviewed and simplified. J P Thomas was given the task of identifying economies that could be made by constructing five sidings to the west of the station for trains of seven-car configuration only and modifying the construction of platforms.

October 1937 brought further change in arrangements at Edgware, revised by A R Cooper to provide a common platform for passengers travelling south. More significantly, alterations to the track layout allowed for trains from Golders Green to traverse the extension although it would still be possible to work Highgate trains through during the off peak hours. But the Board had a problem due to the additional distance of 1.27 miles using the Edgware–Highgate route to the City and West End, compared with the existing route via Golders Green. This disparity of distance would add six minutes to the journey time and J P Thomas was asked to consider whether, by the omission or non-stopping of stations, the journey time on both routes could be equated. Unfortunately, no record of his findings has been traced. Throwing another spanner in the works, the Engineering Committee deemed the latest track plan unacceptable and Cooper was requested to reverse it in order to allow Highgate trains to use the extension by the installation of a flyunder, the common southbound platform being retained.

Cooper's response was swift and his plan met the Committee's mandate in the use of a flyunder to allow the southbound Highgate line to be carried beneath its northbound counterpart. Problems surrounded this latest proposal, for it only provided a single line connection for Golders Green trains running to the depot. In addition, it would cause the reversal of northbound and southbound tracks north of the station, with steeper gradients and difficult access to the sidings. A conclusion was soon reached that no layout could be devised which gave the facilities required without suffering some disadvantage, and consequently Cooper's earlier proposal was recommended for acceptance.

But in the current climate of debate and modification, there could be little doubt that the Chief Engineer's plan would not be without alteration. J P Thomas voiced his disapproval by stating that it did not provide sufficient facilities for reversing the anticipated heavy service at Edgware and prevented access to the sidings planned for the west side of the site. Cooper's new plan, drawn up in order to address his colleague's criticism, allowed use of the existing Golders Green line to reach sidings and a relief platform at Edgware, which was accepted as the best response in meeting all requirements. Graff-Baker then expressed his concern about the existence of lengthy rail gaps, which would delay the acceleration of trains due to a loss of power. In an attempt to reduce this effect, Cooper was asked to work with Graff-Baker who, presumably pacified, was amongst those giving approval to the final track layout on 6th December 1937.

The turn of the year saw further examination of Theodore Thomas's earlier proposals for a significant remodelling of Edgware station forecourt. An alternative was placed before the Engineering Committee on 9th January by V A M Robertson to support his proposal for a cheapening of the project. His scheme, subsequently approved, retained as much of the original station as would not be interfered with by engineering works with remaining sections of the building dismantled and re-erected after completion. This proposal no doubt pleased Stanley Heaps, on whose earlier designs the station entrance and forecourt were based. Heaps observed that the barrel roof installed above the third platform in 1931 was unsatisfactory as the retaining walls did not follow a straight line. In consequence a decision was taken to provide a pitched roof to match those already in situ.

Robertson's revised plan envisaged using the road to the former LT bus garage for taxis and private cars for which provision would be made at the rear of the station buildings. In removing this traffic away from the front of the station, no difficulties were anticipated in using the existing forecourt for the operation of central bus services after the completion of the railway extension.

J P Thomas sent a memorandum to Pick on 1st February 1937 regarding the names for the stations on the extension and thereby instigated a series of exchanges, which was not finally resolved until May of the following year. Thomas's original suggestions were North Edgware for the first station at 0.85 miles

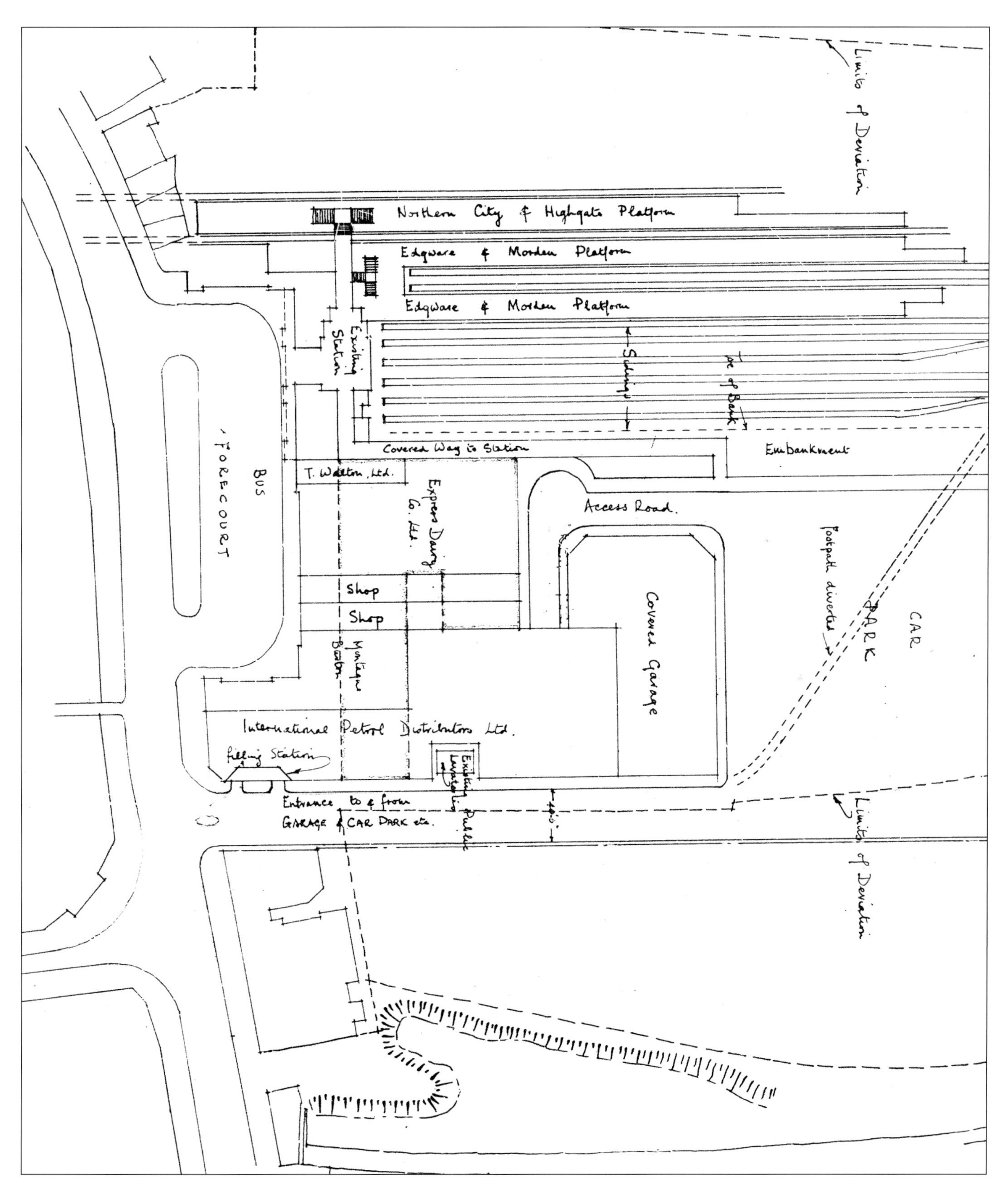
Limits of Deviation
Northern City & Highgate Platform
Edgware & Morden Platform
Edgware & Morden Platform
Existing Station
Sidings
Toe of Bank
Covered Way to Station
Embankment
BUS FORECOURT
T. Walton, Ltd.
Express Dairy Co. Ltd.
Access Road.
Shop
Shop
Covered Garage
Footpath diverted
CAR PARK
Montague Burton
International Petrol Distributors Ltd.
filling Station
Existing Public Lavatories
Entrance to & from
GARAGE & CAR PARK etc.
Limits of Deviation

At the time the LPTB Bill was debated by a Select Committee of the House of Lords, names applied to the stations on the Elstree Extension were still to be settled. Lord Ashfield had suggested Edgebury as a shortened alternative of the three-syllable Edgwarebury. Elstree had yet to gain the suffix 'South' and Aldenham was yet to be renamed Bushey Heath. This map which was provided to the members of the Select Committee and Counsel, shows, with some clarity, the short encroachment of the line into the County of Hertford made necessary by the siting of the terminus at the junction of Elstree Road and the Watford By-Pass. It was this minor incursion that led to considerable debate within the House of Lords, from which Lord Ashfield emerged victorious.

beyond Edgware, and Elstree Hill for the second station located 0.42 miles from the centre of Elstree Village. The actual position of the terminal station was 1 mile from the centre of Elstree Village, 1¼ miles from Bushey Heath, 2 miles from Borehamwood and 3¼ miles from Aldenham Village. A few names which Thomas felt were descriptive of its location were West Elstree, Caldecote Hill (formerly Caldecott), South Aldenham and Aldenham.

The Traffic Committee recommended the stations should be named Edgwarebury, Elstree and Aldenham respectively; all of which were used extensively throughout the planning stage. Thomas was asked to write to the local authorities and other parties concerned with a view to the acceptance of these names. In view of their gift of land for railway construction, the Board's Estate Agent was requested to inform the governors for All Souls College of the proposal to name the first station Edgwarebury, and invite possible alternatives. However, there were some misgivings within the Board regarding the lengthy three-syllable name bestowed upon the first station. Lord Ashfield put forward 'Edgebury' and Pick supported his suggestion replying that it was in the right tradition of the Anglo-Saxon language adding 'always abridge and simplify to help the common people'. Around the time of adoption of this shortened name, the Board's 1937 Bill was about to be considered by a House of Lords Select Committee and it was therefore used throughout the proceedings.

All Souls College had been notified of the Board's proposal to name the first station Edgwarebury and instructed its estate agents Messrs Done, Hunter and Co to approve the name. The agents were soon notified about the Chairman's suggested abbreviation and their reply recorded their client's disappointment that the original name was about to be unnecessarily condensed. Feelings ran high; the College considered the name suggested by the Chairman would have no association with the locality, be mispronounced 'Eggbury' and was no less and indeed more likely to be confused with Edgware than Edgwarebury. The estate agents further suggested that if the name Edgwarebury was definitely ruled out, Brockley Hill might be substituted as the position of the station would then relate to a well-known locality. J P Thomas had some misgivings. He reported to the Board's Traffic Committee that Brockley Hill was one mile distant from the proposed station and might be confused with Brockley on the Southern Railway.

Decisions regarding the names of the stations were not transmitted to the local authorities in view of the initial protest received. Those suggested by the Traffic Committee were used in all issues relating to the planning of the line and it was not until the end of the year that the next round began. On 16th December 1937, the Clerk for Bushey and Watford (Rural) Joint Town Planning Committee, Sidney Payne, wrote to Frank Pick suggesting that the terminal station be called Bushey Heath and Aldenham, if the latter name was to be retained at all.

Frank Pick replied that the name had been selected as all main line railways and the Board were in a common pool of traffic and that it was important for stations to carry distinctive names (conveniently overlooking that the name Elstree proposed for the penultimate station had been duplicated). He also mentioned that the LMS already had a station named Bushey and that, in order to provide an individual name, the Board had been compelled to use Aldenham. In denying the use of either Bushey or Bushey Heath for the station, Pick stated that the Board would not object to the suffix 'for Bushey' or 'for Bushey Heath' being added to its title.

Payne was also in correspondence with J P Thomas on the same topic. He stated that the Council would like the station to be named Bushey and Aldenham, as it would be the only station situated within the Urban District. Bushey and Oxhey station was located in the Borough of Watford and, according to Payne, led to endless confusion – a statement that he failed to qualify.

Whilst the Battle of Bushey continued, a general consensus of opinion arrived at the name Brockley Hill for the station at Edgwarebury, the reason for the alteration being attributed to possible confusion with Edgware in the minds of the travelling public. Pick strongly suggested that the station be named All Souls. However, Alec Valentine, now Commercial Manager, could not agree stating that All Souls did not appear a very happy name. He also tried to diffuse the disagreement surrounding the naming of the terminus by suggesting Lake or Lakeside, due to its proximity to an expanse of water.

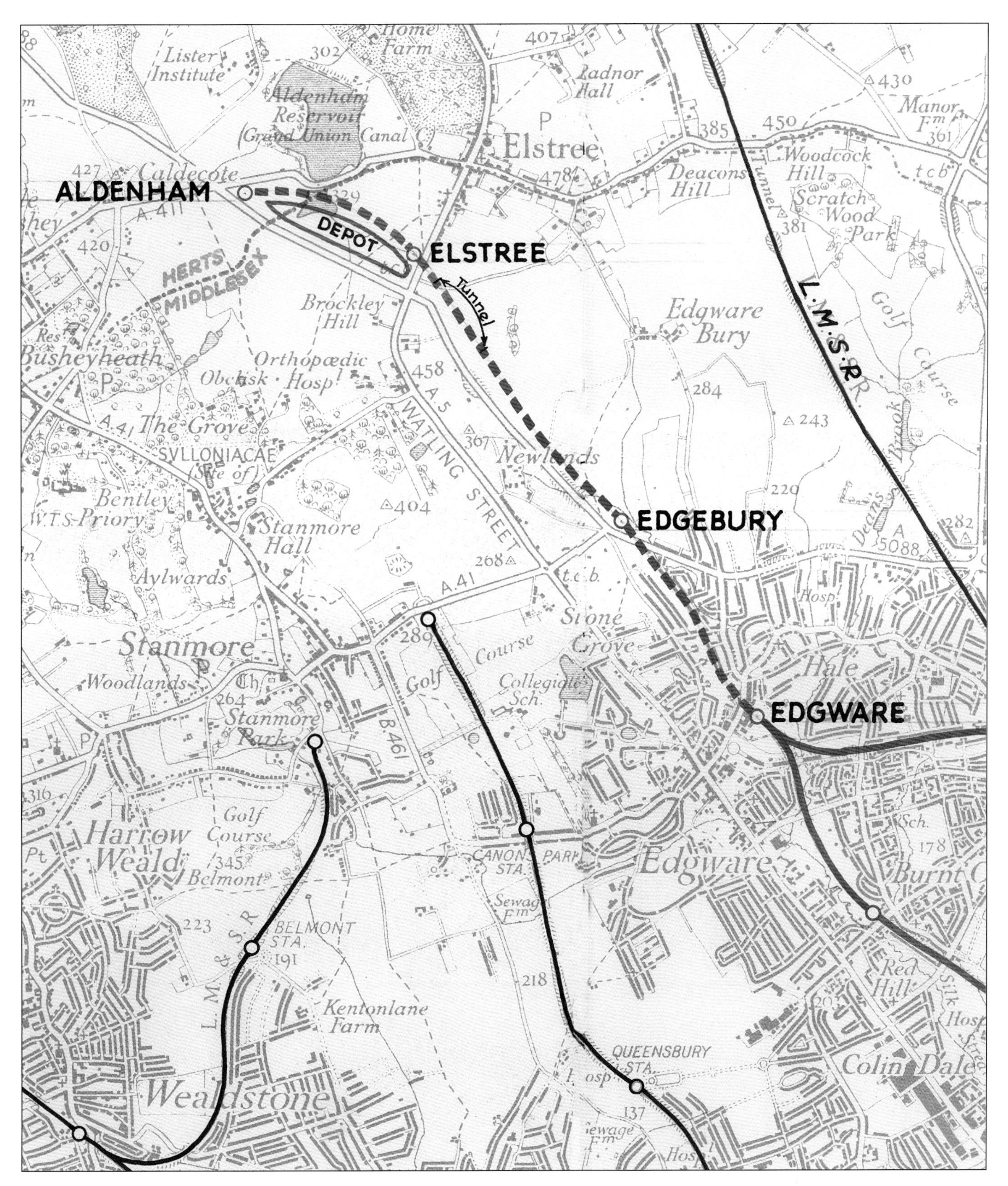
ALDENHAM
DEPOT
ELSTREE
Tunnel
HERTS
MIDDLESEX
EDGEBURY
EDGWARE
L.M.S.R
Elstree
Aldenham Reservoir
Stanmore
Harrow Weald
Wealdstone
Edgware
Colin Dale
BELMONT STA.
CANONS PARK STA.
QUEENSBURY STA.
WATLING STREET
Busheyheath
Stanmore Hall
Edgware Bury
Newlands
Deacons Hill
Woodcock Hill
Scratch Wood Park
Brockley Hill
The Grove
SVLLONIACAE (Site of)
Aylwards
Bentley Priory
Lister Institute
Radnor Hall
Hale
Red Hill
Burnt

Lord Bethell then pinned his colours to Bushey Urban District Council's mast and a meeting of the Watford Rural District Council, when invited by the LPTB to recommend a name for the planned terminus, recorded that Aldenham was totally inappropriate. One member, amid laughter, did suggest Profit Grabber's Paradise.

Finally, at a meeting of the Board's Traffic Committee on 5th January it was agreed that the terminus should be called Aldenham (for Bushey). At the same time, the name for the first station on the extension was discussed. In this context, J P Thomas was asked to ascertain the origin of the place name Canons Park. If no reasonable objection arose, it was decided that this station should be called Canons whilst that bearing the name Canons Park, on the Stanmore branch, be renamed Whitchurch.

By the end of the month Sir Denis Herbert, the local Member of Parliament had entered the terminus title debate. The Board relented and on 14th January 1938, it was decided that the name Bushey Heath should be adopted. On 1st March 1938 the name Brockley Hill was once more back in the frame. The final change occurred at the beginning of May when it was decided that Elstree should become Elstree South to avoid confusion with the station of the same name on the LMS line.

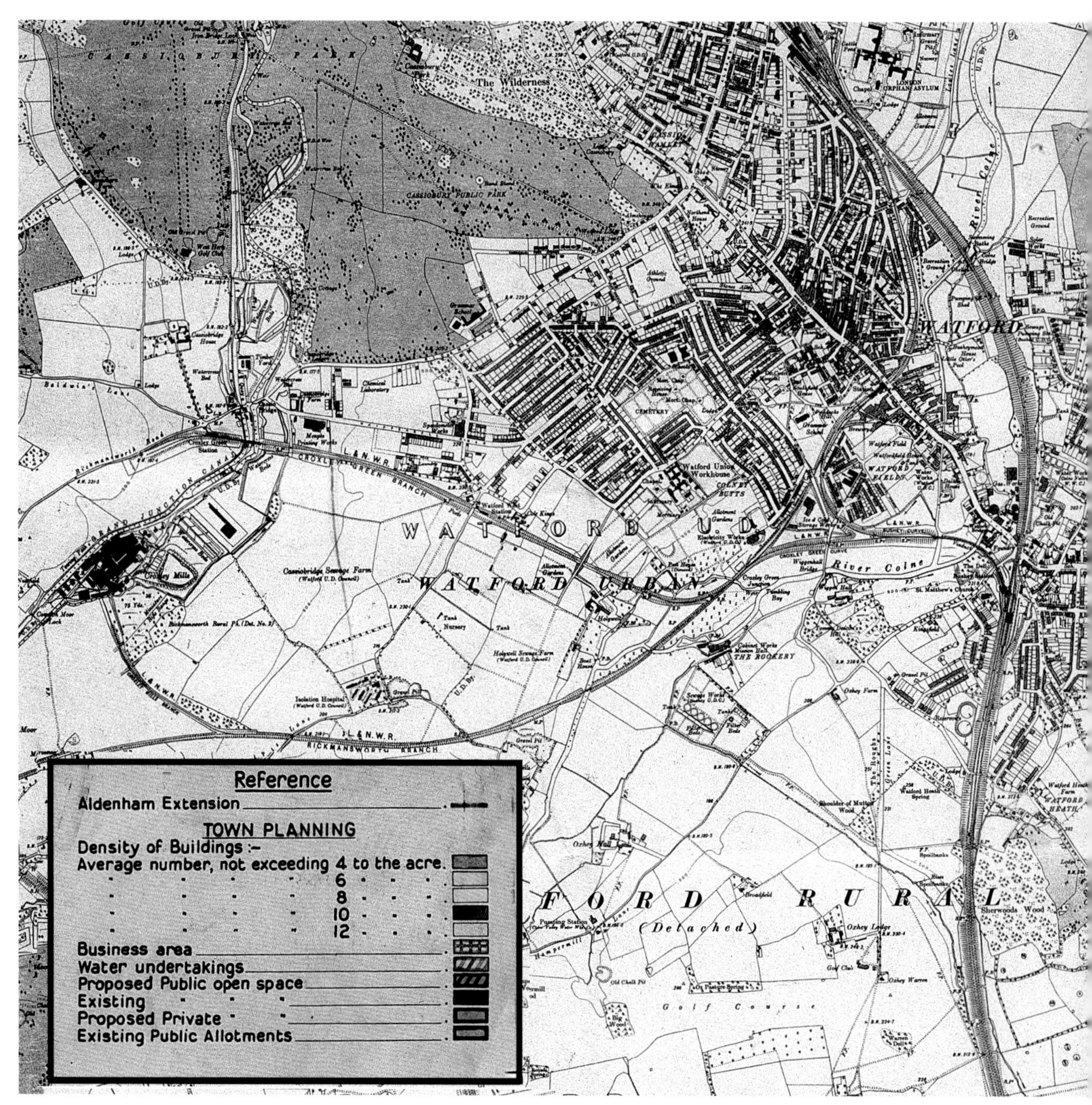

Town planning of the Bushey area had been undertaken in 1925 and 1934. The latter revision followed a move supported by Hertfordshire County Council, which gave Bushey UDC administration of an area originally within the rural district of Watford. Substantial development was planned north-west of the station that the LPTB proposed to build at Aldenham. Members of Bushey Council were led to believe that Hertfordshire County Council had been expecting for some time construction of the Board's Tube railway along the route of the 1903 Watford and Edgware Railway. This concept was partially supported by Frank Pick in an address to officials from local councils and other interested parties in January 1937. He stated that financial constraints dictated that the line must terminate at Aldenham, but if there were a possibility of further projection then it would be extended to Bushey but nowhere else. Sydney Payne, with whom Pick would later cross swords regarding the name of the terminus, suggested a site within the neighbourhood of Coldharbour Lane, the Town Plan including such a provision.

During the period of negotiation with petitioners against the 1937 Bill before the initial House of Lords debate, the layout at the station beyond Aldenham Depot had been the subject of continuous discussion. A large scale plan was subsequently drawn up for use by the Parliamentary Committee showing an area sufficient to accommodate 200 cars and a bus station twice the size of that at Morden. Bus lay-bys were to be built in Elstree Road. A roadhouse based on the plan of the Comet at Hatfield would be constructed on the triangle opposite the station. The plan also showed Elstree Road moved closer to the railway line in order to provide room for trees to be planted between the road and the reservoir as required by the Lords' Select Committee.

Benskin's Brewery had already been contacted in order to stimulate the company's interest in operating the roadhouse. The Board was also represented at a meeting convened to discuss the Bushey Town Plan, which included the erection of shops at the crossroads where the terminus was to be built. By promoting the construction of a low level terminus, A R Cooper considered it possible for subways to connect the booking hall with pavements either side of the Watford By-Pass and Elstree Road, thereby addressing another of the Select Committee's recommendations.

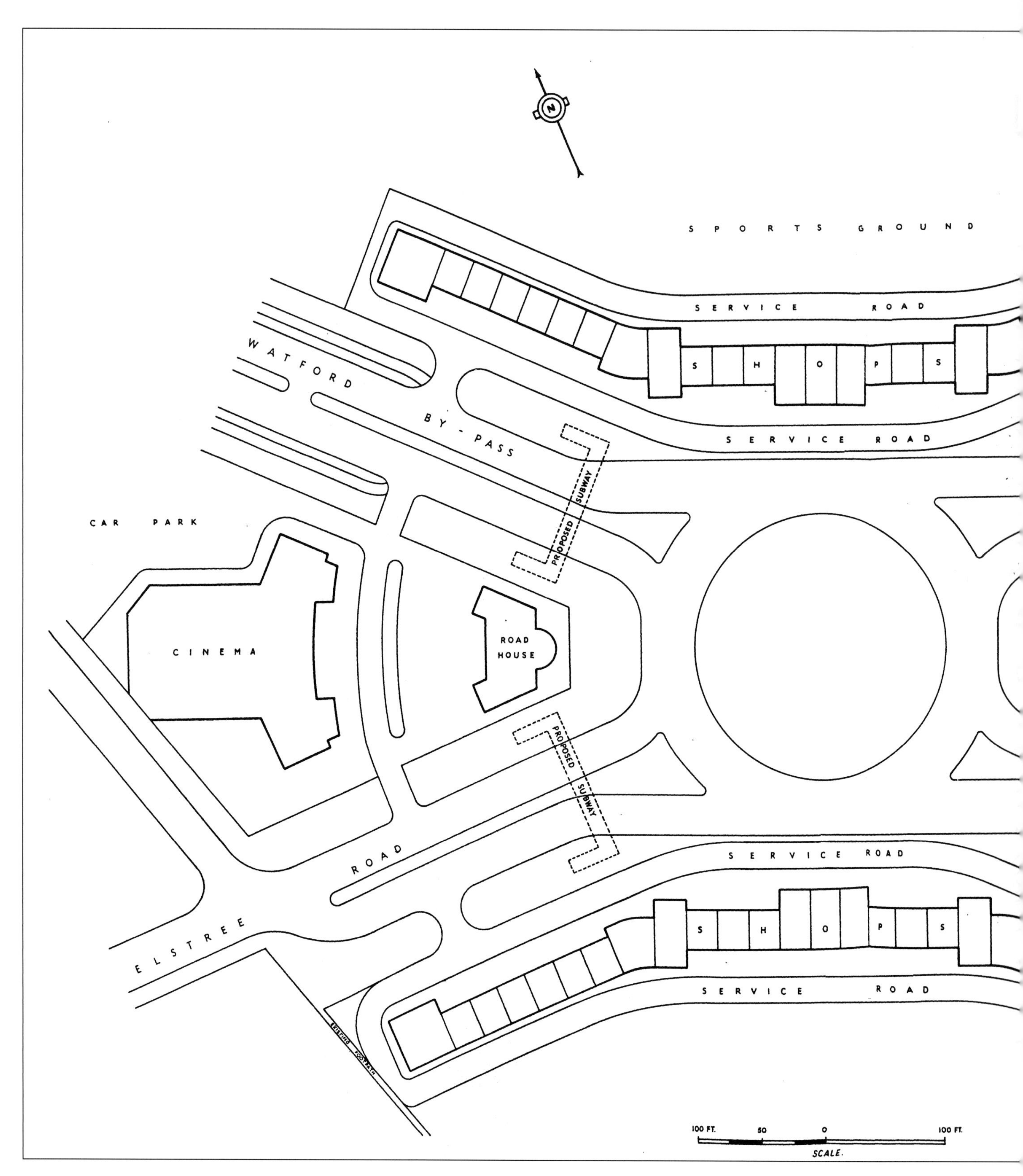
N
SPORTS GROUND
SERVICE ROAD
SHOPS
SERVICE ROAD
WATFORD BY-PASS
PROPOSED SUBWAY
CAR PARK
CINEMA
ROAD HOUSE
PROPOSED SUBWAY
SERVICE ROAD
ROAD
ELSTREE
SHOPS
SERVICE ROAD
EXISTING FOOTPATH
100 FT.
50
0
100 FT.
SCALE.

BUSHEY HEATH. PROPOSED STATION & ROAD PLAN

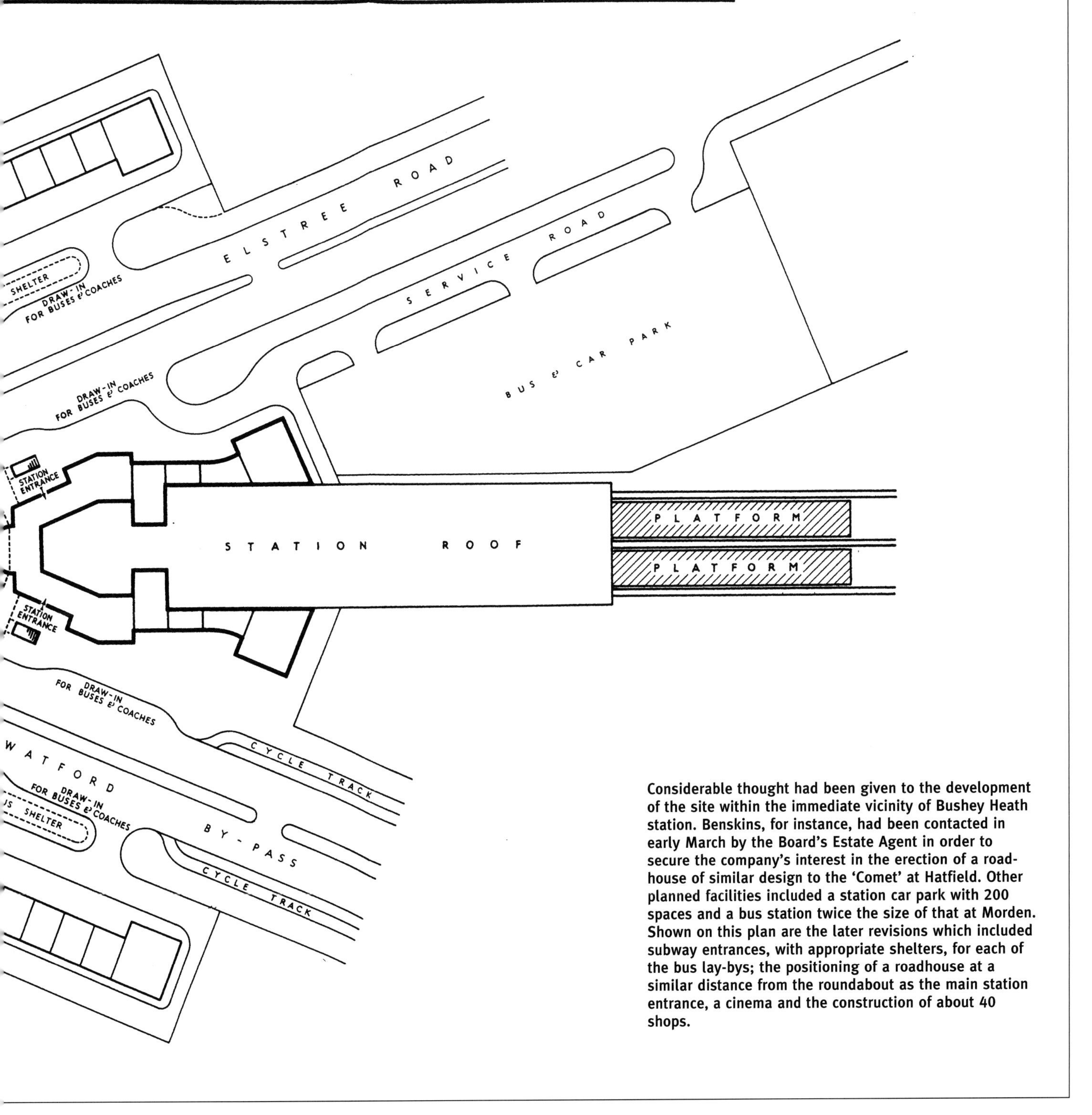

Considerable thought had been given to the development of the site within the immediate vicinity of Bushey Heath station. Benskins, for instance, had been contacted in early March by the Board's Estate Agent in order to secure the company's interest in the erection of a road-house of similar design to the 'Comet' at Hatfield. Other planned facilities included a station car park with 200 spaces and a bus station twice the size of that at Morden. Shown on this plan are the later revisions which included subway entrances, with appropriate shelters, for each of the bus lay-bys; the positioning of a roadhouse at a similar distance from the roundabout as the main station entrance, a cinema and the construction of about 40 shops.

Large scale plans for the Elstree Extension still survive in the Depot facility of London's Transport Museum, being drawn to the scale of 40ft to 1 inch. This example shows the track of the terminal station, which bears its approved name Bushey Heath, although Aldenham appears in parenthesis.

During October 1937, the Bushey Town Planning Scheme became the topic of debate between Frank Pick, the County Surveyor for Hertfordshire, the Surveyor for Bushey Urban District Council and the London Divisional Road Engineer from the Ministry of Transport. The general layout of the cross-roads at the junction of Watford By-Pass and the Bushey Heath to Elstree Road was discussed, with particular reference to the station site.

All parties had previously agreed to the general layout of the station approaches and the junction itself. It then transpired that Bushey Council had zoned the road junction as a shopping area and wished to increase its rateable value, the land on either side of the junction having previously been acquired by the Board. Pick stated that it would be happy to part with the land at the original purchase price, which was set at approximately £800 per acre. But all was not as it may seem. An annotation in the margin of the Board's copy of the proceedings reads: '*almost one acre is the cheap £100 per acre land and we are asking £800 per acre for it all*'. The Board were reluctant to endorse the construction of buildings, a reluctance that did not meet with the approval of the Bushey Council Surveyor. However, the London Division Road Engineer concluded that the creation of a shopping area at the cross-roads was undesirable and proposed to recommend that no access be approved, especially as the Watford By-Pass would soon become a trunk road.

On 19th October 1937, the Engineering Committee met and approved in principle a new layout for the terminal station site. This was subject to:

Lay-bys for buses being provided on the main carriageways with subway entrances located on the adjacent grass strips. A shelter for bus passengers would be combined within each entrance.

The proposed roadhouse being brought forward so that its exterior and that of the station were similar distances from the road frontage.

The construction of a cinema behind the road house.

A limit being set on the shop development by a break in the building line.

A plan encompassing these proposals was produced on 29th November.

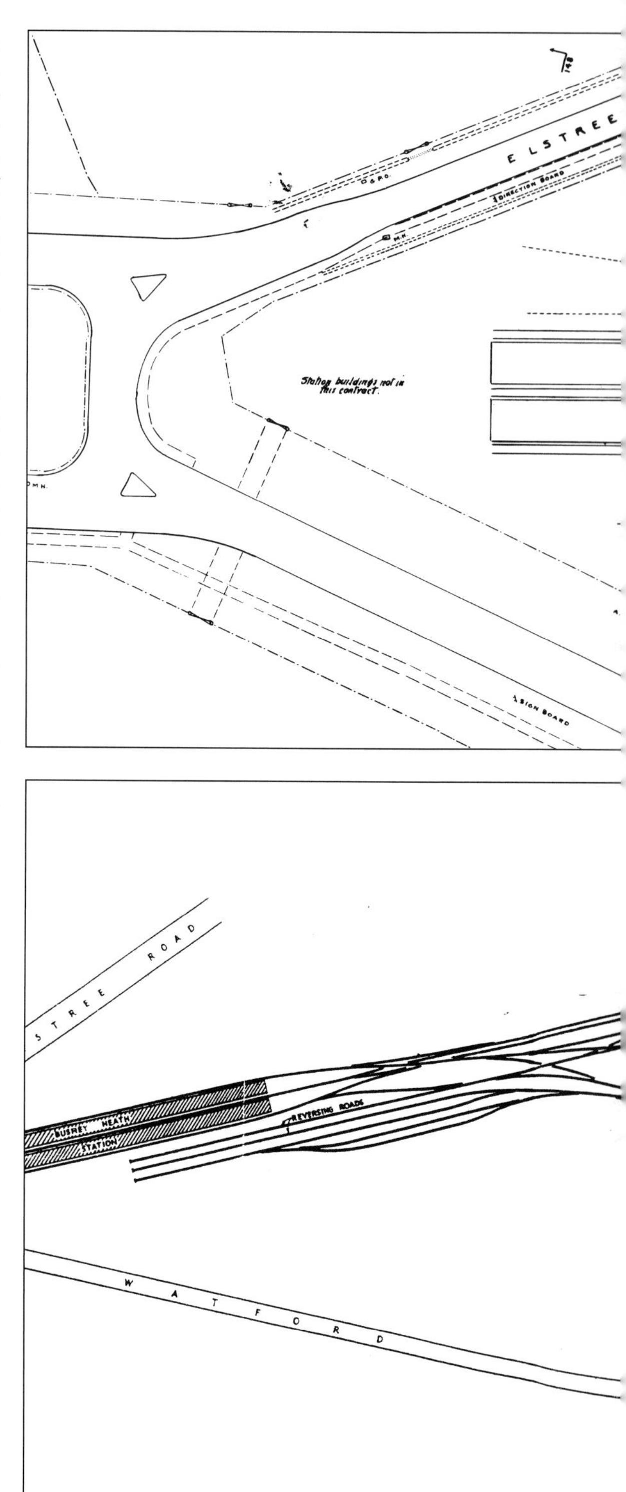

Plans prepared in 1938 showing the layout of Bushey Heath station and what was referred to as 'Bushey Heath Works'. The track level at the terminus was to be 14 feet below road level.

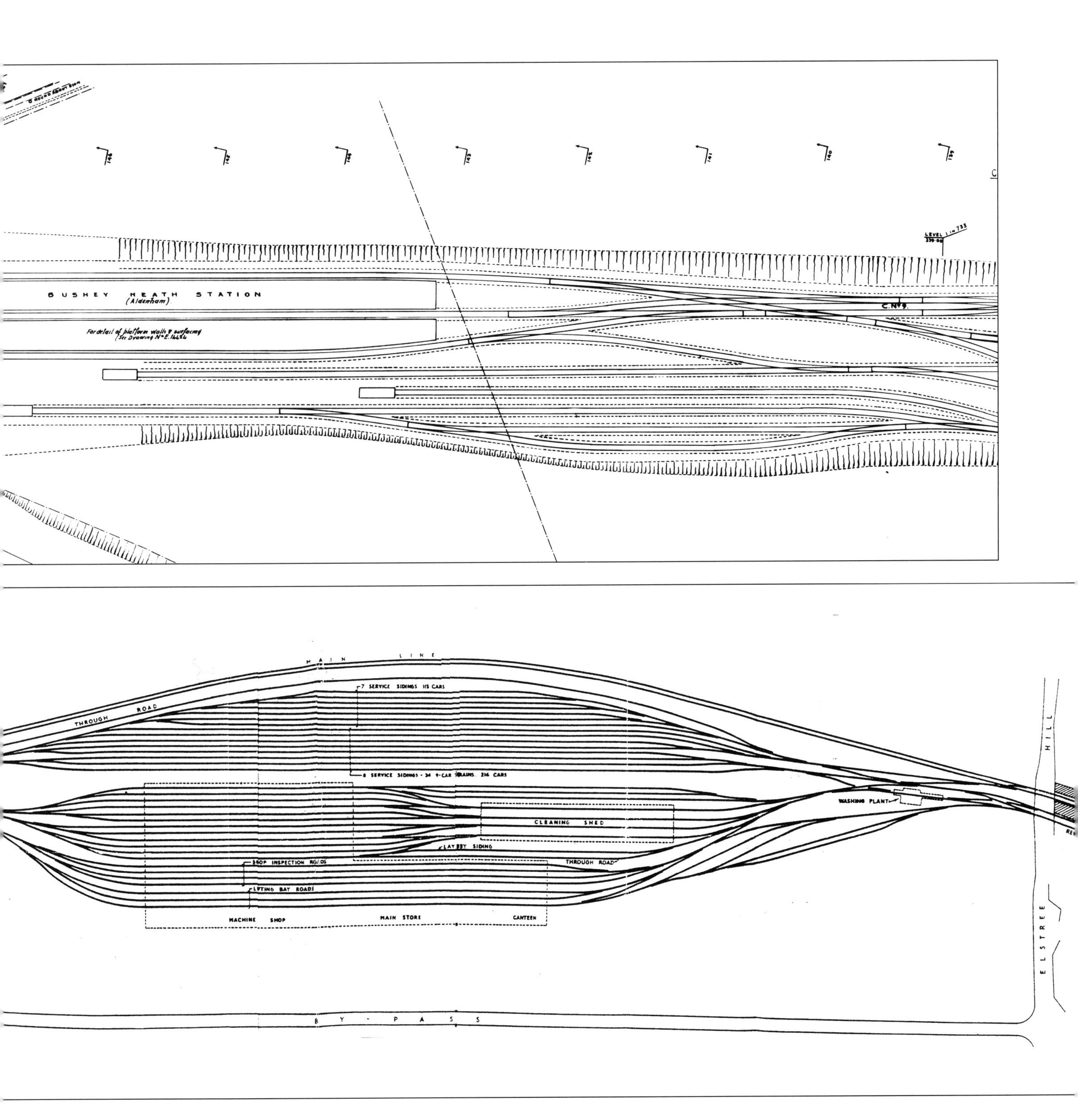
BUSHEY HEATH STATION
(Aldenham)
For detail of platform walls & surfacing
(See Drawing Nº E.16424
C.Nº9.
MAIN LINE
THROUGH ROAD
7 SERVICE SIDINGS 113 CARS
8 SERVICE SIDINGS - 24 9-CAR TRAINS. 216 CARS
CLEANING SHED
LAY BY SIDING
SHOP INSPECTION ROADS
LIFTING BAY ROADS
THROUGH ROAD
WASHING PLANT
MACHINE SHOP
MAIN STORE
CANTEEN
ELSTREE HILL
BY-PASS

Another factor to have some influence on the layout for the terminal station hinged on the possibility that the LCC might establish a county school on land west of the Watford By-Pass. The Board did everything possible to secure an early decision from County Hall in view of the necessity of having to deal with school traffic at the station. It was not until February 1938 that the LCC officially stated that the land was insufficient in area for its requirements.

During the summer of 1938, planning for the area around Bushey Heath station reached an advanced stage following discussions with the local surveyor. In order to improve transport facilities the road that ran from Caldecote Hill to Bushey Heath station would be made suitable for double-deck bus operation.

Some criticism was levelled at Harrow Urban District Council whose town planning of the areas either side of the new depot would introduce indifferent housing and spoil the neighbourhood. The Surveyor of Bushey Urban District Council subsequently took the matter up with the Hendon Council in an endeavour to secure a revision.

Happy to promote the development of the Green Belt, the Board suggested that steps should be taken to connect Harrow Weald Common, Stanmore Common and the land to be used for the Green Belt at Aldenham Reservoir by green strips. These would not be less than 100 yards wide in order to secure a definite line of country at Bushey Heath, that linking Stanmore Common and Aldenham Reservoir being in the form of an arc around Caldecote Hill.

The Board still considered it unlikely that the railway would be extended beyond the proposed Bushey Heath terminus further into the Bushey Urban District and suggested that all town planning for the area should be based on this assumption. Consequently, as its lands were released from railway requirements, the Board agreed to confer with the Council regarding disposal. This statement might be viewed with some degree of scepticism, as some consideration continued to be given to further extension of the line. Supporting the idea of allowance being made for further projection, it is interesting to reflect that terminating the extension at Elstree South was never seriously considered by the Board, especially after the Ministry's rejection to the establishing of a significant shopping area around Bushey Heath station. Two precedents for depots being sited beyond terminal stations existed at Upminster and Morden, the latter being further from the southern terminus of the Northern Line than Aldenham Depot would have been from Elstree South. Nevertheless, a proposal for extending the line beyond Bushey Heath was not to be part of any serious planning by the LPTB at any time.

During December 1938, the Ministry of Transport released details of a scheme for the diversion of the Watford By-Pass away from the site proposed for Bushey Heath station. The Ministry was concerned that the new roundabout in front of the station would impede the flow of traffic, the diversion having been planned to carry traffic originating from the A5 and A6 roads and the existing By-Pass. The Board was totally opposed to the Ministry's proposals, which could result in a breakdown of negotiations with the Brewery Company and Hertfordshire County Council and would affect the planned development of the area.

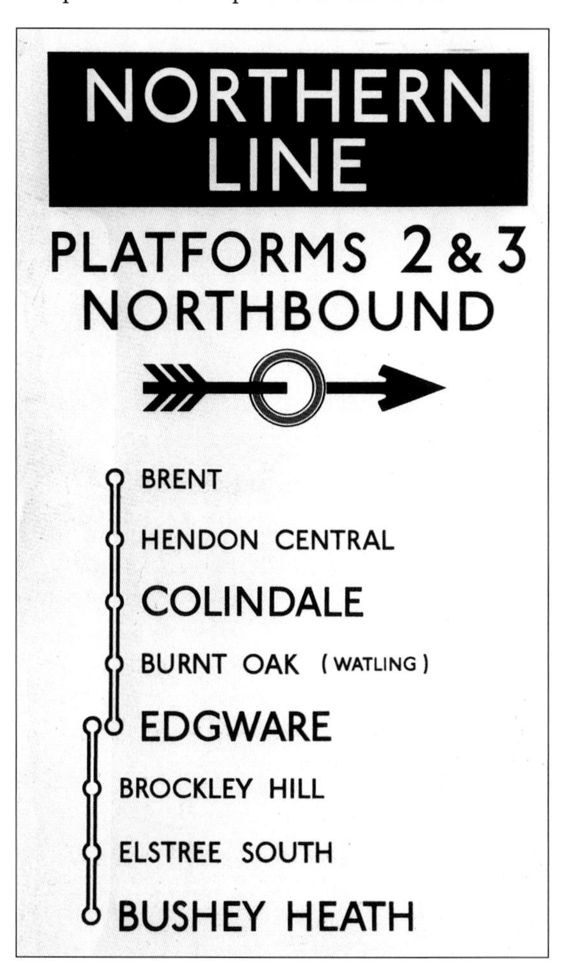

This enamel sign was displayed at Golders Green station and could be used to support the theory that the Elstree Extension might have operated as a separate shuttle. However, if the service on to the branch was planned to operate via Highgate, passengers wishing to travel beyond Edgware would in any case be required to change there.

A revised plan was submitted by the Ministry in July 1939 that proposed a flyunder at Bushey Heath station which would enable traffic on the Watford By-Pass to travel below the surface road junction. As a result, the LPTB's Chief Civil Engineer, V A M Robertson, put forward a number of points for consideration by the Works Committee. These included the deletion of pedestrian subways below the By-Pass, now unnecessary as the fast traffic would be at low level; a subway below Elstree Road to provide direct access to the booking hall and a further subway with ramps under Elstree Road on the west side of the roundabout.

Although the Board had recorded its intention not to extend the line beyond the terminus, this was not reflected in Robertson's report. He noted that, as the track level was to be fourteen feet below the road service, the sub-surface By-Pass prevented easy further extension of the railway.

MEMORANDA

ROAD	FRONTAGE	LENGTH OF ROAD	Nº OF HOUSES
TOWN PLANNED Rº	1180	985	46
HILLTREE AVENUE	1575	760	55
BEAUFORT RISE	2105	1180	80
THE AVENUE	2710	1590	106
GREENFIELD GDNS	1540	910	58
ELSTREE HILL	815	650	31
	9925	6075	376

TOTAL AREA 31·4 ACRES – PLUS HALF WIDTH OF ELSTREE HILL – 32 ACRES – DENSITY 12 HOUSES PER ACRE = 384 HOUSES

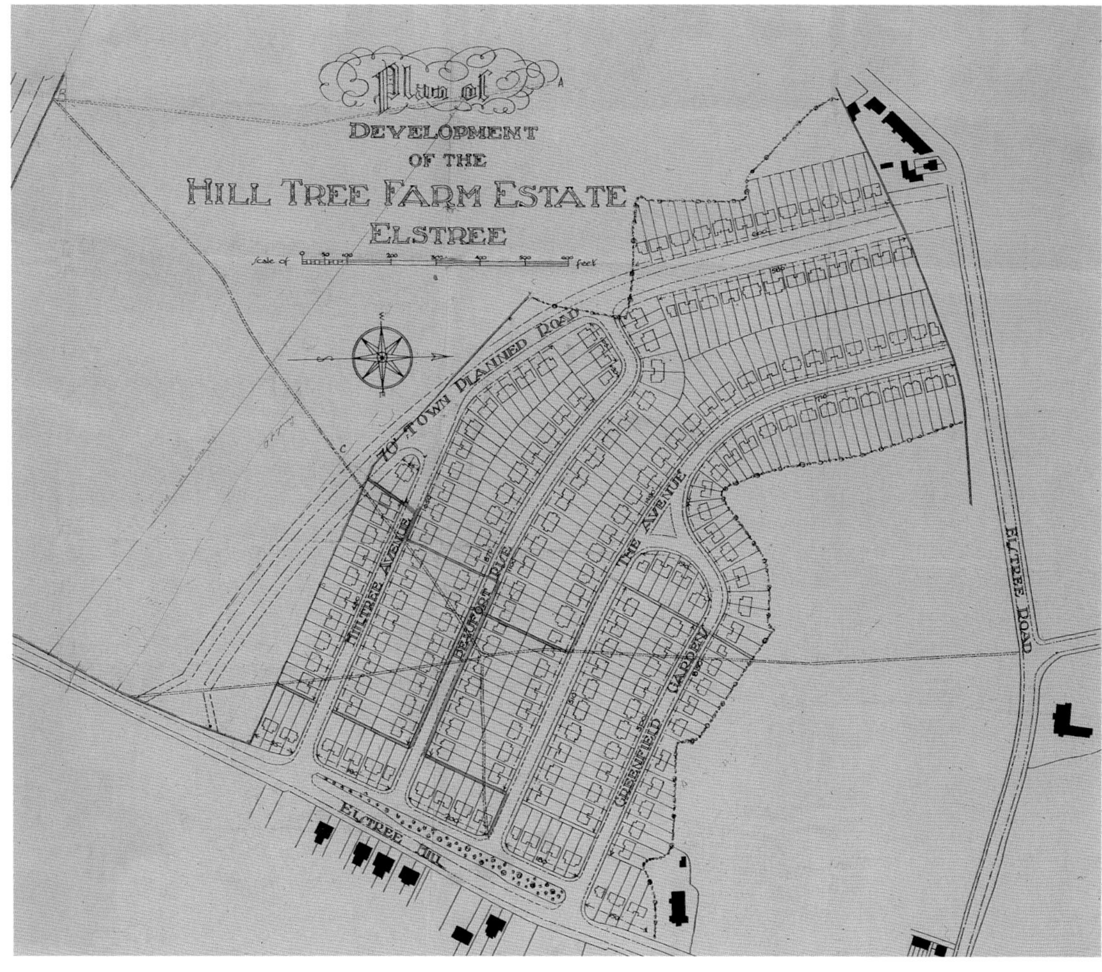

The first planned residential development following the authorisation of the Elstree extension was on the west side of Elstree Hill. Hill Tree Farm Estate was never built, though another development on the same land took place after the war.

Plans for the first station beyond Edgware were also being carefully considered. It was to feature prominently in the development of the adjoining estate to be known as All Souls. Those present at a meeting held on 10th February 1938 were able to study two sketches of the existing Spur Road, south west of the railway, laid out as a shopping centre. It was agreed that the station platforms should be of nine-car length, a principle being applied to the other stations on the extension. The original plan had been for a single island platform to be constructed which involved a reverse curve south of the station. Modifications to this arrangement placed a platform at either side of the tracks, obviating the need for the curve and saving £12–15,000.

Two flights of stairs would lead down to a resited ticket hall situated under the bridge designed to carry the line over the proposed extension of Spur Road. There would also be provision for escalators to be installed at a later date. The forecourt was to provide standing room for 20–25 private cars and space for three buses on through services and four buses terminating. No documentary evidence has been found of any plan to extend trolleybus route 645 from its nearby Canons Corner terminus.

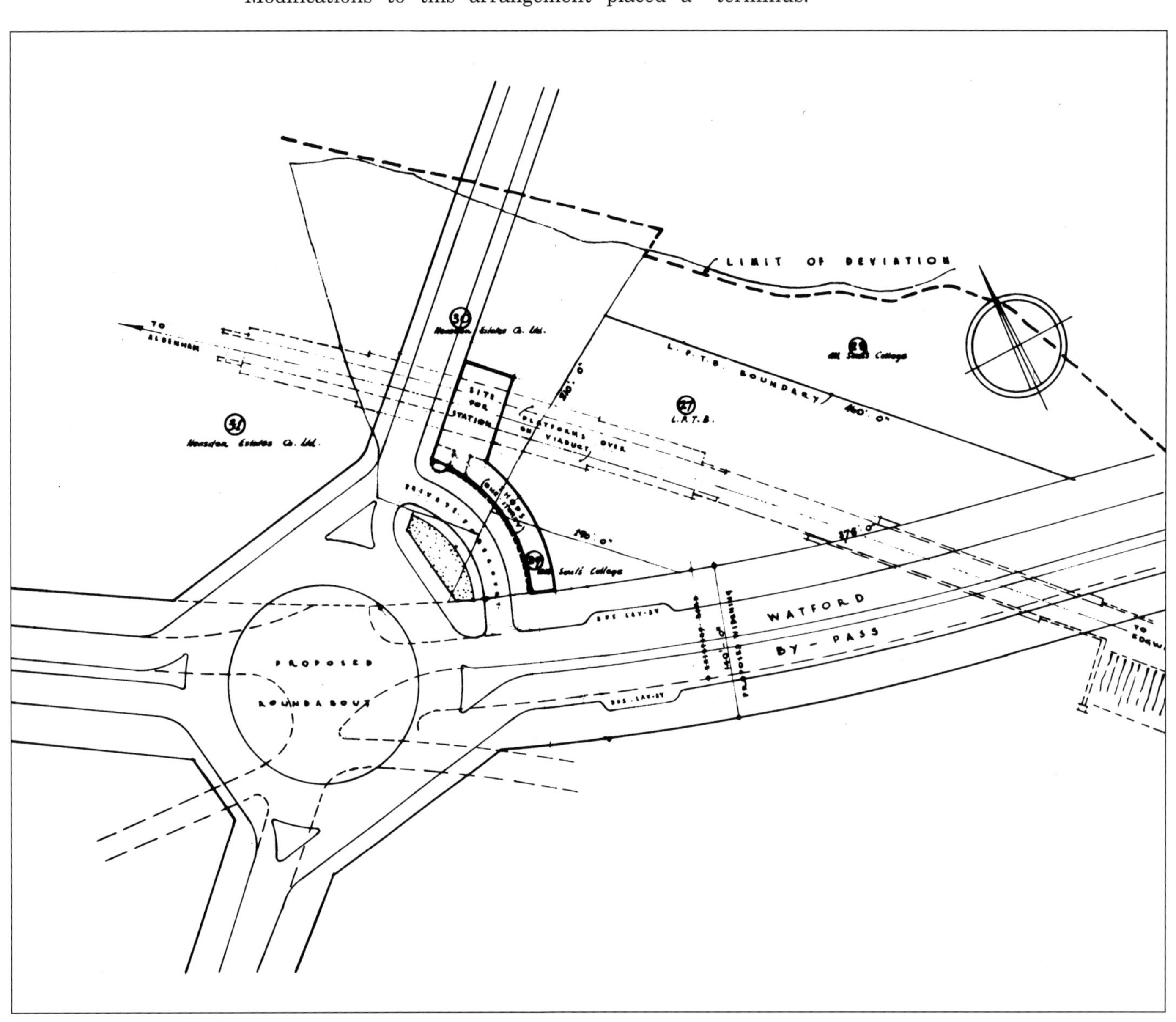

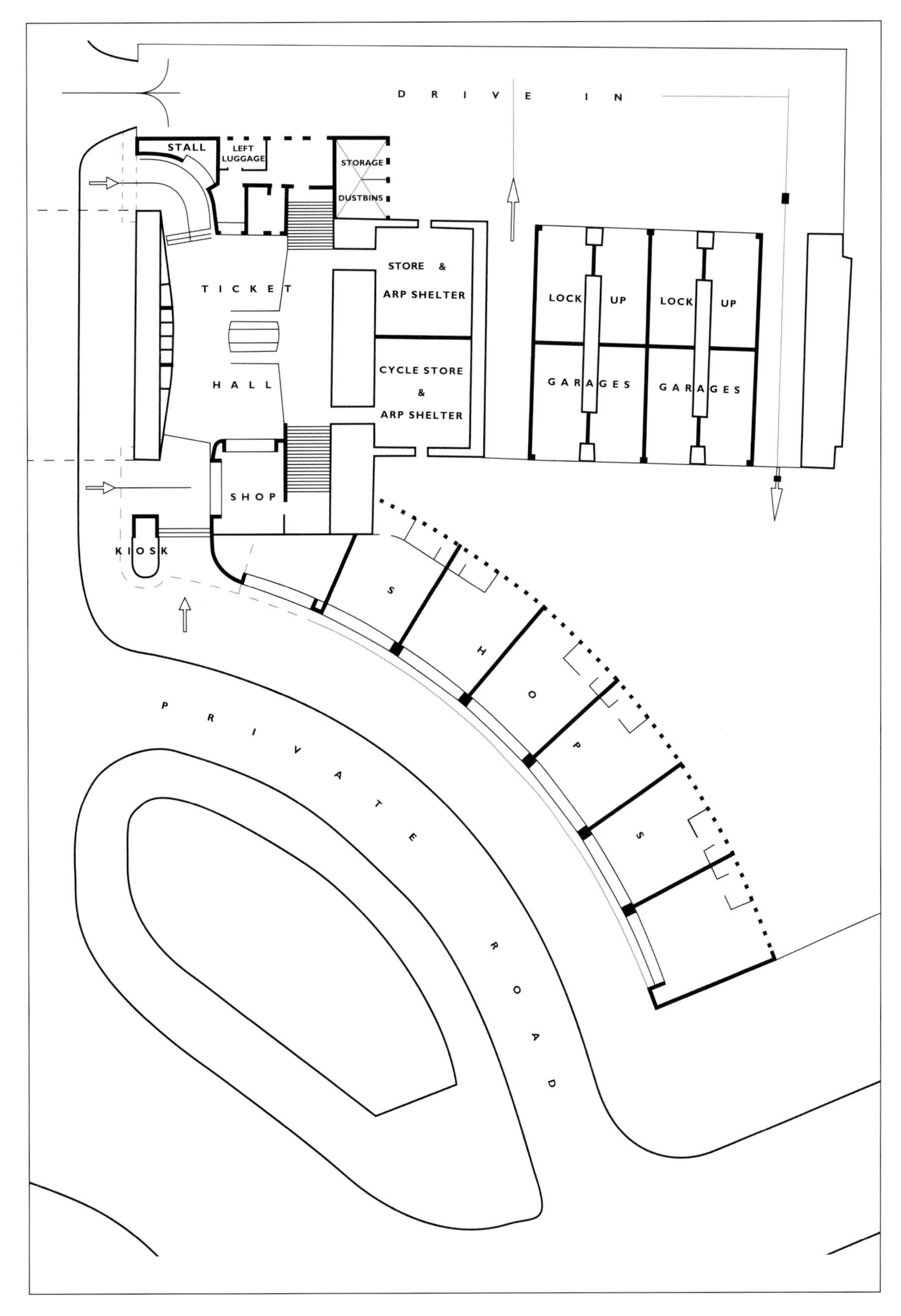

Facing page **Situated approximately three quarters of a mile from Edgware, the first station on the branch was bestowed with the title Brockley Hill after a number of names had been suggested, adopted and later disregarded (*see text*). The initial layout provided for a booking hall situated beneath a bridge spanning an extension of Spur Road that necessitated the construction of a roundabout to provide a junction with the Watford By-Pass. Some of the land in the immediate area of the station had been acquired from All Souls College, Oxford, whose estate agents were planning to establish a shopping centre on the existing section of Spur Road, for which plans were being established to allow a start to be made in the summer of 1938.**

Left **With the Country having been placed on a war footing, Air Raid Precautions became of prime importance. At Brockley Hill station, two air raid shelters were planned for installation in the arch adjacent to the booking hall. The ARP Control Room was sited to the side of the booking hall area, necessitating a resiting of the station telephone kiosks in order for personnel in the room to have a clear view of the street.**

Little was available in sketch form to act as a basis for this painting of Brockley Hill by Barry Pearce especially commissioned by Capital Transport. However, by producing a three-dimensional model of the proposed station using architect's drawings, it has been possible to recreate a view of the station and its surroundings. Records held by London Transport show that yellow stock bricks were to be used for building work throughout the Elstree Extension.

NO EXIT

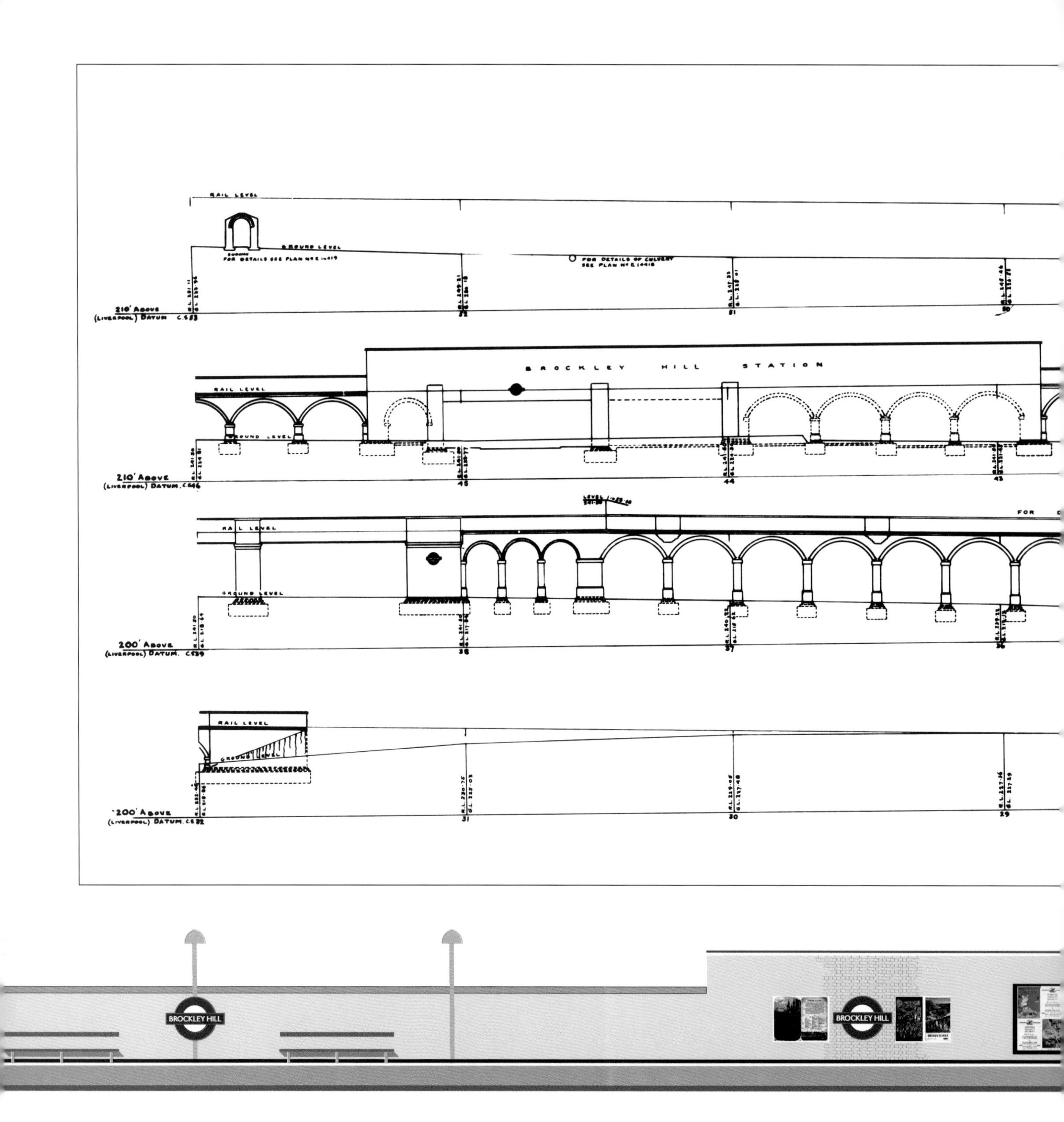

Elevations dated 1st April 1939 of the planned building work in the Brockley Hill station area including the unbuilt bridge over Edgware Way and the unbuilt arches south of Edgware Way. The computer-generated colour image is based on the final drawings for the planned platforms.

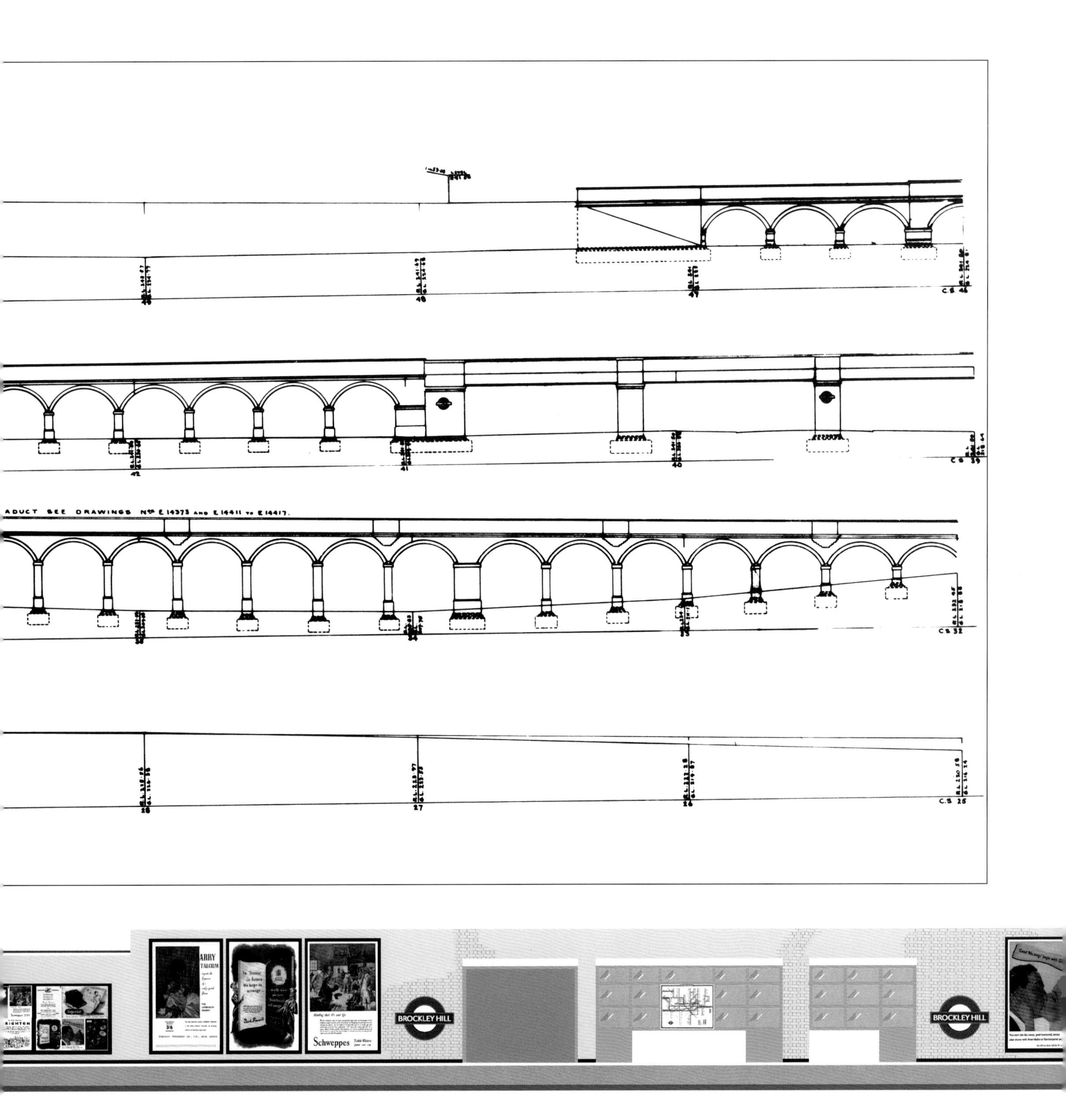

ADUCT SEE DRAWINGS No E 14373 AND E 14411 to E 14417.
C.S 32
C.S 25
BROCKLEY HILL
Schweppes
BROCKLEY HILL

Elstree South station, at the side of the Elstree Hill (then the A5), north of its junction with the Watford By-Pass caused little concern. A scheme had been drawn up which would establish the A5 as a trunk road with its width increasing from 29 feet to 100 feet in the process and it was thought prudent that the railway should be built to allow for this expansion. In October 1939, the Board approved an exchange of land near the station with Far Hills Estates Ltd in order to straighten out a boundary on the north east side of the depot. This replaced an earlier proposal for a development to be known as Hill Tree Farm Estate comprising 376 houses built on four roads one of which was town planned and was to have provided a new link between Elstree Hill and Watford Road. The land acquired by Far Hills was appended to that which it already owned for the construction of 256 houses on five roads off Elstree Hill and within walking distance of the station.

The design of Elstree South station was entrusted to Charles Holden whose initial design is seen as a perspective sketch opposite. The proximity of the station to the site of the Roman settlement of Sulloniacae was an influence for the installation of a centurion statue on the roof of the building.

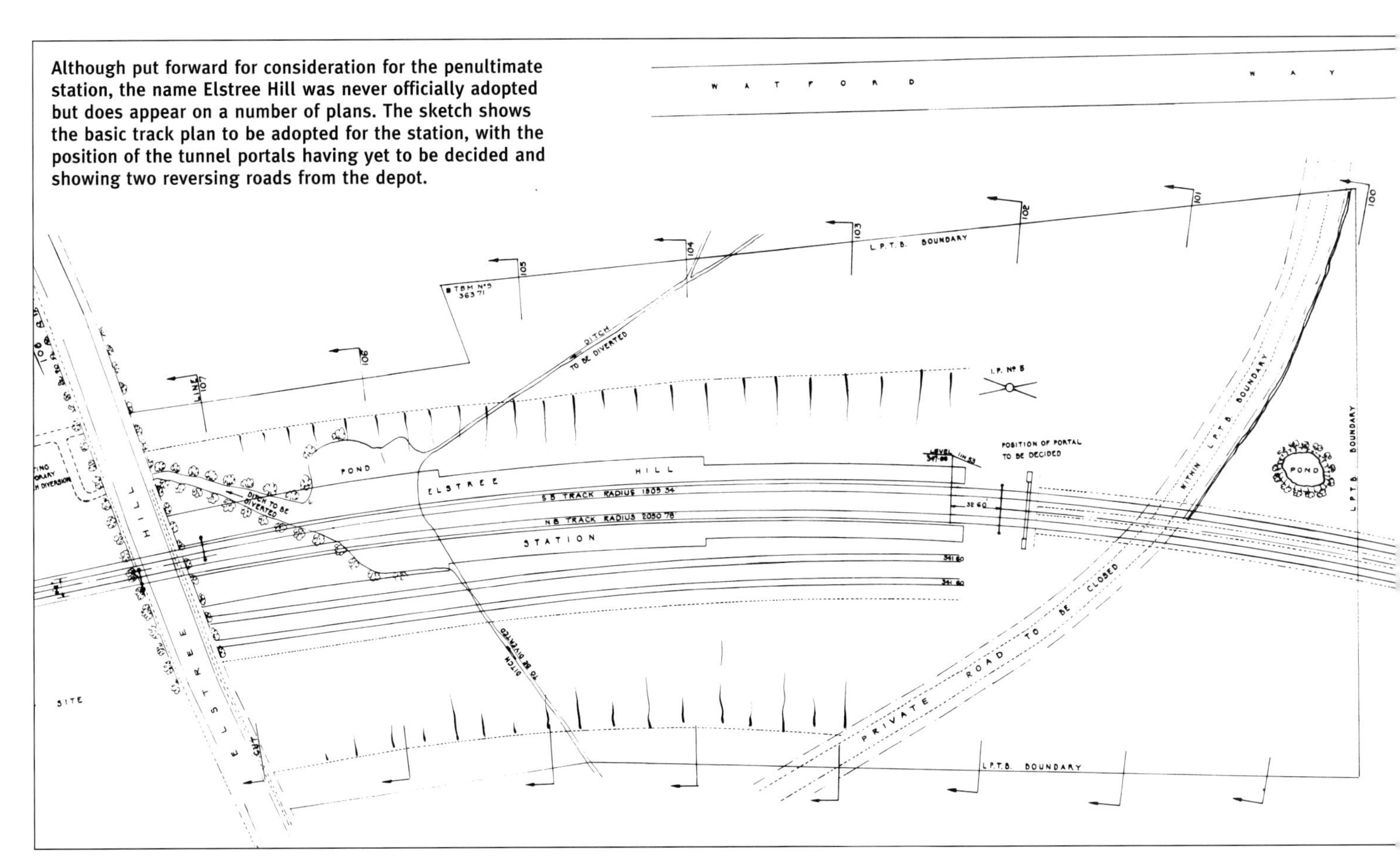

Although put forward for consideration for the penultimate station, the name Elstree Hill was never officially adopted but does appear on a number of plans. The sketch shows the basic track plan to be adopted for the station, with the position of the tunnel portals having yet to be decided and showing two reversing roads from the depot.

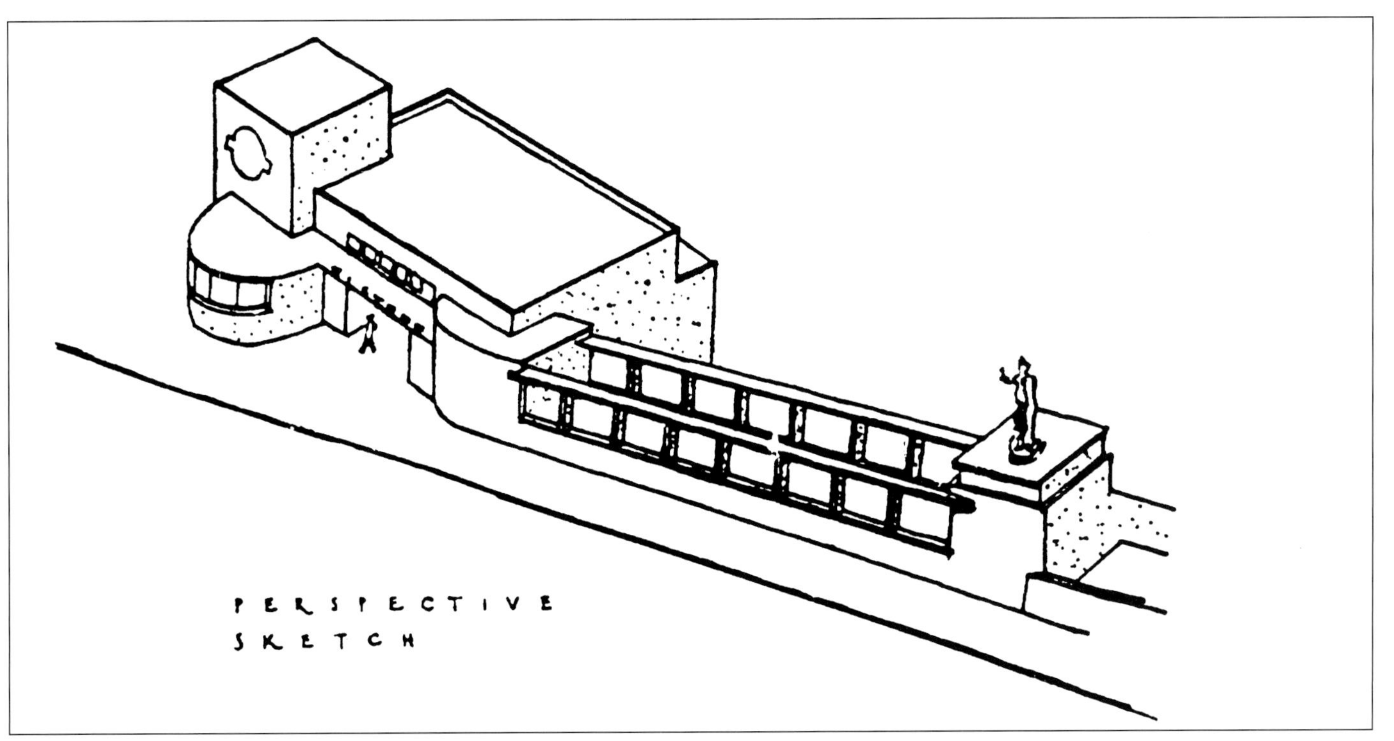

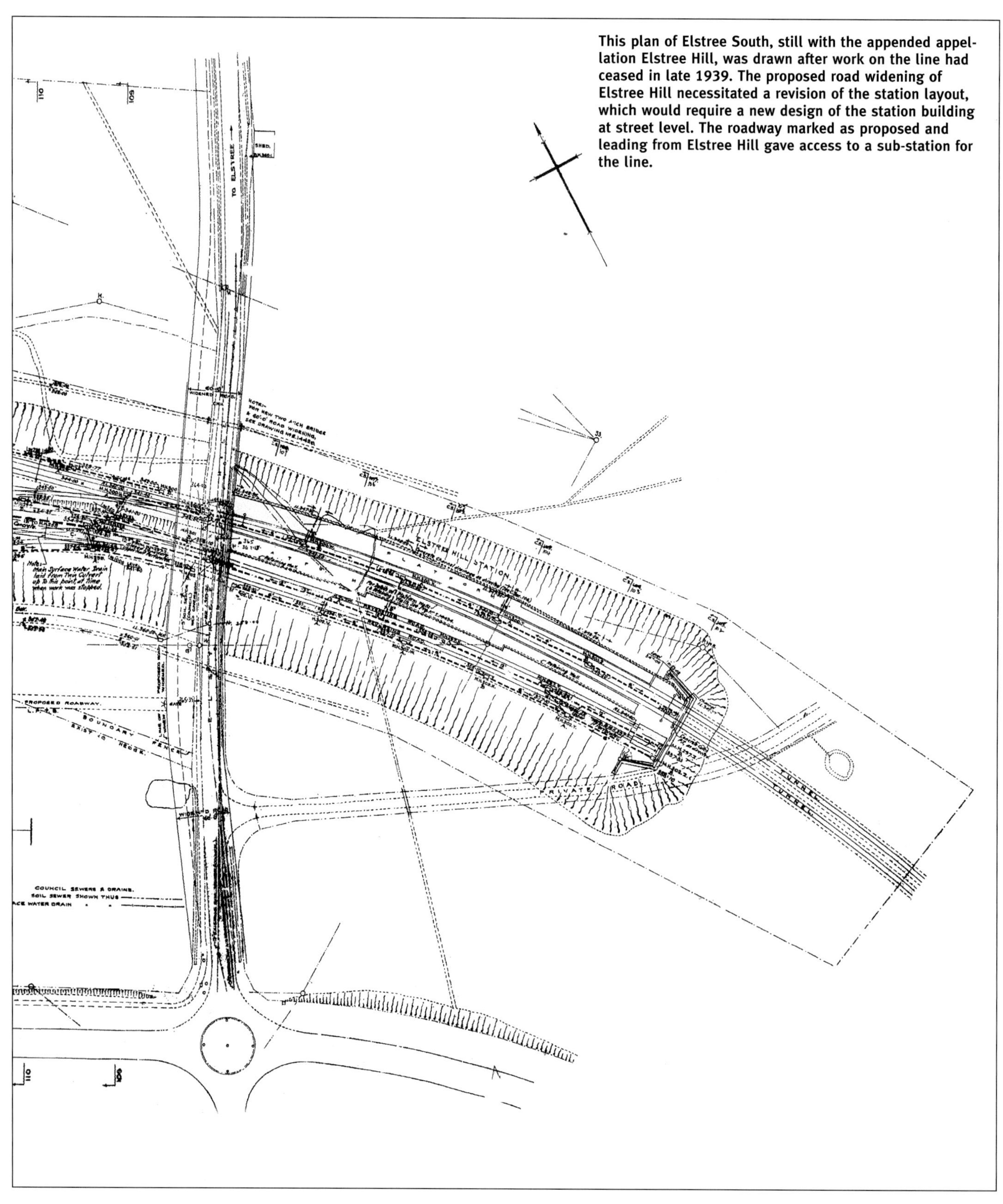

This plan of Elstree South, still with the appended appellation Elstree Hill, was drawn after work on the line had ceased in late 1939. The proposed road widening of Elstree Hill necessitated a revision of the station layout, which would require a new design of the station building at street level. The roadway marked as proposed and leading from Elstree Hill gave access to a sub-station for the line.

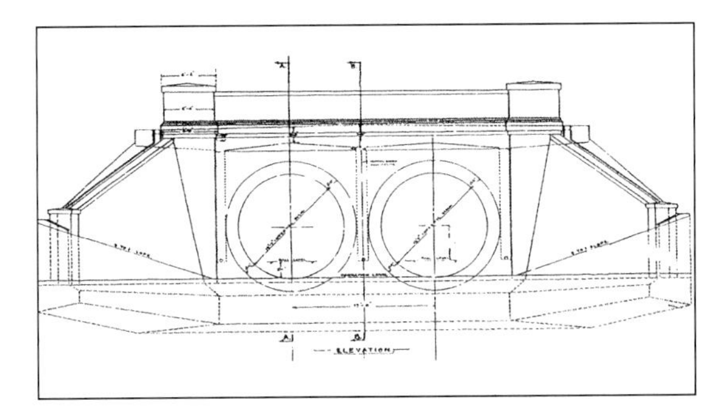

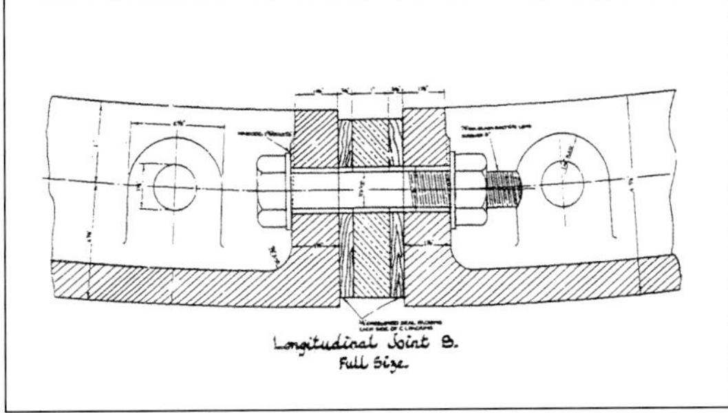

The tunnel beneath Elstree Hill was commenced from the southern end during the summer of 1939. The cast iron segments had been made surplus by the lengthening of stations on the Central Line and required an increase in size to bring them to current standards. The deficiency in diameter was addressed using a sandwich of treated wood and cast iron at four points around the circumference of the segments.

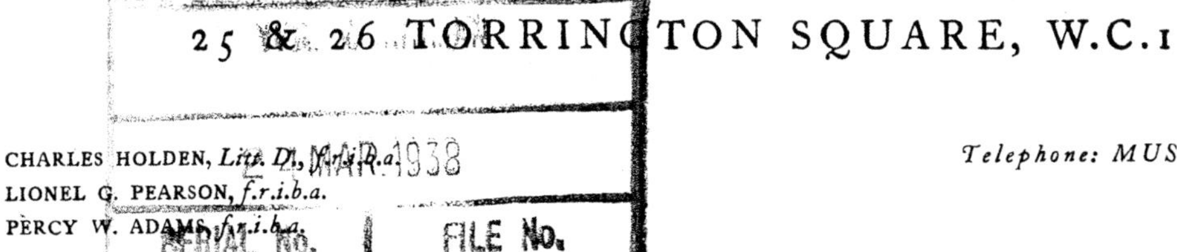

ADAMS, HOLDEN, & PEARSON, *ARCHITECTS*

25 & 26 TORRINGTON SQUARE, W.C.1

CHARLES HOLDEN, *Litt. D., f.r.i.b.a.*
LIONEL G. PEARSON, *f.r.i.b.a.*
PERCY W. ADAMS, *f.r.i.b.a.*

Telephone: MUSEUM 3033-4

25 MAR 1938

SERIAL No. 3193 | FILE No. 124/B

CH/EH.

24th March, 1938.

Frank Pick Esq.,
55, Broadway,
S.W.1.

Dear Mr. Pick,

Bushey Heath Station.

I thank you for your letter. I will visit the site and prepare a preliminary scheme for the layout of the station and surroundings.

I hope to submit this proposal shortly.

Yours sincerely,

Charles Holden

Charles Holden's letter confirming his commission to design Bushey Heath station is carefully preserved amongst many similar items of correspondence in the vaults of the Archive and Records Management Service at 55 Broadway.

The remodelling of Edgware station fell to Stanley Heaps, where the Italianate façade he designed for the opening of the station in 1924 was about to be partly demolished in connection with the extension work, whilst the Board's architects in consultation with All Souls College and Estate Developments would assume responsibility for Brockley Hill. Adams, Holden and Pearson were entrusted with the architectural design of Elstree South and Bushey Heath stations. Holden's design for Elstree South might have included a statue of a Roman centurion on its roof, justification for this being its proximity to the site of the Roman settlement of Sulloniacae.

But all these elaborate plans were about to pale into insignificance, as they had been conducted against a background of developing international unrest which would eventually cause significant changes of fortune for the Elstree Branch.

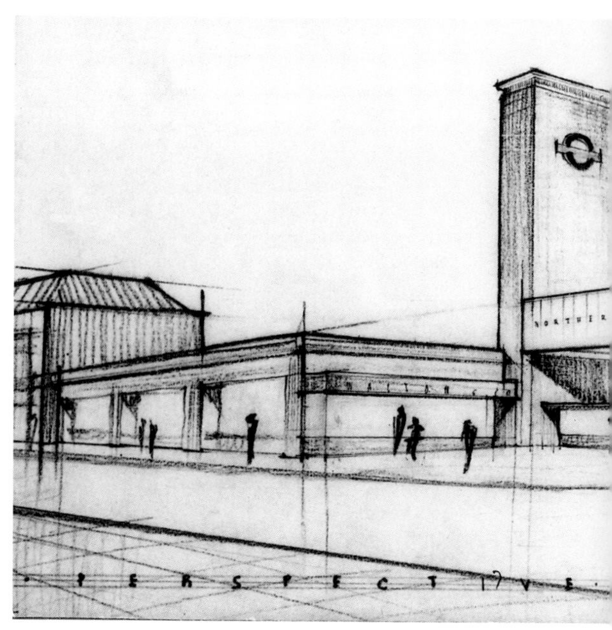

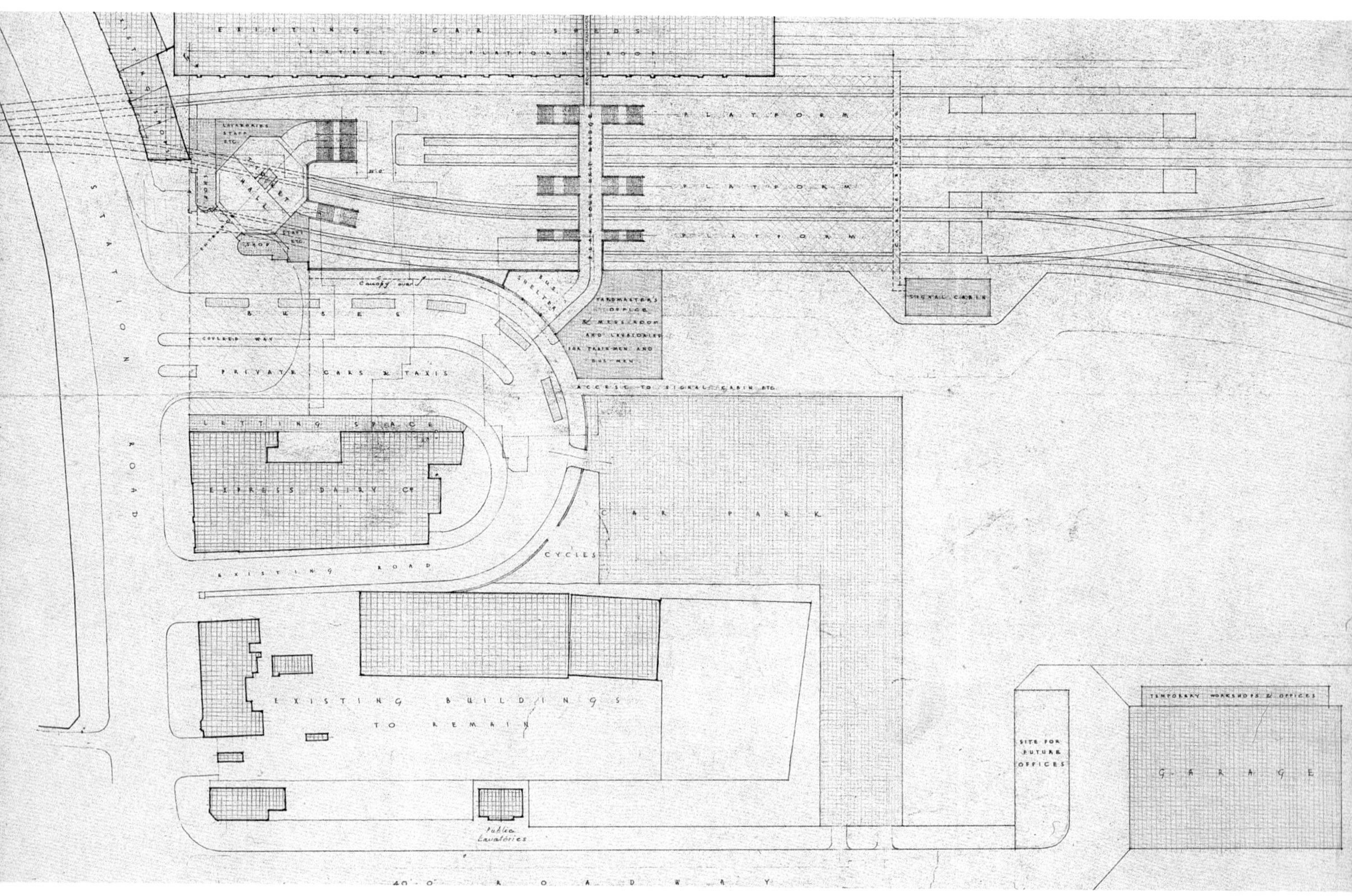

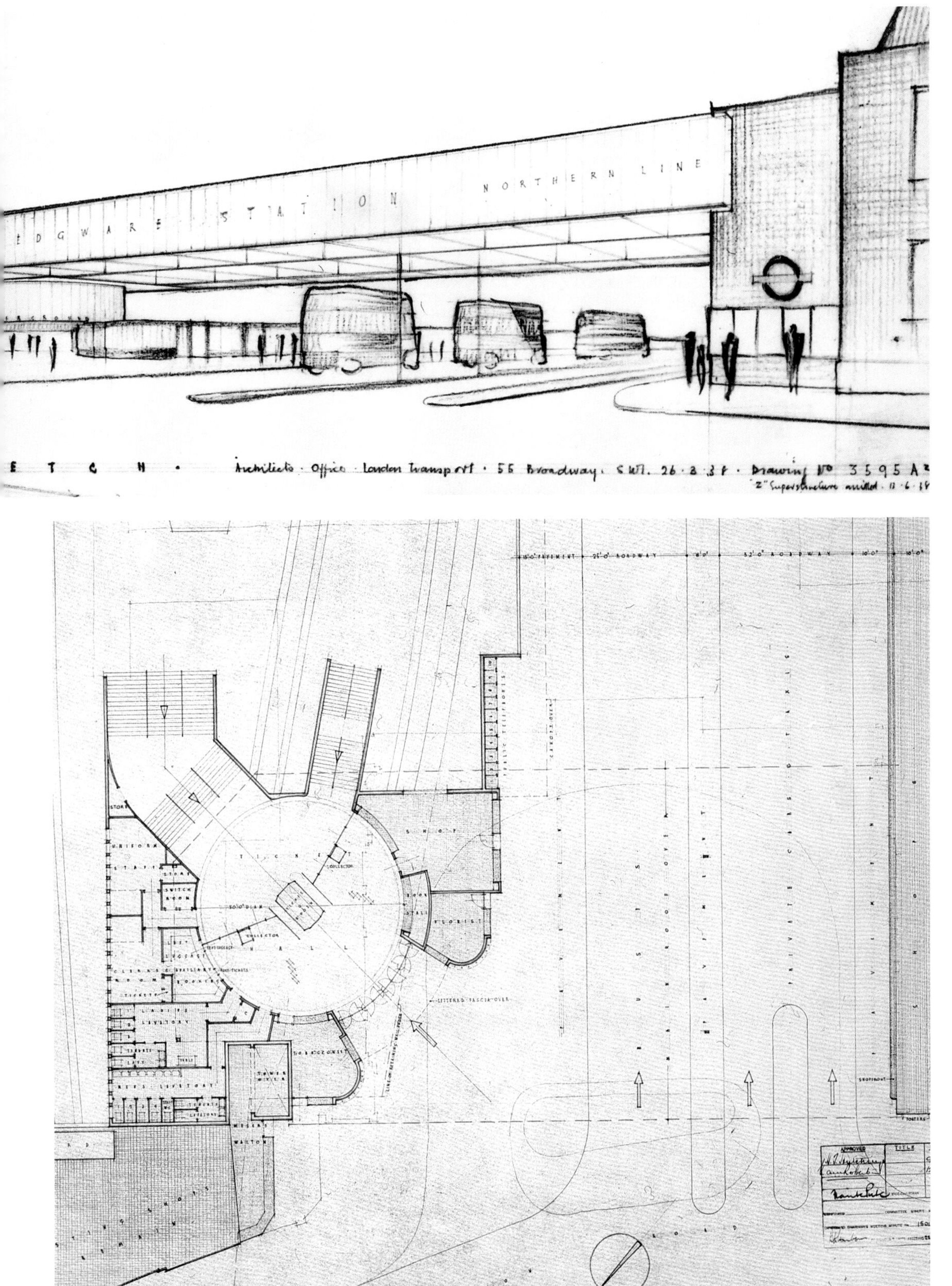

Left **A drawing dated 26th March 1938 of the planned redevelopment of Edgware station in connection with the extension.**

Facing page **Much thought was given to redesigning Edgware station for the extension to Elstree, this plan being dated 5th March 1938. Gone would be the Italianate façade designed by Stanley Heaps for the opening of the extension of the Hampstead Line to Edgware in August 1924, its ticket hall being replaced by an hexagonal example situated above the new line to Bushey Heath. Spaces for six bus stands and a separate lane for private cars and taxis was provided in a new road layout, the front section of which would be covered.**

Left **Another plan originating from the Architect's Office at 55 Broadway on 12th May 1938 shows a second radical and again unadopted scheme for the revision of the street level buildings at Edgware. In gaining Frank Pick's signature as part of the approval process, the plan provided for a circular ticket hall and also a tower following plans for similar landmarks at Elstree Hill and Bushey Heath stations. The site of Stanley Heaps's booking hall and that of the original road layout are shown in light relief against the proposed covered lanes for buses and private cars and taxis.**

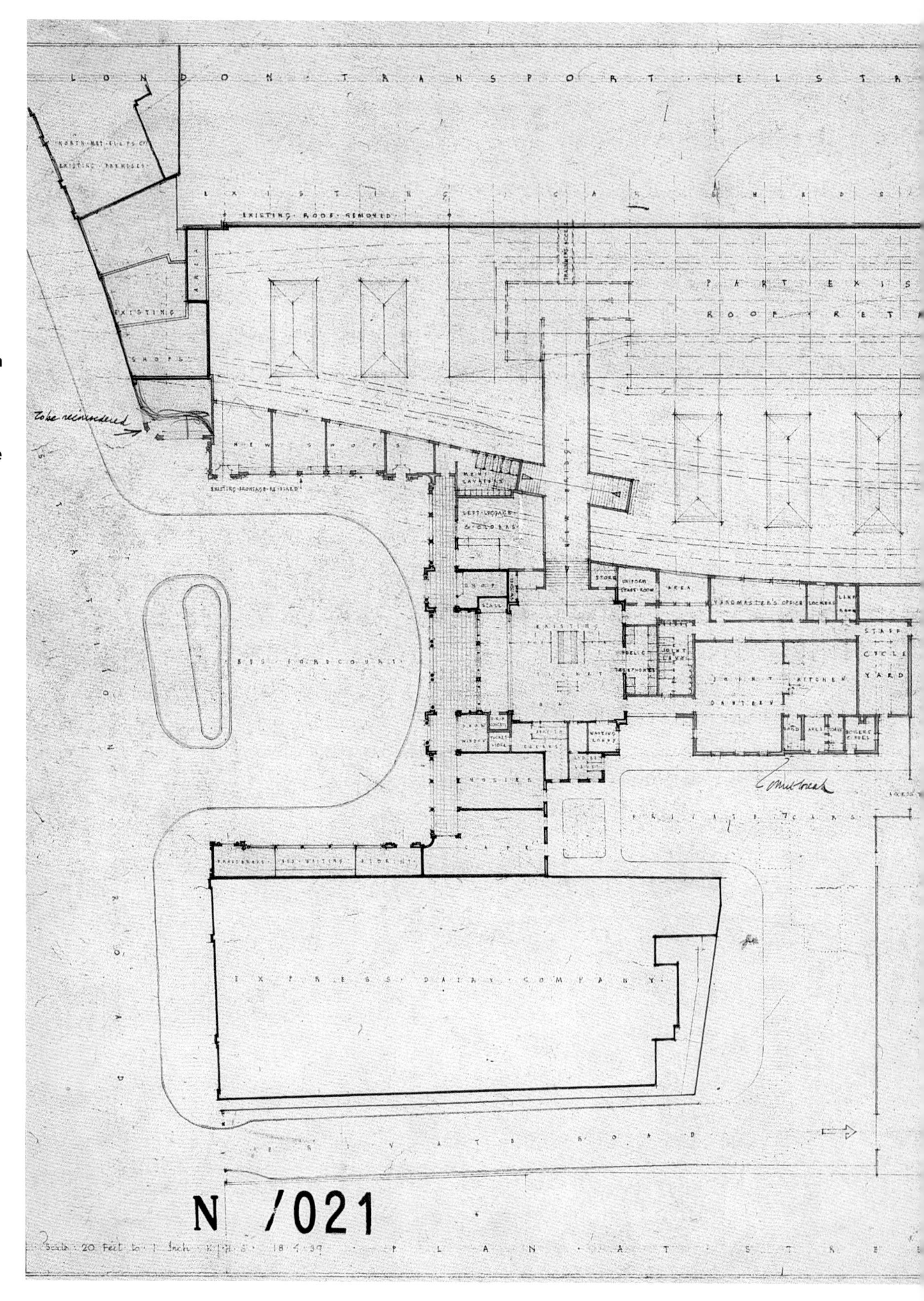

The final version of the revised street level layout for Edgware station is not as severe as those proposed a year earlier. The majority of Stanley Heaps's façade would remain, only the north east wing being demolished although the plan is notated 'existing frontage to be reused', presumably in an attempt to maintain some degree of symmetry. Two revisions were apparently necessary before final approval took place, some ten months later. In appending his signature on 27th February 1940, Frank Pick has added the comment 'subject to minor adjustment' to cover the two hand alterations to the plan. Just three weeks earlier, on 4th February, Pick had indicated that he would not be seeking a further term of office on the Board, departing its service on 17th May.

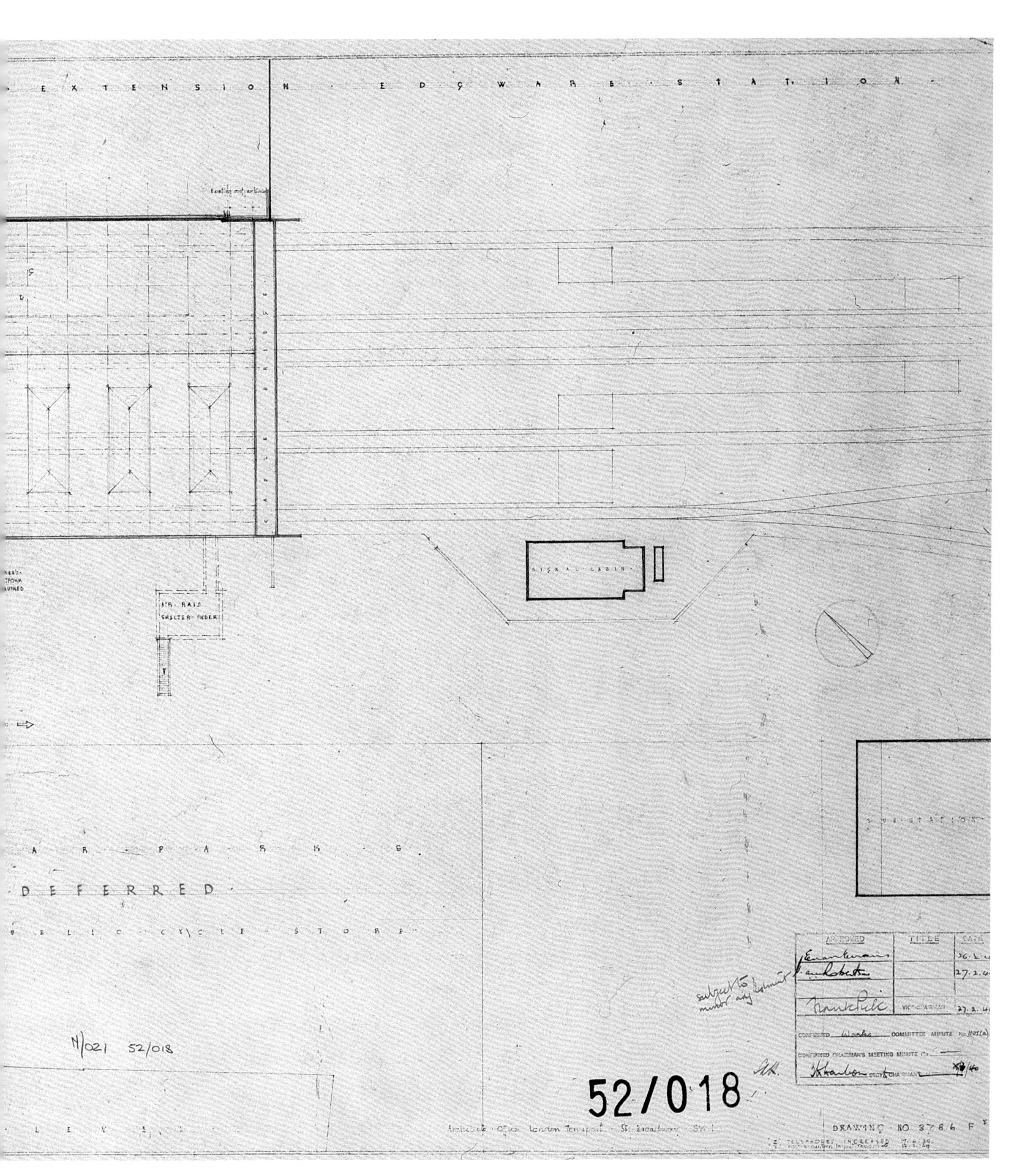
EXTENSION · EDGWARE · STATION
SIGNAL CABIN
SUB-STATION
DEFERRED
DRAWING · NO 3786 F
52/018
N/021 52/018

CHAPTER SEVEN

Postponement

The rise to power of Adolf Hitler as the German Chancellor on 30th January 1933 had been immediately followed by a programme of German rearmament. This provoked Winston Churchill into bringing this to the attention of Parliament in an overstatement that was designed to stress the Dictator's readiness for war. The British Government begrudgingly responded and by the time of the Munich Crisis in September 1938, an effective rearmament of Britain was taking place. The Nazi leader failed to be appeased by the Prime Minister of the day, Neville Chamberlain, and the famous paper-waving demonstration at Heston airfield did little to divert the inevitable. By the end of 1938, the security of the civilian population was being addressed and this had resulted in the establishment of Air Raid Precautions (ARP). Expenditure on Civil Defence expanded dramatically from £9.5 million in the year before Munich to £51 million, (including the fire services) from 1939–1940.

As far as the extension to Elstree was concerned, the plans for Brockley Hill station were studied during February 1939 by members of the Board's Station Committee. They noted that it would not be possible to obtain a clear view into the street from the ARP control room, which had been by then added to the list of facilities at the station. The plans were duly amended by moving the proposed location of the telephone kiosks and sales stall to the sides of the ticket hall to maintain uninterrupted observation of the entrance. Provision for a passenger air raid shelter would be made in the arch of the viaduct adjacent to the ticket hall, the remaining arches serving as lock-up garages.

Despite such an attention to detail, no contracts for the branch had been issued. Moreover, the fact that Britain was on a war footing had not been the major cause for delay – there was simply no funding available. This situation had arisen because the Elstree Extension had not featured in the original New Works Programme estimates drawn up in 1935 for improvements to the Northern Line (the name applied the Northern City Line and Morden–Edgware Line and proposed projections from late August 1937). The subsequent additions to the Programme might have been included in 1935 had the Board been able to consider its original submissions in greater depth. At the time, the Elstree Extension and depot had yet to be finalised, and consideration had first to be given to the two alternative sites mentioned earlier.

In early October 1937, shortly after parliamentary powers had been obtained for the extension, the Treasury was advised that Lord Ashfield was seeking a meeting with the Governor of the Bank of England. This was an attempt by Ashfield to secure an additional £5,000,000 in order to complete the amended programme, although not all of this amount was required for LPTB projects. Of the £5,000,000, the cost of building the Elstree Extension was placed at £1,140,000 (to which a further £90,000 would be added for its rolling stock) and was amongst a list of works considered essential to the completion of the 1935–1940 New Works Programme. Other projects within this category, which accounted for nearly half of the amount requested, included the extension of Acton Works to provide for the overhaul of additional rolling stock and the electrification of the routes from Fenchurch Street to Stratford and Loughton to Ongar. The remainder of the sum would be utilised to finance additional works that comprised the electrification of Ruislip to Denham (and rolling stock), reconstruction and improvements to some of the Board's central area stations and the substitution of trolley-buses for trams over 52½ route miles. Some savings from the original £40,000,000 loan had been identified by the removal from the scheme of the need to lengthen platforms on the Morden–Edgware line, rendered unnecessary by the introduction of improved rolling stock.

The Bank expressed some surprise at this move, it being aware that the Board had already a committed allocation of £28,000,000 from the original £40,000,000 guaranteed by the Government. The remaining £12,000,000 had been allocated to the LNER and GWR at the ratio of 25% and 5% respectively. The Governor suggested his noble lordship raise the capital when required and without Government intervention, a near impossible circumstance for each of the three parties. Eventually the Treasury vaguely responded that the amount could be provided when the Government's rearmament programme slackened off, new railway construction being considered as a slump activity. In August 1938, a letter sent by the Ministry of Transport to the Treasury referred to a statement made by the Standing Joint Committee that the extension of the Northern Line to Aldenham remained essential to the whole project. The Treasury then exercised its penchant for procrastination by requesting additional information despite pleas for a speedy decision.

Ashfield continued to press his case for a loan supplemental to the original agreement. His campaign, during which he enlisted the assistance of part-time member of the Board and director of the Bank of England, Patrick Ashley Cooper, took some considerable time to produce appreciable results. In November 1938 an exasperated Ashfield wrote to the Minister of Transport, Leslie Burgin to inform him of the Board's intention to apply for a further £5m in the forthcoming session of Parliament for the completion of the New Works Programme, the Board's current financial position rendering it impossible to raise any additional capital for the New Works Programme or other projects. Using the tactic of coercion, Ashfield concluded that any consideration of schemes for extending or improving transport facilities would be deferred in the London area until the financial position of the Board improved.

The Standing Joint Committee continued to maintain its support for additional funding to complete the New Works Programme, and once sensing victory, there can be little doubt that Ashfield acted in advance of legislation being received. In consequence, the Board awarded its first contract for work on the line to W & C French on 9th February 1939 for a wall to protect the railway embankment where it passed through the area of the Aldenham Subsidiary Reservoir. On 18th July 1939, the Minister of Transport finally gave his support to further funding being made available by writing personally to the Chancellor of the Exchequer, although there was insufficient time for parliamentary action before the end of the current session.

Tenders had already been invited for the construction of the actual railway. For such purposes, the major works on the line were divided into two sections.

The works on Section One included the long retaining walls from the commencement of the line opposite the station at Edgware, earthworks and cuttings, a footbridge at Purcells Avenue and a viaduct 525 yards long which included a four span bridge over Watford Way and a 55ft span bridge above the service road just north west of Brockley Hill station. Also included were sundry culverts and drains.

The works in Section Two included earthworks on embankments and in cuttings from the north end of the viaduct to the terminus and the whole earthworks for the depot site. Also contained in this section were two shield-driven 12ft diameter tunnels at a point two miles from Edgware with tunnel portals at either end; a footway underbridge and a road-bridge of two arched spans at Elstree Hill; the construction of station platforms at two stations; one access road to the car shed at the depot; sundry stream diversions, culverts and all land and track drainage.

Robert McAlpine successfully tendered for both sections submitting £89,095 for Section One and £133,436 for Section Two. The contract was issued on 26th May 1939 and sealed on 31st August.

In October 1939, a report on progress made with the depot buildings at Aldenham established that the smaller car-cleaning shed was almost complete and that some of the steel framework had been erected for the larger maintenance shed. This view of Aldenham, dated 1st June 1940, shows construction work on the lifting bay for the maintenance shed in the foreground and the exteriorly complete car cleaning shed. Beyond is the trackbed levelled for the main line connecting Elstree South and Bushey Heath stations. By August, due to constant revisions to the original plans, De Havilland would start to take up occupancy of the smaller unit and begin preparations for building fuselages for Mosquito aircraft.

By April 1939 Haymills (Contractors) Ltd had been earmarked to receive the contract for the depot, having carried out similar constructions at Neasden and Grange Hill. At the time, the company was engaged in building Ruislip depot for the Central Line extensions and the Board agreed that a new contract based on that used for Grange Hill should be issued. The 10th August 1939 saw the sealing of a contract with Haymills for the construction of 'various buildings at Aldenham'.

Some revisions had taken place regarding the construction of the depot to take into account current building trends following the Munich

Taken from the reverse angle, the three-track wide lifting bay appears not so well developed as in the previous view. When complete this structure and the adjacent shop inspection bay would extend 1,036 feet, being twice the distance of the framework already erected. By the end of July the Board had been appointed as managing agents for the London Aircraft Production Group but had yet to determine which parts of the completed depot would be required.

crisis. A clerestory roof installed over the workshops was considered more effective in providing protection against the effects of air raids than the pitched glass roof installed at other depots. The outer wall of the workshop would be built to a height of six feet with a continuous window above, which would be carried along through the length of the offices and stores. Additional protection in the form of a brick wall between the workshop and the main car shed was also to be incorporated into the design as this would also facilitate the heating of the workshop. As an anti-blast measure, wired glass would also be installed throughout.

Another view of the car maintenance shed looking towards the site of the proposed terminal at Bushey Heath showing in the foreground, the foundations of a block of five connected outbuildings, the first on this side being a lavatory. It had not escaped the planners' notice that the wartime workforce employed at Aldenham would be far in excess of that for which it had been designed and a commensurate increase in facilities was provided.

Below **Taken from the bridge carrying the LNER tracks above the 'new' line to Golders Green, this August 1940 view contains many items of interest. In the far-left background can be seen the water tower at the LNER Edgware station and to its right the replacement bus garage built to replace an earlier structure which impeded the development of the station area. The bridge in the foreground did not form part of the original plans for the station and was built at the suggestion of J P Thomas who expressed concerns regarding the problems caused by the proposed track layout for the station. The tracks beneath the bridges never saw their intended use, remaining as No. 17 and 18 sidings until they were finally taken out of use in September 1964. The retaining wall on the left marks the end of the site where four sidings were to have been established.**

As recorded in Chapter 4, provision for the doubling and electrification of the line from Finchley to Edgware had been included in the LNER (London Transport) 1936 Bill as part of the New Works Programme. This original line to Edgware had been operated by the GNR until 1923, the company being among those grouped to establish the LNER under the Railway Act of 1921. The contract for this section was given to Fletcher (Contractors) Ltd in November 1937 and work began the following year. In May 1939 the LNER Works Committee received a report that the embankments and cuttings on the branch were proving particularly unstable. Despite meticulous care having been taken in carrying out the widening operation, slips continued to occur and additional funding was made available for restorative work.

A report was produced on 11th August 1939 regarding progress made on the Elstree Extension, work having commenced on 6th June. At Edgware, the new platform wall and earthworks were in progress and construction of the covered way under Station Road had been started. Permanent way works had progressed to allow the first changeover on 26th August when new shunting necks would be brought into use.

On the branch some £30,000 worth of contractors' plant was then in operation, the whole of the railway having been cleared of shrubs and trees, and all culverts and cross drains under embankments having been installed. Between Edgware and Brockley Hill viaduct, about 20% of the general excavation had been completed and about 100 yards of the Edgware retaining walls were under construction. The whole of the brick piers and abutments of the viaduct north of the Watford By-Pass were complete up to arch springing level and a start had been made on three of the brick arches.

On the southern side of the Watford By-Pass the concrete for the six viaduct pier foundations was proceeding. Between the viaduct and Elstree Hill some 10% of the excavation in cutting had been completed, equivalent banks formed, and the driving of the northbound tube tunnel had just been commenced. A start had also been made on the erection of a sub-station near the site of Elstree South station. About 30% of the general excavation of the depot site was in hand. In addition, a substantial start had been made on the foundations for the depot buildings. A report issued on 17th October regarding Haymill's progress determined that the car-cleaning shed was nearing completion and the steelwork for the main depot building was being fabricated. The construction of the signal and permanent way cabins at Edgware and Elstree was assigned to Ekins and Company.

Platform construction at Edgware appears complete in this view dated 6th August 1940. The left-hand side of the new island platform was to be used for terminating trains, cross platform facilities being provided with trains departing for Bushey Heath. The signal cabin built to replace the example that can be seen at the end of the covered train shed remained out of use until 1957. Burrowing work has also begun beneath Station Road, an area subsequently used as an air-raid shelter for the station.

At its meeting held on 21st September 1939, the Board received notification of the contracts sealed with Sir Robert McAlpine and Haymills and at the same time received information relating to war emergency procedures. In consequence, certain parts of the New Works Programme had suffered a general deceleration and in some instances ceased completely. This was due to the whole of the Board's engineering staff and building contractors being required for special tube protective measures. In some cases, the Government had commandeered contractors' plant, transport and labour for its own work. It was also conjectured that recruitment into the armed services, delay in the delivery of structural steelwork and lighting restrictions caused by the blackout would adversely affect the progress of the works. Nevertheless, attempts were made to arrange special priority for the manufacture of materials to finish a few of the projects in hand, even though the demand for some commodities was at a premium due to Britain's re-armament programme. Eventually an agreement with the Fairfield Shipbuilding and Engineering Company was signed, but not until 23rd May 1940. Fairfield's contract was for the supply of steelwork for the footbridge at Purcells Avenue, station platforms, the bridges at Watford Way and Brockley Hill station (including the ticket hall roof. The Board's Works Committee agreed to Fairfield's suggestion that the company should store the steelwork at its Chepstow premises for the duration of the war.

Despite its efforts, the Board quickly accepted the inevitable and decided that in the current climate the Elstree Extension was inessential and that work should be halted. Arrangements were put in hand for the recently issued contracts to be terminated and the building sites to be made safe. One factor no doubt influencing the Board's decision was the unlikelihood of funding being made available now that war had been declared. The Ministry of Transport ratified the Board's decision in December, but there is a strongly held theory that the project had already been closed down by the end of September. The Treasury then put its cards on the table and proposed that the entire New Works Programme should be abandoned, a view not shared by the Board.

Although work to complete the Extension was unceremoniously halted, there was still some hope of completing the reconstruction of Edgware station. The new track layout would consist of two island platforms with the inner faces alongside terminal tracks. This would be created using the original platforms dating from the 1924 opening and that constructed in 1932, the latter having a second, outer face added for through trains to Bushey Heath and not totally swept away, as some sources believe. The only new platform was a single island with northbound interchange facilities on the west side of the site. Built on land originally occupied by the five sidings laid down in 1931, the eastern face of the platform paralleled and would give access to trains for Bushey Heath, a terminal track being laid between its western face and a new retaining wall. The new track layout had necessitated the demolition of the Board's Edgware bus garage and a contract for its resited replacement was issued in July 1938, the new premises opening in January 1939.

The steam service operated by the LNER from Finchley to its own terminal station at Edgware had been suspended from 11th September 1939 in order to accelerate the work in hand, which could be more swiftly undertaken when there were no trains in operation. The proposed date for the opening of this section was 1st April 1940 but engineering difficulties delayed the completion of the Board's Edgware station to allow the introduction of an electric service by that date. V A M Robertson, the Chief Engineer, therefore put forward a suggestion that the reconstruction of Edgware station should be completed apart from the final stage involving the diversion of the LNER's line into the Board's station. This, he conjectured, could be put in hand as soon as possible and until the connecting junction and associated signalling was installed it should be possible to provide an electric shuttle service to the LNER station at Edgware. He anticipated that this temporary projection could be brought into use on 14th April 1940 to coincide with the opening of the electric service to High Barnet.

However, the Works Committee decided that the electrification of the Edgware branch to Finchley should be held in suspense until work was sufficiently advanced to enable its trains to run into the Board's station. This decision was taken at the end of January 1940 when it was considered that a twelve-month deferment would enable some advancement to be made on the eastern extension of the Central Line. Even so it was reported that the LNER proposed, as opportunity offered, to proceed with the permanent way doubling of their Edgware branch.

By February, the Committee had decided that should it be impractical to complete Edgware station for terminating trains from the Finchley route during 1941, then such facility should be shelved until after the war.

In view of this resolution the Works Committee's attention was drawn to the inadequacy of reversing capacity at the south end of the Board's Edgware station, now that it was to be used as a terminal for all trains during the war period. The installation of an additional single crossing was adjudged necessary for trains that would use the tracks ultimately projected towards Bushey Heath. The most convenient position for the additional facilities would be north of the station, again echoing the proposals considered in 1931, involving the continuance of civil engineering ground work under Station Road and beyond to provide a siding. Despite the engineering work being approved, the escalation of developments on the war front brought about its cancellation.

However, a brave attempt was made to plan for peacetime in the midst of war. The inaugural meeting of the Post War Planning Committee was held on 18th December 1942 to produce its own terms of reference for each of the Board's spheres of operation. For the benefit of the Committee, the New Works Programme 1935–40 was divided into three sections:

1. Those schemes already commenced.
2. Those schemes not yet commenced.
3. Those additional to either of the aforementioned schemes.

The Elstree Extension was amongst a list of nine contained in the first category, the remit for which comprised four sections, all requiring consultation with the LNER, GWR and other main line railways:

a. To review those schemes commenced as part of the New Works Programme 1935–40 which had yet to be brought into service and upon which appreciable expenditure had been incurred. Proposals for modifications would be made in consideration of anticipated traffic needs after the war, but more significant would be the stage of construction reached at the time of closure.
b. To review the aforementioned works from operating, engineering and architectural viewpoints, and suggest any modifications to plans including standards of construction and the design of stations and depots.
c. To review and report on the train services yet to be introduced over the new extensions.
d. To report upon the expenditure estimates required for any modifications over and above the sum already raised to finance the programme.

Although this diversion of the main running lines from Golders Green was approved in September 1936 to give trains direct access to the Elstree Extension, work was late in starting and depicted here is the extent of work achieved by 18th December 1939. One of the main factors no doubt influencing the path of this new route was the existence of the bridge from which this view is taken. The LNER route to Edgware would have proved an expensive obstacle to overcome but with Dean's Brook recently contained (left), the bridge could be used to span the new link.

The Post War Planning Committee was established when victory in Europe was still some two and a half years in the future, with such horrors as the Baby Blitz of 1944 and the bombardment of London by Hitler's V-Weapons still to be endured. At that time current thinking reflected on the urgency to complete the works already commenced as soon as the war ended, having regard for the large amounts of capital expenditure already consumed. An early review of the works was therefore thought necessary and subsequently taken to an advanced stage before the conclusion of hostilities, urgent action deemed necessary as fresh Parliamentary powers might be required to cover any modifications.

No doubt in anticipation of the Elstree Extension being built, the Board's Architects produced future plans of the extension. Brockley Hill was one of the first sites to be the subject of amendment in May 1942, which showed a repositioned station entrance amid a parade of shops serving the bus terminus. A survey of the whole line produced further new drawings in October 1942, these updating an earlier set created when tenders for the construction of the line were invited during early 1939.

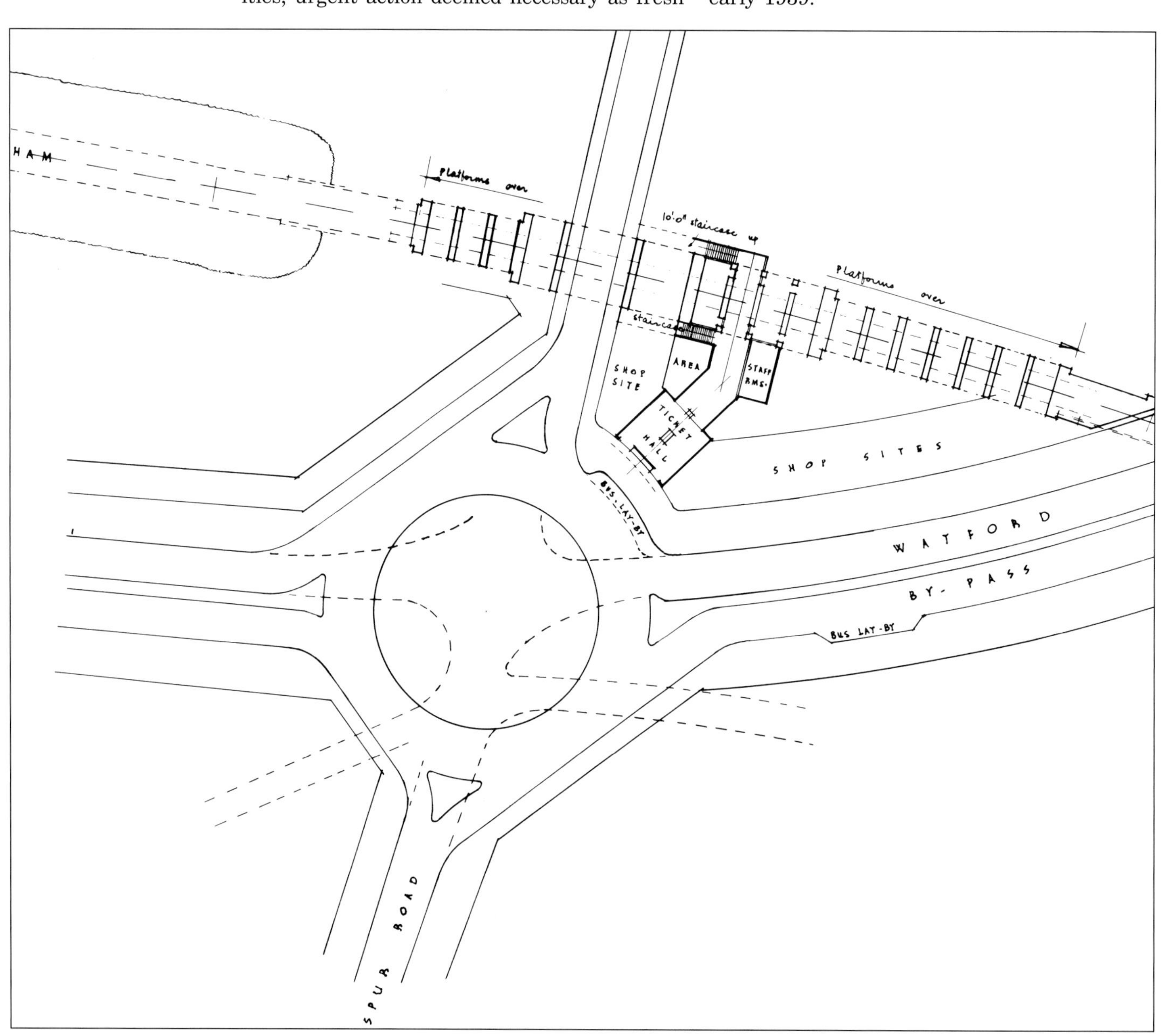

Despite the onset of war, plans for stations on the extension continued to be revised. This layout for Brockley Hill dated 1st May 1942 shows the ticket hall resited between two groups of shops, having been brought closer to the proposed roundabout and adjacent lay-by. By this time, work on the extension had been abandoned, but not before construction work had begun on the supporting arches.

Though dated August 1943 this layout of Elstree South station is based on the design by Adams, Holden & Pearson just before the war (see page 79 for perspective sketch).

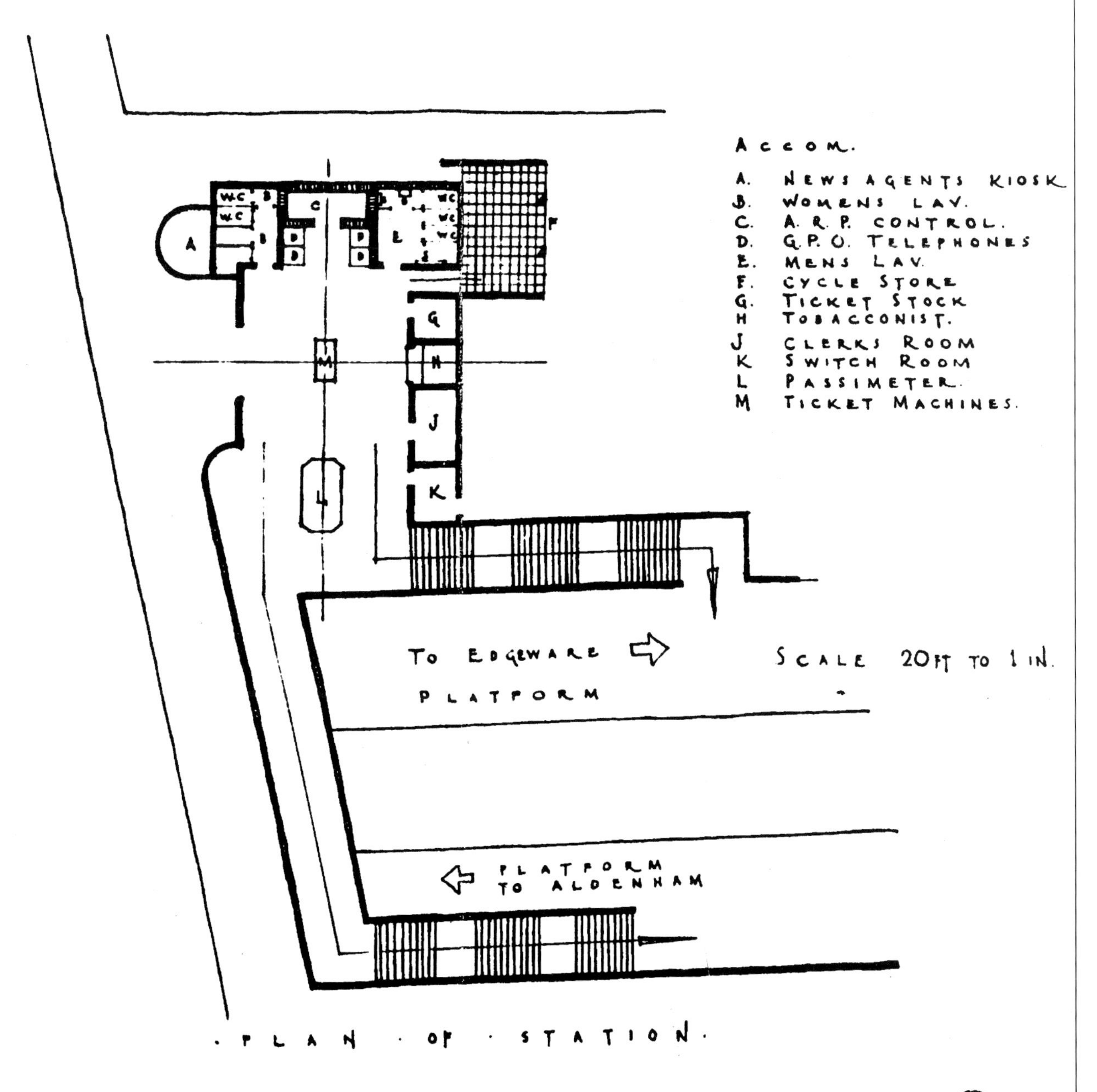

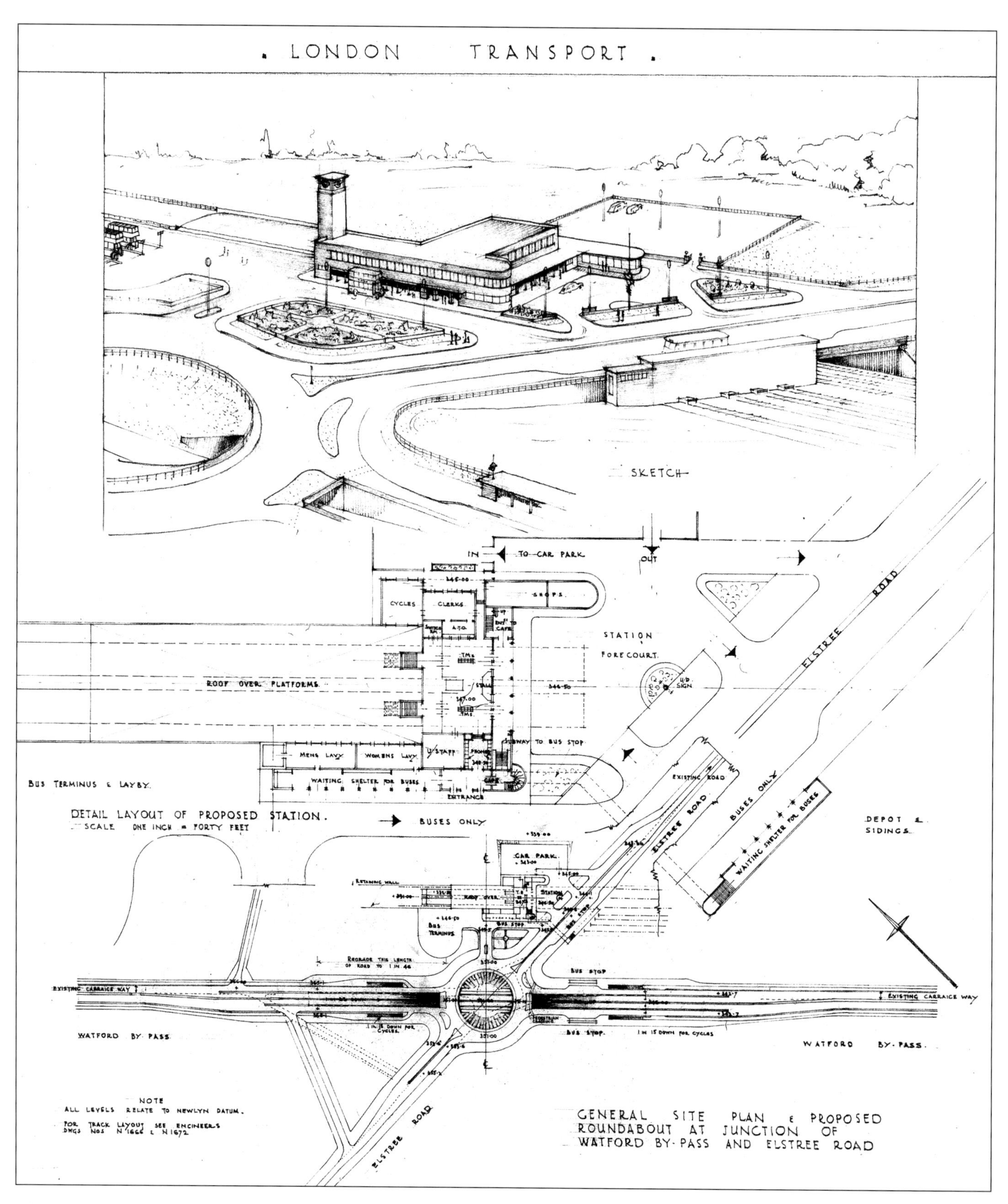
. LONDON TRANSPORT .
SKETCH
IN
TO CAR PARK
OUT
CYCLES
CLERKS
SHOPS
STATION
FORE COURT.
ROOF OVER PLATFORMS
SUBWAY TO BUS STOP
MENS LAVY
WOMENS LAVY
WAITING SHELTER FOR BUSES
ENTRANCE
BUS TERMINUS & LAYBY.
DETAIL LAYOUT OF PROPOSED STATION.
SCALE ONE INCH = FORTY FEET
BUSES ONLY
ELSTREE ROAD
EXISTING ROAD
BUSES ONLY
WAITING SHELTER FOR BUSES
DEPOT & SIDINGS
CAR PARK
BUS TERMINUS
BUS STOP
EXISTING CARRIAGE WAY
WATFORD BY PASS
WATFORD BY-PASS
NOTE
ALL LEVELS RELATE TO NEWLYN DATUM.
FOR TRACK LAYOUT SEE ENGINEERS DWGS NOS N 1666 & N 1672
GENERAL SITE PLAN & PROPOSED ROUNDABOUT AT JUNCTION OF WATFORD BY-PASS AND ELSTREE ROAD

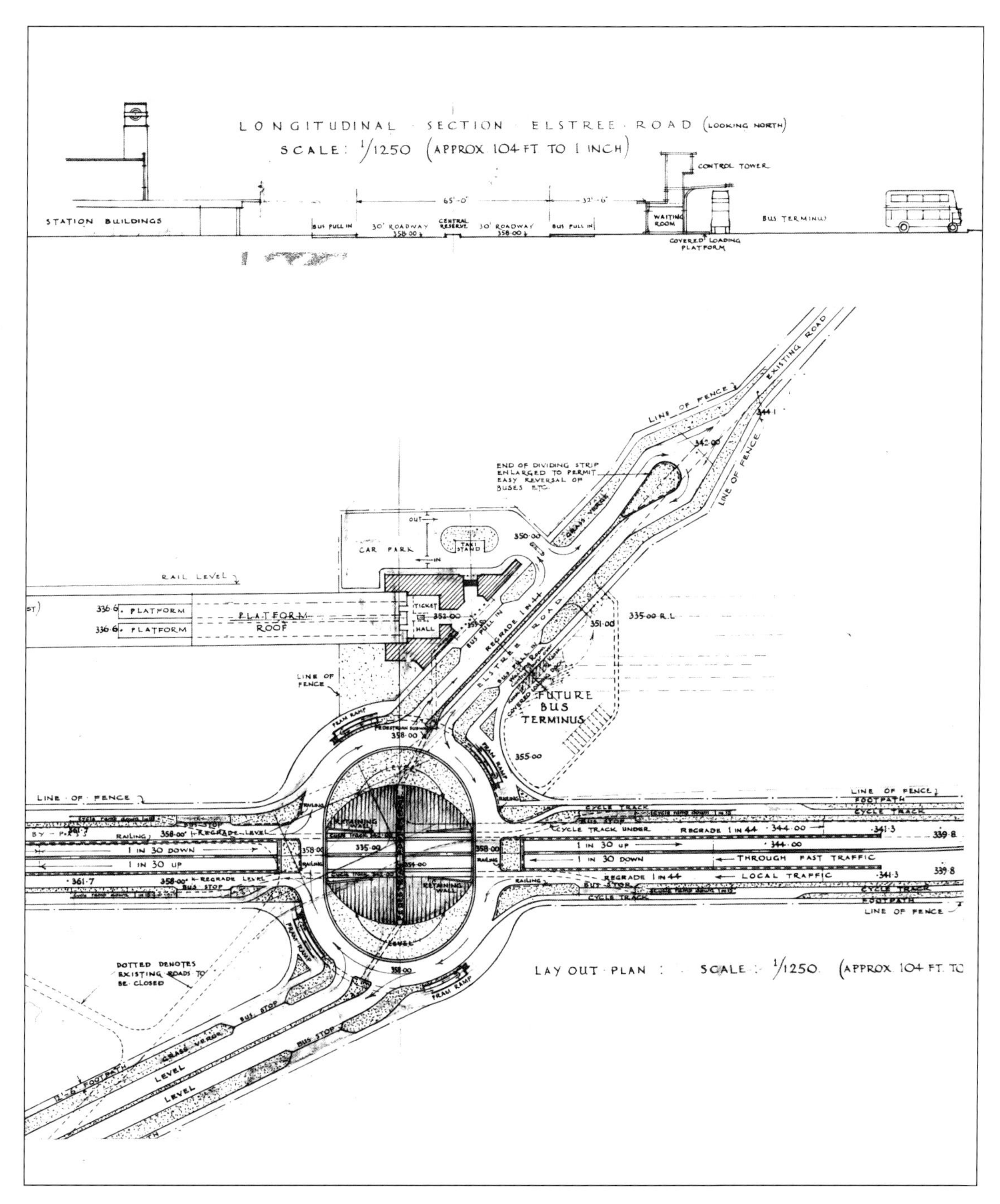

Facing page **Revisions to the original plans for the Elstree Extension continued throughout the years of conflict. This plan of Bushey Heath was produced in December 1943. The principal purpose for such radical thinking lay in the proposal to create a flyunder for the Watford By-Pass beneath the roundabout in front of Bushey Heath station. The LPTB were aware that such construction would preclude any further development of the line and consequently a repositioning was undertaken of the terminal which was then capable of providing through station facilities.**

Left **A further suggested revision to the shape and the access points of the roundabout in front of Bushey Heath station followed in early 1944. The plan included a cross-section of Elstree Road and provides detail of the proposed bus station, complete with control tower, linked to the tube station by one of the subways skirting the circumference of the roundabout.**

Bushey Heath and Elstree South stations were also the subject of layout amendments following the formation of the Post War Planning Committee. During December 1943, plans were issued showing the terminus at Bushey Heath sited on the opposite side of Elstree Road in order to take in a widening scheme that also involved the construction of a new roundabout and flyunder at its intersection with North Western Avenue and the Watford By-Pass. Although Bushey Heath remained the terminus of the Elstree Extension, the amended design for the station allowed for further projection. Another road-widening scheme involved Elstree Hill and initiated a new layout for the area immediately in front of Elstree South station, for which plans were produced in December 1944.

This painting of Elstree South by Barry Pearce is based on the revised sketch for the station produced in December 1944, which encompassed a road widening scheme planned for Elstree Hill. An example of 1938 stock is seen leaving the station for Bushey Heath.

An early post-war photograph of the route between Brockley Hill station and Edgware. The arches and piers each side of Edgware Way show the extent of building work here when work stopped. The buildings between Brockley Hill station arches and the main road are probably farm buildings put up when the LPTB land was used for farming during the Second World War. Farms here and at Bushey Heath grew food to help supply the board's 135 canteens.

Another remit of the Post War Planning Committee centred on railway depots and required a report on the standards of construction and design of existing installations. Recommendations could then be made regarding the equipment and facilities that should be introduced to ensure the highest degree of operation and maintenance whilst providing satisfactory working conditions for the staff. The standards produced would also include a review of the original plans prepared for the depots in the New Works Programme 1935/40 situated at Aldenham, Ruislip and Grange Hill. Proposals and estimates could then be submitted for any modifications that would be practical or desirable when work was restarted on these depots after the war.

But now we must return to the period immediately following the decision to close down work on the Elstree Extension. A report issued on 17th October 1939 to determine progress being made at Aldenham noted that the car-cleaning shed was nearing completion and steel framing for the main depot building was in the course of being erected. Pick therefore requested that the War Office, Air Ministry and other Government departments be contacted to ascertain their interest in using the depot buildings. If such an arrangement were entered into, construction would continue in order to complete the buildings as far as possible for their new role. Should the opposite apply, then the construction of the larger shed would be halted and delivery taken of such steelwork that had been fabricated, which would then be stored in the car cleaning shed.

Initial interest in using the premises came from the Board itself. On 2nd January 1940, the Chief Engineer (Buses and Coaches), A A M Durrant reported to the War Emergency Committee that once delivery had been completed of the 150 2RT2 buses, the spare fleet of

unlicensed buses suitable for service would number 400 vehicles. In conjunction with the Estate Agent, Durrant had endeavoured to locate additional under-cover storage for the spare vehicles. A space for 50 buses had been found at a garage in Clapham Road owned by Red and White Coaches, and 93 were being stored at the Board's properties, giving a balance of 257 vehicles still without homes.

Durrant was opposed to the idea of building temporary structures and proposed that the remainder of the unlicensed fleet should be stored in garages considered more vulnerable to enemy air attack such as Sidcup, Grays, Dartford and Northfleet where the normal peacetime complement of buses had been reduced. Alternatively, it was considered that space might be made available by the dispersal of obsolete and redundant vehicles currently located at Walthamstow in the former AEC works and Chiswick Tram Depot.

The Committee agreed with the Chief Engineer's second proposal but suggested that he consider the use of the partly finished depot at Aldenham. After examining the plans, Durrant considered that the shop bay would be the most suitable and suggested this building should be constructed in accordance with original specification. Mindful of the use for which Aldenham had been designed, Durrant proposed the addition of a temporary wall to finish the building and the laying of an ash floor instead of concrete. Pick directed Durrant to submit a considered proposal, with expenditure estimates.

Barely a week later, on 8th January 1940, Frederick Handley Page reported to the Air Council Committee on Supply that the London Passenger Transport Board was in the process of establishing a depot near Elstree. What then occurred was to become the next instalment in Aldenham's chequered history.

CHAPTER EIGHT

From Underground Depot to Aircraft Factory

During the official opening of the bus overhaul works in 1956, a plaque was unveiled. The 200 guinea marble slab (now to be found in London's Transport Museum's 'Depot' at Acton) recorded the fact that the original buildings on the site had been used by London Transport, as part of the London Aircraft Production Group, for producing 710 Halifax bombers for the Royal Air Force.

Although essentially correct, a number of factors have come to light which reveal that, had the original wartime plan for Aldenham been adopted, then London Transport would certainly never had made such a major contribution to the country's war effort.

It was most fortunate that the partly constructed depot was discovered by Frederick Handley Page so early in the war. Up to the point of the contract being closed down, Haymills had successfully erected the smaller of the two main buildings, with a floor space of 38,000 square feet, intended for the cleaning of rolling stock. The second structure, for car maintenance and with an area of 262,000 square feet, existed in skeletal form only. Its shape was that of a reversed 'L' and, when complete, would provide nineteen roads with covered accommodation. Of the nineteen, seven roads were to have been laid through the extended section, twice the length of the remainder of the building and paralleling the Watford By-Pass for a distance of 1,036 feet. Here overhead lifting facilities would be installed over the three outer roads where the height to the eaves was 25 feet; 15 feet being standard for the rest of the depot.

Handley Page set up its aircraft building business in Dagenham during 1908. In response to an Air Ministry specification calling for a two-engine bomber, as part of the country's rearmament programme during the mid-1930s, the company set about redesigning one of its earlier projects. This met with the approval of the Ministry and a further development contract was awarded in April 1937. This was quickly withdrawn when the Rolls-Royce Vulture engines, that were to have powered the aircraft, began suffering design problems, resulting in the issue of a revised specification calling for the installation of four Merlins. The company responded and began construction of a prototype in January 1938, its maiden flight at RAF Bicester taking place on 25th October 1939.

Although a number of teething troubles occurred during flight testing, the Government decided that the new aircraft, upon which the name Halifax was bestowed, should become a front line bomber. Arrangements for manufacture were therefore initiated and Frederick Handley Page, the company's Managing Director, was asked to oversee the construction of a factory at Stoke. This would be used for the construction of Halifax aircraft in addition to the company's own premises at Claremont Road, Cricklewood. In order to accelerate construction even further, Handley Page suggested that a sub-contracting scheme should be established within the London area under the control of the De Havilland company.

In the first few months of the war, the De Havilland company's contribution to the country's call for arms mainly centred on Tiger Moth, Dominie and Oxford aircraft together with its Gypsy series engines and variable pitch propellers. There was also a private venture on the drawing board for a high-speed bomber reconnaissance aircraft built to Government specification B1/40, a token order for 50, to include six unflown prototypes being issued in March 1940.

De Havilland stated that it would be happy to assist in setting up Halifax production but reasoned that any sub-contracting would best be left with the parent company. Frederick Handley Page then wrote to the Air Ministry and stated that, should his company be required to assume the role of sub-contractor then it might be necessary to relinquish control over the construction of the factory at Stoke.

On 10th January 1940, De Havilland were asked by the Ministry to proceed with the preparation of an aerodrome at Leavesden, near Watford, and its associated aircraft assembly sheds. Once built, the sheds would provide one million square feet of covered accommodation for the construction of Halifax aircraft, in addition to Handley Page's own airfield at Radlett. At the same time as this agreement was reached, the Ministry entered discussions with Frank Pick regarding the use of the Aldenham site. In realising the urgency to finish construction of the depot, Pick opened negotiations with the Ministry of Transport to advance the finance necessary for its completion and under the terms of the original Government guarantee. The Board would then let the premises to the Ministry for Aviation Production for the remainder of the war.

It was planned that the depot should be finished in accordance with the original plans, but with a number of modifications including the installation of improved heating and lighting. The erection of temporary buildings would extend the premises to the size required and the ever-resourceful Pick offered to arrange for the transfer of labour from Watford and Edgware. Even at this early stage there was a hint of the Board's involvement, as Pick was reported as being undecided as to whether the LPTB could usefully assist in Halifax production. From November 1939, the Board had been seeking to obtain war work for its Chiswick Works but there was an important hurdle to overcome. The London Passenger Transport Act of 1933 precluded the Board from undertaking any emergency manufacturing other than for its own purpose. Once there appeared to be some relaxation of this regulation on the horizon, a contract was sought for the construction of lorry bodies and cabs for Thornycroft Ltd, although this subsequently failed.

The Air Council Committee of Supply interviewed Frederick Handley Page on 16th January and secured an agreement that he would proceed with his commitment to oversee the construction of the Stoke Factory that was due for completion in July. At the same time, it was agreed that the Watford Aircraft Factory Project, under the management of De Havilland, should continue as planned. This would be subject to any reductions in size, which might be agreed between the Director General of Aircraft Production, De Havilland and Handley Page in consequence of the allocation of Aldenham Depot to the scheme.

Any sub-contractors in the London Area recruited by Handley Page would supply the company's aircraft factory at Radlett, where an increase in space was suggested to cater for the additional output. Handley Page had already received an order for 200 Halifax aircraft from the Ministry with a further order of 200 to be completed by the Stoke factory, once this installation was up and running. However, the company's entrepreneurial Managing Director suggested a different arrangement. In order to secure the largest possible output of aircraft, the initial order placed with his company should be increased by a further 200. All aircraft would then be constructed at the Cricklewood and Radlett factories, supplemented by a further order of 200 to be built at Stoke when that facility became available.

From a contractual viewpoint the Air Council Committee on Supply had no objection to diverting an order for 200 Halifax aircraft for manufacture by the London sub-contractors, which it hoped had been selected as being suitable and efficient. This would be on the understanding that Handley Page became legally bound to give the necessary manufacturing data, advice and assistance. The scheme was also advantageous to the Air Ministry inasmuch as Handley Page would not be entitled to profit on the cost, as it would if the work were sub-contracted by the company. Conversely, Handley Page was entitled to claim for the use of his design on the direct orders placed by the Ministry.

In normal circumstances, the manufacture of aircraft is usually contained on a single site. In order to produce an aircraft at a range of locations the principle of construction had to be one of complete standardisation of parts. What the Halifax lacked aesthetically was certainly compensated for in its ease of assembly.

On 22nd January 1940, Lee Murray, General Manager of the Aircraft Division of the De Havilland Company wrote to the Air Supply Board to confirm his organisation's involvement in the erection of a factory at Watford (Leavesden) Aerodrome. He also reported that discussions were due to take place with Frank Pick regarding the use of Aldenham Depot for the construction of Halifax bombers. If it were found possible to accelerate the programme further by LPTB's involvement, then the floor space occupied by De Havilland would be reduced accordingly. This was the second reference in as many weeks to the likelihood of the Board becoming involved with war work, although the minutes of its meetings fail to reflect such interest. Nevertheless, in his memorandum dated 2nd February Pick suggested that, due to the war, land adjacent to Bushey Heath and Elstree station sites might be cheaply available, having decreased in value. The area could then be used to provide an aerodrome where aircraft built at the Board's aircraft factory at Aldenham could be test flown!

The Watford/Aldenham Scheme subsequently became part of the Government's 'Shadow Factory' initiative. Despite this seemingly sinister reference, the purpose behind the plan was to establish factories at Government expense to supplement the output of aircraft from factories already in existence. Frederick Handley Page made a most controversial pronouncement in stating that shadow factories only made a relatively minor contribution to the aircraft production programme. To his mind, these units only stood to serve as reserves, further expansion or accommodation should existing factories be bombed.

A comprehensive survey of Aldenham Depot was also requested; discussions between the Board's architects and those employed by De Havilland having reached an agreement relating to the state of the buildings upon hand over.

The resulting report described the buildings as being generally of steel frame construction, with brick infilling and steel purlins carrying patent glazing with wired glass and cement asbestos troughing. The total area of the site was in the region of 88 acres and had cost £35,000. However, the area leased was to be limited to immediate requirements, with the building work taking an estimated eight months to complete. It was agreed that there would be some reduction in the cost of the original building contract, nominally £270,000, as certain works, which related to the requirements of the LPTB were included which were unnecessary. For instance, steel shutters would have normally been used to close each end of the building for which brickwork walls would be substituted. Large and small doors for aircraft production purposes would be required, and panic doors would be installed to facilitate the swift evacuation of the premises in an emergency.

A revised estimate of £175,000 for the erection of the buildings was provided by the Board and the rent was based on this figure. Agreement was reached with the Ministry of Aircraft Production based on a five-year occupancy from 1st August 1940 or until the end of the war, whichever was the shorter period. At the end of the term the Ministry, at its own expense, would be required to reinstate and restore the premises in accordance with agreed plans. This was to include the removal of any equipment or additional buildings although the Board reserved the right to purchase such structures upon giving notice.

No railway track had been laid in either of the two buildings. By excavating the some areas of the maintenance shed floor to be level with the base of the inspection pits, additional height could be gained. A new floor was also to be installed in the car-cleaning shed.

In order to adapt the depot for its new role many additional items were required, including items for ARP services such as a trailer pump, shelters, camouflage and an air raid siren.

It must be recorded that as an underground depot, Aldenham would have possessed a workforce far fewer in number than that anticipated for the construction of aircraft parts. Therefore an increase in facilities above those originally planned, such as additional toilets and canteen facilities, would be necessary – temporary buildings being required for this purpose. A complete boiler and heating installation would also be provided, albeit using second hand equipment.

Arrangements for the supply of electricity were made with the Northmet Company for a temporary supply from the National Grid. As originally planned, power to the depot would have been provided by the live rail and a supply from the substation at Elstree South.

On 24th January, Handley Page wrote to the Ministry of Aviation Production and requested to be released from his responsibility to oversee the construction and management of the Stoke Factory, citing a shortage of materials as the main reason. This situation was deemed responsible for delaying the start of Halifax bomber production at the company's Cricklewood and Radlett factories, which now apparently demanded his full attention. Handley Page also stated that resources would also be taxed by the calling up of a number of employees into the armed services and his involvement in setting up the London subcontract organisation.

Naturally the Ministry were disappointed at Handley Page's decision, but a further demonstration of manoeuvring by the company chairman was set to follow.

The Ministry had been led to understand that of the order for 400 bombers placed with the company, 200 would be constructed using components supplied by the London subcontractors. But Handley Page requested the release of a separate order for 200 aircraft to be built by the London Group, having previously queried the future of the contract for the same number that would be built at the new Stoke factory. At this point, it could be easily construed that Handley Page had an ulterior motive in becoming disassociated with the Stoke project. However the Air Council had previously decided that the allocation of 400 aircraft to be built by the company should stand and the order for 200 to be constructed at Stoke would be deferred until the management of the factory had been settled.

On 9th March, De Havilland entered into discussions with the Air Council regarding the possibility of bringing a Halifax operation into existence based on three sites. These comprised the old Alliance Depot at Western Avenue in Acton, Aldenham with final assembly taking place at Watford (Leavesden) Airfield. On 12th March 1940, the Council issued De Havilland with an order for 150 Halifax bombers to be built at these sites.

On 15th March Handley Page was interviewed by the Air Council during which he put forward his proposals for the manufacture of major components of the Halifax by six large firms in the London Area. Handley Page confirmed that his company would be prepared to undertake technical supervision of the whole organisation, but not financial responsibility due to the number of risks involved. In order to resolve the situation, he suggested that the firms involved should become direct contrators of the Air Ministry but after further discussion implied that his company might manage the enterprise on a shadow factory basis.

The Air Council failed to accept either of Handley Page's proposals and stated that if the company were not prepared to accept normal management responsibilities, then alternative arrangements would have to be considered.

During early February 1940, A A M Durrant had met with representatives from Handley Page with regard to the Board undertaking work under contract for the Air Ministry at Chiswick Works. Such was the magnitude of the assignment that it was considered impractical to take on additional projects at Chiswick. The Board agreed that there was an urgent need to obtain additional work for its West London plant to enable the factory to function efficiently and requested that discussions be brought to an early conclusion. But it was not until 15th April that Durrant was summoned to discussions with the aircraft company. Also in attendance were representatives from Express Motors and Body Works of Enfield; Chrysler Motors of Kew; Duple Bodies and Motors of Hendon; and Park Royal Coachworks. This was the initial meeting of the London Aircraft Production Group, Handley Page informing those assembled that his company would act as main contractor and that an order for 200 Halifax bombers had been received from the Ministry.

A follow-up communication from Handley Page was sent to all members of the embryonic London Aircraft Production consortium. This was written confirmation that instructions had been received from the Air Ministry authorising the company on behalf of the Secretary of State for Air to place contracts for the delivery of components for 200 Halifax bombers. The letter sent to the Board contained details of the component to be entrusted to its workshops. This comprised the central fuselage complete with the inner flaps and all equipment for which an agreed schedule and details of assembly were being drawn up. Similar letters detailing other sections of the aircraft were sent to the other constituent companies.

Handley Page agreed with the Ministry that the provisional output of the Group should be 32 Halifax bombers each month in addition to 16 per month being produced by Handley Page itself. Assembly would take place at Radlett and an estimate of £625,000 was submitted for additional facilities to be installed at the airfield to meet the potential monthly output of 48 aircraft. However, the Battle of Britain had yet to be fought and the country's role was mainly defensive, the first LAPG product not being expected until the winter of 1941/42.

Originally the Group was to consist of six organisations, but the requisitioning of the premises used by Strachans in North Acton reduced the number to five. Strachans were due to manufacture all hydraulic equipment required for undercarriage retraction and other units similarly powered such as the tail unit, flap control and undercarriage doors. Handley Page therefore turned to the Board with a request for it to take on the additional task of producing these components. In its letter of confirmation that followed, the company noted that the works at Aldenham, then currently booked for work by De Havilland could be used by the Board to undertake this extra commission. Although De Havilland were accountable for arranging all adaptations to Aldenham Depot to make the premises suitable for aircraft production, its contract to build Halifax bombers was terminated on 20th May 1940 and superseded by another for the construction of Albemarle light bombers.

The Armstrong Whitworth Albemarle can hardly be described as one of the most outstanding aircraft of the Royal Air Force. Operating mainly as a troop carrier or glider-tug, the aircraft was designed with a structure built mainly of wood and steel for bomber reconnaissance when a shortage of light alloys was thought likely. In view of the Ministry's decision, all three De Havilland sites at Watford, Aldenham and Acton were reclassified to the lowest priority 'Z', and consequently any further construction work was postponed.

In centring its wartime manufacturing operation at Chiswick Works, the LPTB would have at its disposal some 140,000 square feet that would be dedicated to Halifax component production. The area had been used for the manufacture and repair of bus bodies, some of this work still to be undertaken. There would be, of course, some necessary adaptation in order to establish a self-contained unit, it being anticipated that some of the existing machinery could be used, augmented by the acquisition of additional plant.

It was estimated that six sets of components could be produced on a weekly basis. Such an output would require a staff of around 1,200, payment being made using a 'time and line' bonus scheme similar to that in operation in the Handley Page factory. Initial expenditure for various adaptations was expected to be about £50,000, for which the Ministry would be responsible, together with necessary alterations completed by the Board's building department. The Ministry was also asked to give an undertaking that it would be responsible for restoring the property to its original condition at the cessation of wartime manufacturing activities.

But a major obstacle remained to be surmounted. The Board had no experience in the field of aircraft production, and it was agreed that the first twenty sets of components should be constructed as an educational order. This would allow experience to be gained and consequently be able to set realistically the cost of production of the remaining 180 sets that formed the balance of the initial order.

However, there was to be a sudden turn of events, which originated at a special meeting on 29th July 1940 and convened at the Ministry of Aviation Production. In attendance were L C Hawkins, the Board's Comptroller, E C Ottaway, then Acting Works Manager at Chiswick, and Major Buchanan together with other Ministry officials. Early indications had suggested that the Ministry was about to appoint Ottaway to administer the London Aircraft Production Group but, in the event, the Board was asked to assume this role. In turn, the Board appointed Ottaway to manage of the scheme on its behalf. This subtle difference was no doubt prompted by the Minister's behest for the Board to become wholly accountable for administering the scheme; the area of responsibility laid on Ottaway's shoulders was nevertheless far reaching. Under his direct control would be the Chiswick aircraft factory, the administration of all contracts, co-ordination and expedition of the work of all sub-contractors and the delivery of components for assembly before final construction. Frederick Handley Page recorded his approval of the appointment and agreed to provide all the necessary technical data.

It was not until the following month that the sweeping changes made by the Ministry in the management of the London Aircraft Production Group became known. Handley Page, it transpired, had been issuing contracts to members of the Group on behalf of the Secretary of State for Air without possession of an instruction from the Ministry to proceed. The Board expressed uncertainty about its recent assignment, as it was felt that such action might have repercussions amongst the sub-contractors whose confidence had suffered as a result of being misled by Handley Page.

An immediate worry for Ottaway and his team was that there was now a requirement to fix a price for each aircraft provided by the Group, calculated using the costings supplied by the sub-contractors. His major cause for concern was that there might be some financial loss should one of the companies be unable to complete work on a particular section of the aircraft due to enemy action.

The London Passenger Transport Board finally received a report on the action taken on its behalf during the summer, at its meeting held on 5th September 1940, although Lord Ashfield had received notification on 31st July. The Board subsequently approved all contracts made with the Ministry of Aircraft Production, which contained arrangements for progress payments to be made at stages of manufacture by the sub-contractors and for the components constructed by the LPTB. These contracts would replace those issued previously by Handley Page, the Company continuing to undertake final assembly at its Radlett Airfield factory.

The allocation of Halifax component construction, as originally defined by Handley Page, was maintained. This resulted in the Chrysler Car and Dodge Truck factory being given responsibility for assembling the rear fuselage in addition to manufacturing trucks for the Ministry of Supply. Duple Bodies and Motors Limited, better known for building luxury coach bodies and, later in the war, bodies for utility buses, was contracted to provide fully equipped front fuselages. The Express Motor and Body Works, then undertaking engineering work for the Carter Paterson fleet and producing specialised truck bodies, was charged with the erection of the intermediate wings and tail units. Park Royal Coachworks, widely known in the field of bus body construction (of which some would later be built to utility specifications), were to fabricate the outer wings and outboard engine cowlings. The remaining elements of the aircraft would be manufactured by the LPTB.

A change in the fortunes of the De Havilland Aircraft Company was also about to take place. The private project built to Ministry specification B1/40 had now been become DH 98 in the Company's list but more importantly bestowed with the charismatic name 'Mosquito'. The maiden flight of the prototype, which was being built in secret at Salisbury Hall Farm, had yet to take place. However, such was the confidence in the design that an order for fifty bomber/reconnaissance variants was placed for construction at De Havilland's Hatfield Plant. To supplement Mosquito production, a shadow factory scheme was set up under the title of the Second Aircraft Group. This would comprise the factories, which the Ministry originally allocated for Albermarle construction situated at Western Avenue, Acton, Aldenham and Watford (Leavesden) Airfield. Construction to complete the factories at these locations was given the highest priority by the Air Supply Board, the scheme being reclassified from 'Z' to 'A'. De Havilland therefore set about converting the car cleaning shed at Aldenham for Mosquito fuselage construction and at the same time abandoned responsibility, for overseeing adaptations to the car maintenance building.

Early in September 1940, Ottaway contacted the Director of Aircraft Production to report that the increased amount of work envisaged for Chiswick would require further shop space. He therefore requested that the remaining shed at Aldenham be allocated to the London Aircraft Production Group.

Haymills contract had been renegotiated and signed on 20th June 1940, the finance for the project having been made available by the Treasury. By August the first members of the De Havilland workforce, in their capacity as employees of the Second Aircraft Group, moved into the car cleaning shed to begin work in establishing a production line. But now the question of space allocation at Aldenham was in urgent need of being debated by all parties involved.

At the invitation of the Director of Aircraft Production, a site meeting was called for 6th November 1940 with representation from the LPTB, De Havilland and Haymills. The Director was of the opinion that, due to its vulnerability, the Aldenham site should only contain two small units. This was to prove a rather controversial statement in view of the subsequent development of the site, earlier meetings having concluded that all buildings would be constructed as planned but to meet Air Ministry requirements. The Second Aircraft Group representatives announced that the first fifty aircraft fuselage shells would be completed by the end of January 1941. Although no confirmation of further orders had been received, it was agreed that the space in the car-cleaning shed should be retained by the Group with a view to an eventual output of fifty units each month.

Ottaway announced that he would required some 75,000 square feet of space for the production of Halifax centre sections and would like to utilise the extended side of the car maintenance shed. Here an overhead crane would be installed, which could be utilised to move parts of the aircraft. However, as Haymills' building operations were far more advanced in the larger area of the building, it was agreed to take up occupancy here, the facilities afforded by the overhead crane still being available. The whole building would eventually be built to original specification but the unused portion would be partitioned off and not provided with services, although it was agreed that the main heating boilers should be installed as if supplying the whole factory.

De Havilland was anxious to relinquish financial administration for the building construction and alteration at Aldenham. However, the whole area already formed part of the shadow factory scheme, the instigation of which pre-dated the Board's involvement with the site. In these circumstances it would be necessary for De Havilland to remain at the helm whilst the various projects were completed. By January 1941, all such arrangements had been changed. De Havilland's enforced hold on the purse strings was relaxed and given over to the LAPG, which became responsible for the expenditure incurred in adapting its own area and the installation of common services for the whole site.

As the speed of the country's munitions output moved up another notch, factory space stood at premium. Not surprisingly, a use was soon found for the unused section of the maintenance shed at Aldenham. This came in the shape of the well-established firm of Napier Ltd of Acton, which had been in the business of producing aircraft engines since the Great War. Towards the end of 1935, the company had embarked upon the production of a 2000 horsepower engine that incorporated a number of radical improvements. The engine named the Sabre had suffered many problems during its development stages. A test conducted for the Air Ministry during March 1940 confirmed that further revisions were necessary before the power plant was ready for active service.

The main Napier factory was situated in Acton but additional accommodation was soon secured within the Renault factory in Western Avenue, Park Royal. Due to demands from the Admiralty and Ministry for Aviation Production, for the Company to effect repairs to other engines from its range, floor space at the Western Avenue location for Sabre engine repairs was correspondingly reduced. The company therefore looked to the Aldenham site where it hoped to create 40,000 square feet of space in two hangars especially erected.

The proposal was duly presented to the Air Supply Board at its meeting on 17th December 1940. The Director of Repairs and Maintenance being requested to investigate the possibility of using space currently available to avoid the construction of new buildings. Thus the remaining section of the maintenance shed was offered to Napier for the repair and overhaul of the recalcitrant Sabres; the Minister agreeing to defray cost of the building work estimated at £16,500. Amenities including canteen availability for the Napier workforce would be provided by the London Aircraft Production Group but additional ARP shelters would cost £5,000.

One final facility was established at Aldenham, near to the proposed location of Bushey Heath station. The De Havilland Company had secured a contract for the repair of Rolls-Royce Merlin engines and had looked to the site in order to erect six testing cells to supplement those at the company's Hatfield plant. Later in the war, with De Havilland repairing Merlin engines at the rate of sixty each week, additional testing cells were considered necessary to replace those at Hatfield, which by then had been declared in need of rebuilding due to an infringement of fire precautions. The move was considered more convenient for De Havilland's repair shops in Finchley. However, the plan, which was drawn up in April 1944, was initially postponed and then finally withdrawn in September.

Building operations on the site began. An earlier decision taken by the Works Committee had determined that bricks already delivered to the site of the Elstree viaduct should be used to complete the depot at Aldenham.

Yet there was still to be another major turn of events within the structure of the London Aircraft Production Group. When the LPTB had been asked to take over the control of the Group, it was on the understanding that all components manufactured by its five constituent companies would be delivered to Handley Page for final assembly at Radlett Airfield. In March 1941, the Ministry of Aviation Production suggested that the Board might take on the erection of Halifax aircraft at Watford (Leavesden) airfield where facilities could be shared with De Havilland. Handley Page immediately voiced his opposition to such a proposal as he felt it unwise for the Board to undertake such a responsibility. In fact, it was widely believed in some quarters that aircraft manufactured by the Board would never fly. Handley Page's protestations were overlooked and on 31st March Lord Ashfield, with the support of Eric Ottaway, committed the Board to the final assembly of components manufactured by the London Aircraft Production Group.

Arrangements were therefore put in hand for the completion of a second flight shed at Leavesden Airfield, where the building contractors George Wimpey were in the process of constructing a building with an identical purpose for De Havilland. The parent company was asked to supply a set of components for a Halifax bomber that would be assembled by the Board's employees as a trial run. A revision was made to the earlier agreement so that the first twenty Halifax bombers built by the LPTB would be classed as an educational order, each aircraft attracting a profit of £2,200.

Building work at Aldenham remained generally disappointing. To add to Ottaway's anxieties, the workforce had only increased by 35 men by the beginning of May 1941 since the turn of the year. The whole of the project had been carefully scheduled so that the most essential parts of the factory could be completed at the earliest possible date. A hutment camp had been established for some of the builders, made necessary by the inaccessibility of the site. However, by the end of May considerable improvement had taken place, with the Board's own employees having been engaged to install jigs, fixtures and stores buildings. Ottaway was then able to record that the completion of Aldenham Depot would not affect the planned production programme. Progress was maintained during June, where work at Aldenham centred on the transfer of certain administrative functions in anticipation of a recently inaugurated spares facility being established at the site. Communications were also improved around this time by the introduction of an internal mail service using a motorcycle despatch rider. Nine staff cars were also acquired around this time for key members of personnel.

Some serious thought was given to installing machine tools at the five companies that comprised the London Aircraft Production Group. This move was considered essential to obviate the restrictive effect on production cause by the total sub-contracting of all machined parts to firms outside the main Group. Although costing some £180,000 to install, this arrangement would allow the members of the Group to manufacture machined parts for their respective components.

During October 1941 the erection of the first Halifax using components provided by the London Aircraft Production Group was proceeding at Leavesden Airfield, alongside a similar machine using parts supplied by Handley Page. Unfortunately production problems had been encountered and a speculative August completion date for the first LAPG-built Halifax had evaporated when Chiswick Works failed to complete the centre section of the aircraft in time. Production of this part of the aircraft would eventually be entrusted to Aldenham but, as the factory had yet to begin operations, the task had been undertaken in west London. Construction of sections for the second, third and fourth machines was well advanced in the other Group factories.

There is no doubt that nothing short of superhuman effort contributed to the completion of the first Halifax bomber built by the Group at Leavesden. Despite insufferable delays, BB 189 (a B/Mk II variant) finally left the ground on 8th December bound for Handley Page's Radlett airfield. During the final months staff of all grades had worked day and night to complete the aircraft. As the sound of four Rolls-Royce Merlin engines faded into the distance on that late autumn day, plans were already being established for an output of 30 aircraft each month by March 1943.

As the London Aircraft Production Group's contract to supply 200 Halifax aircraft gathered momentum, it immediately became apparent that all was not well at Duple, where problems were being encountered with the production of the front fuselage. This section of the aircraft carried the greatest concentration of electrical equipment, space at the coachbuilder's Hendon factory being insufficient to provide the number of workstations necessary to complete the whole procedure.

Duple's Managing Director requested that, as an interim measure, the Board could take delivery of the fuselage shells and undertake the electrical installation. Some weight was given to this request when it was reported that the output from Hendon was trailing some four units behind the number of constituent parts built by other members of the Group. Fortunately contingency plans had been formulated, the layout at Aldenham having been planned with the possibility of such a move in mind, the transfer being considered unlikely to have any serious effect on the programme as a whole. In the short term, some delay was experienced in securing enough units from Duple to build the first ten aircraft. From that point Aldenham took to its additional role using the expertise of some of the key personnel involved in this work at Hendon.

During January 1942 a decision was made whereby the machine tools that were to have been brought into Aldenham would be transferred to Chiswick. Amongst the main factors taken into consideration was that most of the aircraft construction workforce came from the Chiswick area. Moreover, Aldenham was not well placed due to its remoteness and lack of transport facilities for the conveyance of a night shift. The fabrication of centre sections of the aircraft was due to be transferred to Aldenham following the completion of the first ten units at Chiswick, which would provide space for the installation of machine tools. At the same time, an operation that involved the erection of engines was also assigned to Aldenham. So meticulous were the transfer arrangements that there was no disruption in output added to which was the bonus of saving some 300 miles per week in haulage.

Even at this early stage, plans began to be formulated for the Group to increase Halifax production to an astounding 46 aircraft per month by July 1943. In order to meet this target, Ottaway estimated that an additional 75,000 square feet of factory space would be required. He therefore suggested that this might be achieved by the requisitioning of a site for use by the spares department as a store. The total estimated cost of the project, including major adaptations to Leavesden airfield, was £450,000, of which £35,000 would be used for alterations at Aldenham.

When Lord Ashfield first presented plans for such a production increase, the Air Supply Council stated that no further expenditure could be allocated. Yet the Board still pressed for increased production, going so far to revise its estimates in February 1942 and submitting figures of £500,000 for buildings and £100,000 for more machine tools. The decision was a foregone conclusion; the Ministry informing Ottaway that it did not consider the proposed increase to be a viable proposition. By way of compromise, the Ministry put forward a plan for a monthly output of 35 aircraft that involved less ambitious building alterations at Aldenham, Chiswick and Express Motors amounting to £129,000, to which Ottaway gave his approval

In anticipation of the whole production of the front fuselage returning to Hendon, a member of staff from Park Royal vehicles was sent to Duple in an attempt to improve the company's production methods. During April 1942 Handley Page contacted the Board and requested that Duple be permitted to take on this work again. Ottaway refused, opting to keep the existing arrangements at Aldenham with a result that Handley Page resigned from the Group's management team. His reaction failed to earn him any form of rebuke from the Ministry; he was knighted two months later.

I am indebted to Dorothy Skelley for some of her reminiscences of working for De Havilland at Aldenham which, by mid-1942 was in full production with Mosquito fuselage assemblies in the car cleaning shed. When Dorothy applied to the company she was taken on immediately and asked to complete 33 weeks training as a bonder. This took place in one half of the premises where initial work on the fuselage was undertaken. The fuselage was built in two halves by skilled carpenters at Harris Lebus in Tottenham who gave up their peacetime furniture making activities and helped build the Wooden Wonder. Once these sections had been delivered to Aldenham, Dorothy was required to pin a wide copper bonding strip on the inner face of the port side of the fuselage. To this

Halifax centre sections dominate the foreground in this view whilst in the background can be seen the all-important twin level stores unit. By applying techniques that had been used for the construction of aircraft, London Transport was able to instigate a standardised parts system for its post war bus fleet. Ironically the site eventually chosen for its bus overhaul works, where the system would become of great importance, was Aldenham but at the time this view was taken it was expected that the premises would revert to being used as a depot for the Northern Line following the cessation of hostilities.

Aldenham also installed two of each Halifax's four engines and in this view Bristol Hercules XVI power units are being prepared. Engines nearest the camera are mounted on special stands in the low-level section of the building created by excavating the depot floor to pit bottom level. Small gantry cranes then lift each completed unit to a raised area for loading on to a flat bed trailer and transporting to Leavesden Airfield. Beyond the temporary wall is Napiers, the last of the three occupants of the Aldenham site to take up residence. Here examples of the initially troublesome Sabre engine were being examined and overhauled for return to Hawker Typhoon and Tempest aircraft.

strip would be fitted various items of equipment. It then fell to Dorothy to ensure that each was securely soldered in place.

Around the mid-point of the car cleaning shed both halves of the fuselage were joined, and Dorothy then climbed inside to undertake the more difficult bonding work. This involved adopting a supine position and working in extremely cramped conditions with hot lights and soldering irons almost in facial contact. The most difficult areas were to be found in the tail and cockpit. Any faults, found by the inspection team, would require immediate rectification in order that other workers could continue with their allotted tasks.

The completed units were then sent to the 'dope' shop, where each was sprayed with a dark red preservative before being despatched to Leavesden Airfield. The wings for the Group's output were assembled at the Western Avenue site and also transported to Leavesden, to be united with the Aldenham-built fuselage sections and transformed into finished aircraft.

By March 1942, transport facilities serving the Aldenham complex became the subject of a crisis for the Board's Central Bus Operating Department. The number of staff employed by the three resident organisations and their respective daily commencement times were:

London Aircraft Production – 900 staff (7.30 am)
Napier Ltd – 240 staff (7.30 am)
De Havilland Ltd – 300 staff (8.00 am)

The Board's Public Relations Officer compiled a memorandum, which concluded that the situation was not ideal and requested an equal division of the total workforce with two groups of 720 starting at 7.30am and 8.00pm. He reasoned that buses could then be effective for at least two journeys as the round trip from Edgware to Aldenham and back took half an hour to complete.

To make matters worse, the London Aircraft Production Group indicated that it would not consider two starting times, which would supposedly have a detrimental effect on output. Napier compromised with the offer of a 7.45am start although such action only stood to make matters worse from the point of economic operation. At Edgware, the problem of finding space on the special buses became so apparent each morning that staff began finding alternative ways of reaching the site. This situation was exacerbated by many new employees who were sometimes confused by the strangeness of the district. Problems were also experienced at the end of the working day when at least 50 workers were unable to leave the site on the group of buses timed to depart at 6.15pm. This resulted in a wait of at least 30 minutes in what was described as an exposed location.

To counteract the problem, the Central Bus Operating Department agreed to place an additional vehicle on route 18 each morning and evening whilst the Country Bus Department introduced new schedules from 1st April for the Bushey and Watford areas. An extension of route 324 to the factory complex from North Watford via the Watford By-Pass was also planned. However, all solutions could only be for the short term, as the number of workers on the site was on track to rise considerably around the turn of the year. Despite an equal division of starting times, the situation was set to deteriorate again.

Following the flight of the first LAPG Halifax in December 1941, time was taken to get all sites up and running before full-scale production began. Ottaway and his team decided to base their working practices on those of English Electric at Preston, where the bomber was also being built, as opposed to those of Handley Page at Cricklewood and Radlett. The first target of six complete aircraft was fixed for April 1942, which was almost achieved, had one example not suffered a magneto failure. It was no doubt an example of the initial output that made a demonstration flight on 7th May. Arranged as a morale-building exercise, the bomber overflew all sites used by the London Aircraft Production Group so that its employees could see the product of their labours.

Keeping pace with other front line aircraft, the Halifax went through a number of type variations throughout its existence. The initial order placed with the LAPG was for 200 B/MkII, Series 1 aircraft, this model forming the basis of all orders to companies receiving initial contracts. As design changes were made to improve the performance of the bomber, modifications were issued that resulted in variations of the type being in simultaneous production.

The knock-on effect of delays in the supply of Duple's front fuselage sections continued to be felt in June, only thirteen from a target of seventeen being finished, including the sixth from the previous month. By 1st August the

P.M. times are in heavy figures	Leavesden - Watford - Bushey Heath - Borehamwood - New Barnet	306

MONDAY to FRIDAY (TT.6683)

LEAVESDEN *Ganders Ash*	....	....	....	....	....	....	....	....	....	6 35	....	....	....	....
LEAVESDEN *Works*	..	..	..	..	..	..	..	..	..	..	..	..	..	7 1
Watford *Chilcott Road*	....	....	....	....	....	6 9	6 24	....	....	6 39	6 54	....	7 2	7 9
Watford *Gammons Lane*	..	..	..	..	..	6 12	6 27	..	6 35	6 42	6 57	..	7 5	7 12
Watford *Junction*	....	....	....	....	....	6 18	6 33	....	6 41	6 48	7 3	....	7 11	7 18
Watford *Old Market Place*	..	..	..	..	..	6 21	6 36	..	6 44	6 51	7 6	..	7 14	7 21
Watford *High St., LT Garage*	5 40	5 55	5 57	6 10	6 12	6 25	6 40	6 41	6 48	6 55	7 10	7 11	7 18	7 25
Bushey & Oxhey *Station*	5 42	5 57	5 59	6 12	6 14	6 27	6 42	6 43	6 50	6 57	7 12	7 13	7 20	7 27
Bushey Heath *St. Peters Church*	5 52	6 7	6 9	6 22	6 24	6 37	6 52	6 53	7 0	7 7	7 22	7 23	7 30	7 37
BUSHEY HEATH *Windmill*	..	..	..	..	..	..	..	6 55	..	..	..	7 25	..	..
BROCKLEY HILL *Works*	....	....	....	....	....	....	....	....	7 7	....	....	....	7 37	....
Elstree Village *Plough*	6 2	6 17	6 19	6 32	6 34	6 47	7 2	..	..	7 17	7 32	..	..	7 47
Borehamwood *Crown*	6 8	6 23	6 25	6 38	6 40	6 53	7 8	....	....	7 23	7 38	....	....	7 53
BOREHAMWOOD *Warwick Road*	6 12	6 27	6 29	6 42	6 44	6 57	7 12	..	..	7 27	7 42	..	..	7 57
Arkley *Arkley Hotel*	6 24	6 39	....	6 54	....	7 9	7 24	....	....	7 39	7 54	....	....	8 9
Barnet *Church*	6 28	6 43	..	6 58	..	7 13	7 28	..	..	7 43	7 58	..	..	8 13
NEW BARNET *Station*	6 35	6 50	..	7 5	..	7 20	7 35	..	..	7 50	8 5	..	..	8 20

LEAVESDEN *Ganders Ash*	....	....	....	....	....	....	....	....	....	....	....	....	....
LEAVESDEN *Works*	..	7 16	..	7 31	..	7 46	..	8 1	..	8 16	..	8 31	..
Watford *Chilcott Road*	7 17	7 24	7 32	7 39	7 48	7 54	8 2	8 9	8 18	8 24	8 32	8 39	8 47
Watford *Gammons Lane*	7 20	7 27	7 35	7 42	7 51	7 57	8 5	8 12	8 21	8 27	8 35	8 41	8 50
Watford *Junction*	7 26	7 33	7 41	7 48	7 57	8 3	8 11	8 18	8 27	8 33	8 41	8 48	8 56
Watford *Old Market Place*	7 29	7 36	7 44	7 51	8 0	8 6	8 14	8 21	8 30	8 36	8 44	8 51	8 59
Watford *High St., LT Garage*	7 33	7 40	7 48	7 55	8 4	8 10	8 18	8 25	8 34	8 40	8 48	8 55	9 3
Bushey & Oxhey *Station*	7 35	7 42	7 50	7 57	8 6	8 12	8 20	8 27	8 36	8 42	8 50	8 57	9 5
Bushey Heath *St. Peters Church*	7 45	7 52	8 0	8 7	8 16	8 22	8 30	8 37	8 46	8 52	9 0	9 7	9 15
BUSHEY HEATH *Windmill*	7 47	..	8 2	..	8 18	..	8 32	..	..	..	9 2	..	9 17
BROCKLEY HILL *Works*	....	....	....	....	....	....	....	....	8 54	....	....	....	....
Elstree Village *Plough*	..	8 2	..	8 17	..	8 32	..	8 47	..	9 2	..	9 17	..
Borehamwood *Crown*	....	8 8	....	8 23	....	8 38	....	8 53	....	9 8	....	9 23	....
BOREHAMWOOD *Warwick Road*	..	8 12	..	8 27	..	8 42	..	8 57	..	9 12	..	9 27	..
Arkley *Arkley Hotel*	....	8 24	....	8 39	....	8 54	....	9 9	....	9 24	....	9 39	....
Barnet *Church*	..	8 28	..	8 43	..	8 58	..	9 13	..	9 28	..	9 43	..
NEW BARNET *Station*	..	8 35	..	8 50	..	9 5	..	9 20	..	9 35	..	9 50	..

LEAVESDEN *Ganders Ash*	....	....	....	9 16	....	9 36	....	....	9 56	....	10 16	....	10 36	....
LEAVESDEN *Works*	8 46	..	9 2	..	..	..	..	..	..	..	..	..	..	..
Watford *Chilcott Road*	8 54	9 2	9 10	9 20	9 30	9 40	9 50	9 55	10 0	10 10	10 20	10 30	10 40	10 50
Watford *Gammons Lane*	8 57	9 5	9 13	9 23	9 33	9 43	9 53	9 58	10 3	10 13	10 23	10 33	10 43	10 53
Watford *Junction*	9 3	9 11	9 19	9 29	9 39	9 49	9 59	10 4	10 9	10 19	10 29	10 39	10 49	10 59
Watford *Old Market Place*	9 6	9 14	9 22	9 32	9 42	9 52	10 2	10 7	10 12	10 22	10 32	10 42	10 52	11 2
Watford *High St., LT Garage*	9 10	9 18	9 26	9 36	9 46	9 56	10 6	10 11	10 16	10 26	10 36	10 46	10 56	11 6
Bushey & Oxhey *Station*	9 12	9 20	9 28	9 38	9 48	9 58	10 8	..	10 18	10 28	..	10 48	10 58	11 8
Bushey Heath *St. Peters Church*	9 22	9 30	9 38	9 48	9 58	10 8	10 18	....	10 28	10 38	....	10 58	11 8	11 18
BUSHEY HEATH *Windmill*	..	9 32	..	9 50	..	10 10	..	..	10 30	..	..	..	11 10	..
BROCKLEY HILL *Works*	....	....	....	....	....	....	....	....	....	....	....	....	....	....
Elstree Village *Plough*	9 32	..	9 48	..	10 8	..	10 28	..	..	10 48	..	11 8	..	11 28
Borehamwood *Crown*	9 38	....	9 54	....	10 14	....	10 34	....	....	10 54	....	11 14	....	11 34
BOREHAMWOOD *Warwick Road*	9 42	..	9 58	..	10 18	..	10 38	..	..	10 58	..	11 18	..	11 38
Arkley *Arkley Hotel*	9 54	....	10 10	....	10 30	....	10 50	....	....	11 10	....	11 30	....	11 50
Barnet *Church*	9 58	..	10 14	..	10 34	..	10 54	..	..	11 14	..	11 34	..	11 54
NEW BARNET *Station*	10 5	..	10 21	..	10 41	..	11 1	..	..	11 21	..	11 41	..	12 1

Stop	Then at these mins. past each hour							UNTIL				
LEAVESDEN *Ganders Ash*		56	....	16	....	36	....		2 16	....	2 35	....
LEAVESDEN *Works*		..	..	..	..	..	..		..	..	..	..
Watford *Chilcott Road*		0	10	20	30	40	50		2 20	2 24	2 39	....
Watford *Gammons Lane*		3	13	23	33	43	53		2 23	2 27	2 42	..
Watford *Junction*		9	19	29	39	49	59		2 29	2 33	2 48	....
Watford *Old Market Place*		12	22	32	42	52	2		2 32	2 36	2 51	..
Watford *High St., LT Garage*		16	26	36	46	56	6		2 36	2 40	2 55	2 56
Bushey & Oxhey *Station*		18	28	38	48	58	8		2 38	2 42	2 57	2 58
Bushey Heath *St. Peters Church*		28	38	48	58	8	18		2 48	2 52	3 7	3 8
BUSHEY HEATH *Windmill*		30	..	50	..	10	..		2 50	..	..	3 10
BROCKLEY HILL *Works*		....	....	....	....	....	....		....	....	....	....
Elstree Village *Plough*		..	48	..	8	..	28		..	3 2	3 17	..
Borehamwood *Crown*		....	54	....	14	....	34		....	3 8	3 23	....
BOREHAMWOOD *Warwick Road*		..	58	..	18	..	38		..	3 12	3 27	..
Arkley *Arkley Hotel*		....	10	....	30	....	50		....	3 24	3 39	....
Barnet *Church*		..	14	..	34	..	54		..	3 28	3 43	..
NEW BARNET *Station*		..	21	..	41	..	1		....	3 35	3 50	....

27

P.M. times are in heavy figures	Brockley Rise - Croxley Green *Manor Way* Brockley Rise - Watford *Met. Station*	334 334A

MONDAY to FRIDAY

WATFORD-BY-PASS *Suicide Corner*	....	....	....	....	....	....	....	....	....	....	7 33	....
WATFORD-BY-PASS *Aldenham Rd.*	..	..	..	..	..	6 54	7 4	7 14	7 24	7 34	7 44	7 54
WATFORD-BY-PASS *The Dome*	6	6	6 31	6	6 51	7 1	7 11	7 21	7 31	7 41	7 51	8 1
Watford *Market Place*	6 29	6 35	6 45	6 55	7 5	7 15	7 25	7 35	7 45	7 55	8 5	8 15
CROXLEY GREEN *Manor Way*	....	6 49	....	7 9	....	7 29	....	7 49	....	8 9	....	8 29
WATFORD *Met. Station*	6 40	..	6 56	..	7 16	..	7 36	..	7 56	..	8 16	..

WATFORD-BY-PASS *Suicide Corner*	....	8 3	....	....	8 33	....	....	....	9 3	....	....	....
WATFORD-BY-PASS *Aldenham Rd.*	8 4	8 14	8 24	8 34	8 44	8 54	..	..	9 14	..	..	..
WATFORD-BY-PASS *The Dome*	8 11	8 21	8 31	8 41	8 51	9 1	9 11	9 16	9 21	9 31	9 41	9 51
Watford *Market Place*	8 25	8 35	8 45	8 55	9 5	9 15	9 25	9 30	9 35	9 45	9 55	10 5
CROXLEY GREEN *Manor Way*	....	8 49	....	9 9	....	9 29	....	6	9 49	....	10 9	....
WATFORD *Met. Station*	8 36	..	8 56	..	9 16	..	9 36	..	..	9 56	..	10 16

Stop				Then at these minutes past hour							UNTIL
WATFORD BY-PASS *Suicide Corner*	....	....	....		....	....	....	....	....	....	
WATFORD BY-PASS *Aldenham Rd.*	..	..	..		..	..	..	..	..	..	
WATFORD BY-PASS *The Dome*	10 1	10 11	10 21		31	41	51	1	11	21	
Watford *Market Place*	10 15	10 25	10 35		45	55	5	15	25	35	
CROXLEY GREEN *Manor Way*	10 29	....	10 49		....	9	....	29	....	49	
WATFORD *Met. Station*	..	10 36	..		56	..	16	..	36	..	

WATFORD BY-PASS *Suicide Corner*	....	....	‡5 3	....	....	‡5 33	....	%X	....	‡6 3	....
WATFORD BY-PASS *Aldenham Rd.*	..	‡5 4	‡5 14	‡5 24	‡5 34	‡5 44	‡5 54	..	‡6 4	‡6 14	..
WATFORD BY-PASS *The Dome*	5 1	5 11	5 21	5 31	5 41	5 51	6 1	6 8	6 11	6 21	6 31
Watford *Market Place*	5 15	5 25	5 35	5 45	5 55	6 5	6 15	6 22	6 25	6 35	6 45
CROXLEY GREEN *Manor Way*	5 29	....	5 49	....	6 9	....	6 29	6	....	6 49	....
WATFORD *Met. Station*	..	5 36	..	5 56	..	6 16	..	..	6 36	..	6 56

44

ROUTE 18	Aldenham - Edgware - Wembley - Harlesden - Kings Cross - London Bridge —continued	P.M. times are in heavy figures

Stop	MONDAY to FRIDAY First				MONDAY to FRIDAY Last			SATURDAY First				SATURDAY Last			SUNDAY First			SUNDAY Last			
LONDON BRIDGE *Station*	....	....	....	....	....	....	....	....	....	....	....	....	....	....	....	8 30	....	8 56	10 18	....	....
Ludgate Circus *Ludgate Hill*	..	..	..	..	..	..	..	..	..	..	..	..	..	..	..	8 37	..	9 4	10 26	..	..
Kings Cross *Station, Underground*	....	....	....	....	....	....	....	....	....	....	....	....	....	....	....	8 45	....	9 12	10 34	11 6	....
Hampstead Road *Euston Road*	..	..	..	..	..	..	..	..	..	..	..	..	..	..	..	8 51	..	9 18	10 40	11 12	..
Edgware Road *Chapel Street*	....	....	....	....	....	....	....	....	....	....	....	....	....	....	....	8 58	....	9 26	10 48	11 20	....
Harrow Road *Prince of Wales*	..	..	..	..	..	..	..	..	..	..	..	..	..	..	..	9 6	..	9 35	10 57	11 29	..
Harlesden *Jubilee Clock*	....	....	....	....	....	....	....	....	....	....	....	....	....	....	....	9 17	....	9 46	11 8	11 40	....
Craven Park *Junction*	..	..	..	..	..	..	..	..	..	..	..	..	..	..	..	9 20	..	9 49	11 11	11 43	..
Stonebridge Park *North Circular Road*	....	....	....	....	....	....	....	....	....	....	....	....	....	....	....	9 23	....	9 53	11 15	11 47	....
WEMBLEY *Empire Pool*	..	..	6 45	..	..	9 53	..	..	..	6 45	..	..	9 53	..	..	..	..	....	....	....	..
Wembley *Railway Hotel*	5 31	6 18	6 51	....	....	9 59	....	5 31	6 18	6 51	....	....	9 59	....	7 18	9 31	....	10 1	11 23	11 55	....
Sudbury Town *Approach Road*	5 34	6 21	6 54	..	..	10 2	..	5 34	6 21	6 54	..	..	10 2	..	7 21	9 34	..	10 4	....	....	..
East Lane *Watford Road*	5 37	6 24	6 57	....	....	10 5	....	5 37	6 24	6 57	....	....	10 5	....	7 24	9 37	....	10 7	..	..	....
Harrow *Met. Station Approach*	5 43	6 30	7 3	..	..	10 12	..	5 43	6 30	7 3	..	..	10 12	..	7 30	9 43	..	10 14	....	....	..
Wealdstone *Station LMS*	5 49	6 36	7 9	....	....	10 18	....	5 49	6 36	7 19	....	....	10 18	....	7 36	9 49	....	10 20	..	..	....
Canons Park *Station, Underground*	6 0	6 47	7 20	..	..	10 30	..	6 0	6 47	7 20	..	..	10 30	..	7 47	10 0	..	10 32	....	....	..
EDGWARE *Station, Underground*	6 5	6 52	7 25	....	5 40	10 35	....	6 5	6 52	7 25	....	12 53	10 35	....	7 52	10 5	....	10 37	..	..	....
ALDENHAM ✶	..	7 2	..	..	5 50	..	..	..	7 2	..	..	1 3	..	..	..	..	..	..	....	....	..

✶–Junction of Watford By-Pass and Elstree Road.

LIST OF DEPARTURES FROM AND TO ALDENHAM

Aldenham *Works* to Edgware *Station*, MON. to FRI. at 7 5, 7 31, 7 39, 7 47, 7 58, 8 7, 8 27, 8 57 a.m., 4 47, 4 53, 4 58, 5 2, 5 6, 5 17, 5 52 p.m.; SATURDAY at 7 5, 7 32, 7 39, 7 47, 7 58, 8 27, 8 57 a.m., 12 5, 12 10, 12 20, 12 45, 1 5 p.m.

Edgware *Station* to Aldenham *Works*, MON. to FRI. at 6 52, 7 18, 7 27, 7 35, 7 44, 7 55, 8 4, 8 15, 8 45 a.m., 4 35, 4 41, 4 50, 4 54, 4 59, 5 40 p.m.; SATURDAY at 6 52, 7 18, 7 27, 7 35, 7 44, 7 55, 8 4, 8 15, 8 45, 11 53 a.m., 12 32, 12 53 p.m.

As the workforce at the three Aldenham sites increased, so too did the need for an intensive bus service to the works during The morning and afternoon peaks. By April 1942, with production at its zenith, the number of journeys had increased significantly. At this time there were 21 departures from Edgware station to Aldenham on Monday to Friday, augmented by additional buses to cater for the changing weekly shift pattern. These three timetables are from 1946. The central area originally described these works as plain 'Brockley Hill' and later, as illustrated, 'Aldenham', whilst country area route 306 provided a stop at 'Brockley Hill Works'. Factory workers using routes 334 and 334A were obliged to alight at the ominously named 'Suicide Corner', incorrectly referred to as 'Brockley Rise' in the timetable heading.

A wartime advertisement encouraging workers to beat the clock and in consequence Hitler, overlooks the main factory area where a predominance of female workers are hard at work constructing Halifax centre sections. The white painted wall in the background squares off the shop inspection bay, and provides further space for Napiers beyond. The time span between the 'discovery' of the site by Frederick Handley Page and the flight of the first LAPG aircraft was just 23 months. Production was then set to continue for a period of three years, heavy bomber production being halted once the tide of the war had been irreversibly changed at the end of 1944.

thirtieth machine had been test flown, but now the stresses of setting up the Group were beginning to take their toll on the health of its General Manager. Ottaway succumbed and was away from his desk during late July and early August. He returned to find a letter from a Ministry of Labour and National Service inspector, who had visited Aldenham during his absence and observed that the factory was the one weak spot within the London Aircraft Production Group.

The inspector had concluded that Ottaway's once a week visit to Aldenham was insufficient to inspire management and workers with his presence and leadership, and he was asked to think about making the factory his headquarters instead of Chiswick. With an anticipated workforce of around 2,000, the inspector considered that it would be fatal for the workers if they felt isolated from Ottaway's influence. Ottaway replied that moving his headquarters to Aldenham was impractical.

During August, as part of a further expansion of capacity initiative, a factory was opened at White City. The premises to be used consisted of buildings erected for the great exhibitions held before the Great War, and were to be deployed for the manufacture of engine cowlings and a facility for the storage of raw materials.

At the end of September the London Aircraft Production Group's workforce at Aldenham numbered 967 employees, comprising 21 fitter assemblers and erectors, 6 electrical production workers, 61 semi-skilled males and 879 women. In common with the massive increases in Britain's output of war weapons – skilled work was now falling to the fairer sex. The training of those employed at Aldenham had been undertaken by Handley Page at the company's Cricklewood and Radlett establishments.

Production suffered a drop in October when only eleven aircraft were completed and declared ready for service out of the target of fifteen set for the month. Lord Ashfield immediately contacted Ottaway for an explanation, who advised his Chairman that problems had occurred with the hydraulic pipelines installed in each aircraft, each being manufactured to the very exacting requirements of the RAF.

Ottaway also informed his Chairman that the introduction of proper incentive working at all factories within the Group had only just been achieved and as a morale booster the female staff were now paid at the same rate as the men. Moreover, considerable success had already been achieved at Aldenham where the whole factory had been restructured, and consequently there had been a substantial increase in productivity.

Construction of the centre sections of Halifax bombers is in full swing at Aldenham. A temporary wall has been installed at the mid point of the lifting and (neighbouring) shop inspection bays creating a rectangular workshop of some 161,000 square feet. The crane installed above this bay was fitted out with special lifting gear to enable the centre sections to be moved onto specialised transport from a bay constructed at the country end of the depot. In all London Transport built 710 examples of this component. The first ten were built at Chiswick, the remainder at Aldenham. So meticulous were the transfer arrangements that no drop in production was experienced.

Changes in the policy regarding the call-up of men began to be experienced in late November. The retention of labour in factories would be by deferment only and required an application from each individual, it being considered unlikely that such action would be granted for workers below the age of 30. The effect of this policy was thought to be considerable, if applied without discrimination at the factories managed by the Group, with the result that construction work might be reduced or halted altogether. Representations were therefore made, with the emphasis placed on the need to retain skilled labour involved in the production of the Halifax, and some concessions were made.

By March 1943, as the Group's initial order for 200 aircraft neared completion, some wing sets produced by Park Royal failed fatigue testing, and final erection was halted at Leavesden in consequence. In April, a mission visited aircraft manufacturers in the United States of America to observe production methods. From this it was concluded that roof levels in the air-conditioned factories were much higher and illumination about one-third brighter than at Aldenham.

With space at its own installation at Aldenham now at a premium, De Havilland looked to London Transport for assistance in storing Mosquito components. At the time, the company had already been allocated part of Hatfield bus garage but a subsequent offer of space at St Albans garage was declined.

By the end of August 1942, around the time when the 40th Halifax built by the Group had been completed and test flown, some concerns were being voiced regarding the inferiority of the type compared with the Avro Lancaster. Nevertheless, the Group received a second contract to build 250 Halifax bombers to follow the initial batch still to be built to the B MkII Series 1 configuration. However, with effect from the 46th aircraft of the second contract came a type change to B MkII Series 1a, the Group adjusting its production accordingly. Amongst the most obvious changes in the design were the deletion of the front machine gun turret and the addition of a radar blister below the belly of the aircraft. But the most noteworthy was the replacement of original Merlin XX engines with the more powerful Merlin 22 variants. Ottaway was later to record that a single modification could involve changes to anything between 4,000–5,000 parts.

In August 1943, LPTB comptroller L C Hawkins became Joint General Manager of the LAPG with Eric Ottaway. By the end of the month, Ottaway had to report to Lord Ashfield that the production target of 27 aircraft had been reduced by five due to the shortage of tailplane bolts.

This wartime view of Aldenham shows some of the many additional structures that were added to the site to allow the aircraft factories to function. Napiers occupied this end of the main depot, their premises being the extended side of the main depot building, which was 'squared off' at the half way point to provide a larger unit for use by the London Aircraft Production Group. In the background to the right can be seen the roof of the car cleaning shed which provided the Second Aircraft Group with accommodation for the construction of Mosquito fuselages.

One aircraft manufactured by the Group was sent to Boscombe Down during September to participate in comparison trials against one example from each of the other companies involved in the construction of the Halifax. The aircraft was deemed to have the best performance in four out of the five tests used for evaluation. To add to this achievement, the Group succeeded in producing its target of 27 aircraft for the month of November, all other companies failing to complete theirs. Deliveries by the Group then remained on schedule for the ensuing months.

On 20th February 1944, the White City factory was bombed. Although the stores area was unaffected, the manufacture of engine nacelles was temporarily halted whilst a new production line was established in the running sheds at Leavesden airfield.

A further design change was applied to the Group's third contract to build 180 aircraft to the BIII specification. This revision called for another change of engine using Bristol Hercules XVI power units. With an increased wing span of 102 feet 2 inches instead of 98 feet 9 inches, the speed and range of these Halifax aircraft was increased without any reduction in their 13,000-bomb load.

During March, Sir Stafford Cripps, Minister for Aircraft Production, visited Aldenham to view the exceptional effort that was being made. The only other recorded VIP visit is that of HRH the Duke of Kent who inspected all three establishments at the Aldenham factory in early 1942.

By now, the Group was producing bombers at an exceptional rate. All 180 aircraft comprising the third order were built between March and November 1944 during which time production reached a monthly output of 30, but the anticipated 35 aircraft per month put forward in 1942 was never achieved.

A final order for 200 BIII Halifax bombers was placed with the LAPG in November 1944, but by then the tide of the war had irreversibly changed in the Allies' favour and production was halted after the 80th machine was rolled out a Leavesden airfield in February 1945. Information regarding the termination of the final contract after the completion of the 710th Halifax was received by the London Aircraft Production and Joint Production Councils, which issued a statement. This gave an overview of the LAPG, wherein it was noted that components to complete the abbreviated contract existed at two of the factories within the Group. At these locations, there would be complete and immediate redundancies. The statement deplored the fact that the White City factory would be stripped and allowed to become derelict despite an expenditure of £76,000 converting it into a modern factory. There was also mention that the area used by Park Royal Vehicles would become a Government Store. However, the report understood that transport was now a priority requirement and that it was the policy of the LPTB to return to its bus construction as quickly as possible using its own staff at Chiswick. In recognition of their joint management of the LAPG, Eric Ottaway was presented with a platinum watch and Leonard Hawkins with four silver candlesticks.

On 31st January 1945, some indication had been given regarding the future of Aldenham. The Ministry of Aircraft Production had agreed that the whole of the LAPG's assets from all factories involved in the scheme should be concentrated at the site. This action was taken on the understanding that the Ministry's occupation could be terminated on three months notice given by the Board at any time after the term of the existing lease expired on 1st August 1945. The Ministry enquired whether the Board would also be prepared to operate Aldenham as a central store for LAPG material and any similar assets it might wish to store there. Despite having some reservations about the size of the operation in receiving and despatching material to other destinations, the Board agreed to undertake this work at the Ministry's expense. It was realised that the period which Aldenham could be used was governed by the time when it would be required as an Underground depot. Nevertheless, it was assumed that occupation to the end of 1945 was not unreasonable.

The car cleaning shed was duly vacated by early summer 1945 and Napiers departed their section of the maintenance shed later in the year, leaving behind them a latent legacy that would become apparent when the Board's 1947 Bill became the subject to discussion in Parliament.

The final aircraft constructed by the London Aircraft Production Group was named *London Pride* at Leavesden Airfield on 16th April 1945. The unveiling ceremony was presided over by Lord Ashfield and witnessed by hundreds of aircraft workers. The bomber was then handed over to an RAF crew, but was not taken on charge until 3rd November when it entered service with 517 Squadron at Chivenor in North Devon. 517 Squadron used the Halifax for meteorological duties for a brief period, after which it was transferred to a storage and salvage unit for scrap, being struck off charge on 1st November 1946.

CHAPTER NINE

The Post-War Period

As Britain entered the Post War era, London Transport began to pick up the pieces of its 1935–1940 New Works Programme which, it was widely believed, would be completed in accordance with original plans. However, before the London Passenger Transport Board could consider the order in which the construction work was to continue, it received a report from its Chief Legal Advisor. This referred to the contents of a Private Bill submitted to Parliament during the autumn of 1945 by the Colne Valley Water Company.

The Bill sought powers to construct new reservoirs, aqueducts, wells and pumping stations and to acquire lands for such purpose, part of which would be in direct line with any possible extension of the Northern Line from Bushey Heath towards Watford, Bushey or Radlett. Negotiations were therefore opened to protect the Board's position if, in future, it sought power to extend the line. During the ensuing discussions it was discovered that, as the Water Company would require recompense for sterilisation of part of the reservoir land, it might be preferable to leave the decision to Parliament as and when powers for an extension were sought. The matter was allowed to rest when Colne Valley assured the Board that its current proposals for Elstree Extension would suffer no physical interference.

Early in 1946, the Board received a report on the proposed schedule for completing the New Works Programme, from which it was determined that work to extend and electrify the Central Line would be in the first category of a six-category list. Hard on the heels of the Central Line extensions were those of the Northern Line, the aforementioned schedule determining that the route from Finchley to Edgware would be finished between January 1947 and June 1948. The reconstruction of Edgware station was planned to take place between April 1947 to August 1948, with a new layout for trains from Finchley being introduced in June 1948 to coincide with the completion of that section. Both projects had placed in category two, the only project occupying the fifth category being the line from Edgware to Bushey Heath. Although the proposed dates for work on the extension were given as April 1947 to September 1948, there was very little to make it likely that these dates would be met.

There was of course the question of finance for the Programme upon which a figure of £40 million had been placed in 1935. This represented the total cost of construction but at the time no plans had been produced upon which reliable estimates could be based. More precise estimates totalling £42,286,000 were issued in 1936 and submitted to Parliament in connection with the Private Bills promoted by the LPTB, the LNER and GWR for the purpose of obtaining statutory powers. However, the figure of £40 million continued to be quoted as the total cost for the whole programme.

Up to 31st December 1945, the Board had expended £26,827,000 from the pre-war estimate for completing its part of the New Works Programme. A revised estimate was drawn up based on increases in raw materials and labour costs with a result that the amount for

This 1956 view of the route of the extension immediately behind Station Road, Edgware, clearly shows the retaining wall (left) and the service road (subsequently named Rectory Road) bridge. One can only speculate that the narrower construction of the shops and flats beyond the bridge was dictated by the width of the concrete raft constructed to allow the line to be projected beneath.

completing the whole programme from scratch was set at £55,065,000. The Board's share was calculated to be £35,938,000, representing 65% of the total. At the end of 1945, there was still an unspent balance of £5,136,000 from the original pre-war loan and the deduction of a provisional proportion of this amount from the new estimate for completing the Board's projects showed that £7,962,000 still had to be secured.

In its 1946 Report, the Standing Joint Committee carefully considered the possibility of curtailing some of the works in order to bring the cost of the outstanding schemes into accord with the funds already raised. As the New Works Programme formed a co-ordinated scheme upon which considerable sums of money had already been spent, no revisions were put forward. Such action was underpinned by promises made to Local Authorities concerning the completion of the Programme in order to meet the needs of new housing schemes being planned in the Board's area.

The Committee therefore recommended that the whole Scheme should be allowed to progress with the exception of the Ruislip to Denham and, possibly, the Loughton to Ongar extensions on the Central Line, and should be brought to a conclusion as rapidly as possible.

Prior to the production of the report, the Minister of Transport had indicated that first priority should be given to the completion of the Central Line extension. In addition, the electrification of the LNER to Shenfield should be resumed and completed 'with all possible expedition'. Finance for these particular schemes was to be provided from the remaining unspent capital, which only represented about half of the amount required to complete them.

The Ministry of Transport also requested, for the purpose of its deliberations with the Treasury, a statement of urgency for the remaining works in the programme and called for information from the Board and the railway companies. In response the Standing Joint Committee produced an order of priority which included the time for completion of each of the works from a zero date yet to be determined, which assumed a reasonable availability of labour and materials.

Despite appearing on the list, no estimated time of completion was given for the Elstree Extension, the only incomplete Northern Line project not so determined, its future being dependent upon progress made on other sections and the receipt of a date of authority to proceed.

The Committee also stressed that on economic grounds alone, the completion of the programme as a whole should be authorised and commenced as quickly as practicable for three reasons. The first related to the burden of interest charges on idle capital already expended upon projects that had yet to provide revenue; the second to physical deterioration of the uncompleted structures; and, thirdly, by undertaking construction in an uninterrupted sequence, the best use would be made of available labour.

On the assumption that authorisation would be given and funding made available to complete the outstanding works, expenditure for each of the constituent companies' projects was apportioned over a number of years. The Board was allocated the lion's share of £9,111,000 distributed over a five-year period from 1946 to 1950 and inclusive of £1,149,000 that was readily available from the original pre-war loan. The Committee realised that a problem could exist in raising the remaining capital due in no short measure to the fact that repayment dates for the original loan might fail to be met, the earliest due date being August 1950, the latest August 1955. Obviously the war was held responsible for this particular situation; the repayment times having been set in 1935 without any knowledge of the long years of conflict that lay ahead.

In November 1946, the Railways (Maintenance) Division of the Ministry of War Transport sent a confidential memorandum to its Deputy Director, Sir Reginald Hill. The document, which had been compiled at the request of Sir Richard, considered the recommendations made in the Railway (London Plan) Committee's report published at the beginning of the year, and described the problems of starting another round of new works. The report concluded that there was very little chance of carrying through new long term works, due mainly to the present state of the railways, as little headway was being made to overtake wartime arrears of maintenance and renewals. There was also a reference to the uncompleted 1935–40 New Works Programme, wherein some criticism was made of the Board's projection of its tube lines towards the outer suburbs. The preferred alternative was to provide for the through working of main line services which, among other benefits, gave relief to the centre of London where it was primarily required.

The report also reasoned that other proposals by the Railway (London Plan) Committee for a line to Heathrow and improvements at Osterley station for the British Industries Fair (1951) and International Exhibition (1956) in Osterley Park (superseded by the Festival of Britain) would delay completion of the 1935–40 programme. In the light of its findings the Ministry offered a number of alternatives, one of which considered a retardation of the 1935–40 programme and put into question the future of the Northern Line extensions.

On 27th November 1946, the LPTB deposited a Bill in Parliament. Amongst the powers pursued was provision for the resiting of Bushey Heath station under the heading Railway Work No. 1 as detailed in the following submission:

'In the administrative counties of Middlesex and Hertford. A railway of 0 Miles, 6 Furlongs and 2 Chains (approximately 1.25km) or thereabouts situate in the district of Harrow, the parish and rural district of Elstree and the urban district of Bushey commencing in the urban district of Harrow, by a junction with Work No 1 authorised by the Act of 1937 and terminating in the urban district of Bushey at or near the junction of Dagger Lane with the Watford By Pass'.

The Board's minutes of the period provide no indication for such a decision. However, when consideration is given to the powers granted to the Colne Valley Water Company, a few months earlier, a motive begins to emerge. By giving the line scope for further extension, the Board

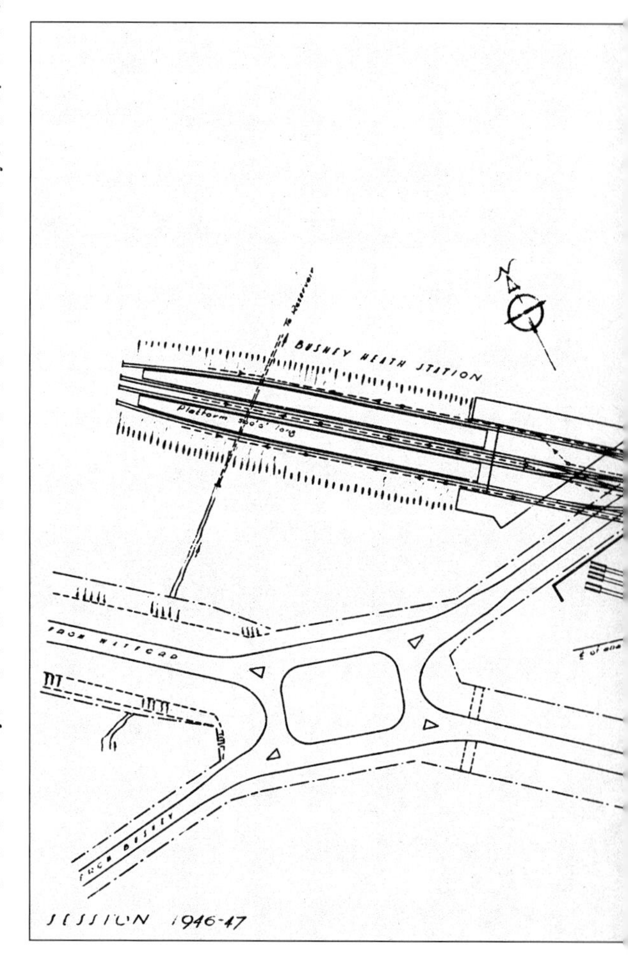

knew that its proposals would bring about objections from the Water Company, which it was now prepared to have debated in Parliament. The 1947 Bill also included provision for the breaking up of Elstree Road in order to build the new railway and the temporary stopping up of this thoroughfare whilst the work was in progress.

As expected, the Board's proposals succeeded in attracting petitions from the Middlesex and Hertfordshire County Councils and, of course, the Colne Valley Water Company. These centred on the resiting of Bushey Heath station, echoing the proposal made in 1944, and other associated works. Proposals to excavate Elstree Road incited a number of concerns from the two local authorities. Hertfordshire County Council attempting to predict the Board's plans by stating that the Council's recent purchase of 1,150 acres known as the Well Hall Estate was at risk. Despite being situated some two miles distant from the proposed new terminus, a straight extension of the new railway would pass through the estate, which had been acquired as an addition to the Green Belt. The severance of the estate was described by the Council as 'having so injurious effect upon the amenities and frustrate in large measure the purposes for which it has been acquired'.

In the weeks preceding the consideration of the Bill in Parliament, the Engineering (Highways) Division of the Ministry of Transport studied the objections raised by Hertfordshire County Council. It was noted that both the Watford By-Pass and Elstree Road would be affected by the resiting of Bushey Heath station. The Ministry therefore supported the Council's insistence for the construction of a temporary carriageway whilst the surface of Elstree Road was being broken up in order for a bridge to be constructed. The bridge was also planned to have a width of 'not less than 33 feet' which the Council stated would give rise to continuous traffic jams and won further support from the Ministry for a road width of 52 feet.

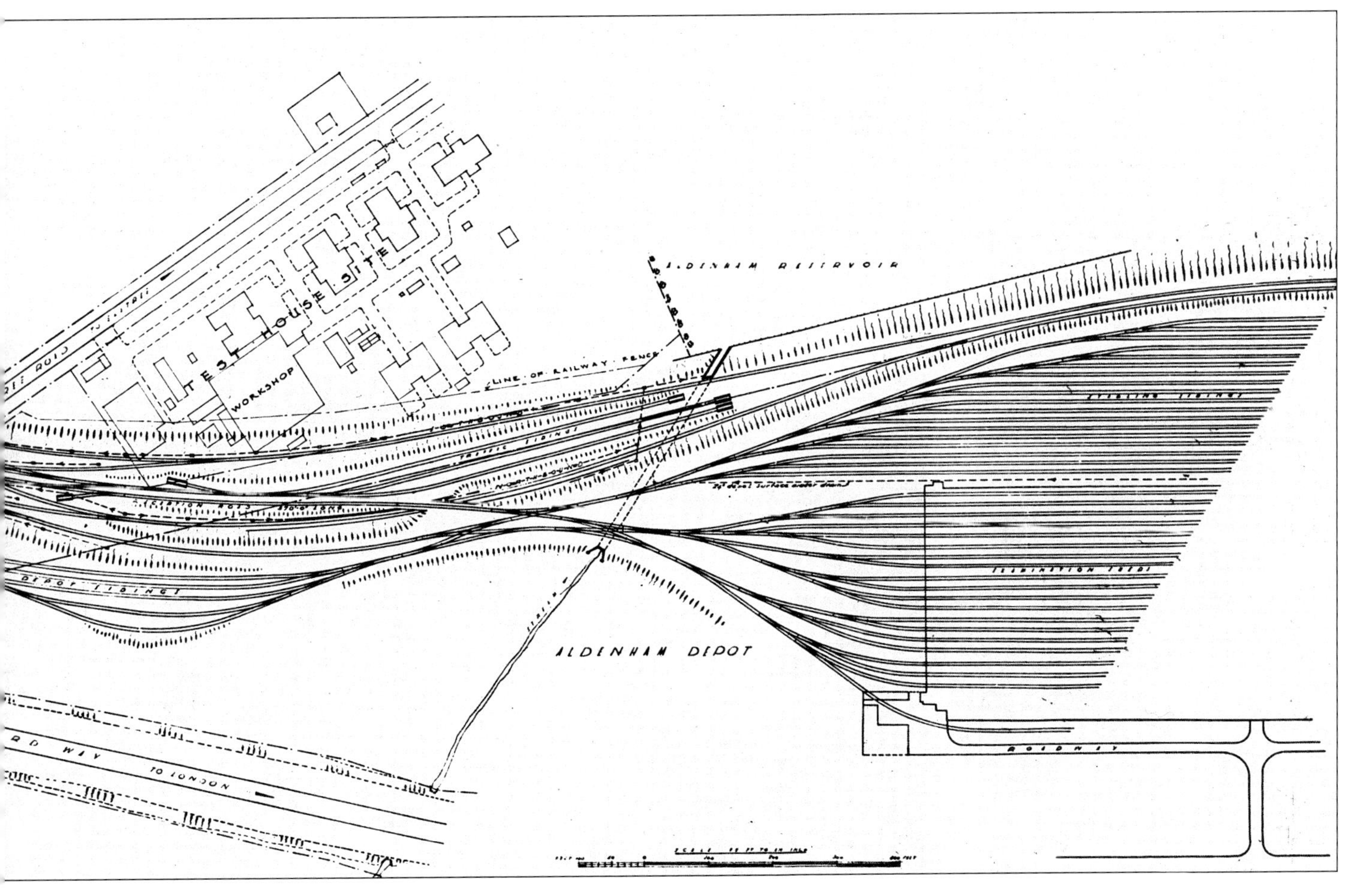

According to the Board's Chief Engineer, Percy Croom-Johnson, the main reason for seeking Parliamentary powers to move the site of Bushey Heath station was to provide improved traffic operational facilities. This would be accomplished by the introduction of adequate reception sidings and space for working traffic back to the depot more easily than had been the case using the layout proposed in 1937. The test houses shown on the plan were constructed for De Havilland for the testing of Rolls-Royce Merlin engines, later becoming a film studio and leased to the Gigi Film Company.

The London Passenger Transport Bill of 1947 sought to transfer the site of Bushey Heath station to the west side of Elstree Road. The Board's Chief Engineer, Percy Croom-Johnson, informed the Parliamentary Select Committee that there was no intention to continue the railway in a straight line beyond Bushey Heath station and cross the site of the proposed Hilfield Park Reservoir, yet he did not completely rule out any further projections. The installation of temporary weirs for oil skimming was necessitated by an objection raised by the Colne Valley Water Company, due to the excessive amounts of aviation lubricants that had permeated the ground during the war.

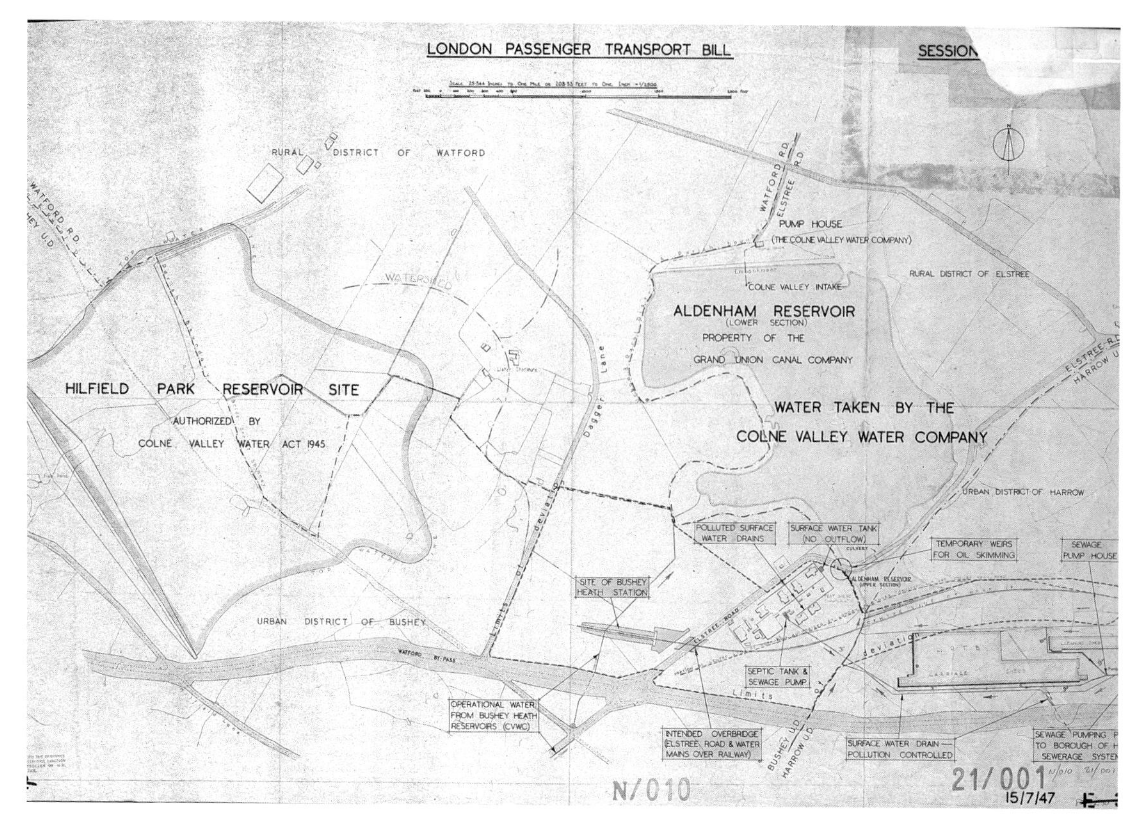

On 8th May 1947, the section of the London Passenger Transport Board Bill that covered proposed railway works came under the scrutiny of a Select Committee of the House of Commons. Only the petition of the Colne Valley Water Company remained, those of Hertfordshire and Middlesex County Councils having been withdrawn by earlier negotiation. From the statements made by the Board's Chief Engineer, Percy Croom-Johnson, it is possible to determine the 'official' intention for the resiting of Bushey Heath station. When asked a question appertaining to this subject, Croom-Johnson stated that the main purpose was to afford improved traffic operation facilities by the provision of adequate reception sidings in the space between the station and the depot. Apparently, this would not have been possible using the track layout proposed in the 1937 Bill. To clarify the situation further, Croom-Johnson confirmed that, if it was decided to stable a train or take it out of service, it could return via the accommodation sidings to the reception roads until depot space was available. A movement such as this could now be made without interfering with the main line passenger tracks. It was therefore concluded that the extension would provide more space and elasticity for working trains back to the depot.

The Committee then moved to the petition of the Colne Valley Water Company, and Croom-Johnson was asked to give an indication of the Board's intentions regarding plans for the line, the design of the relocated Bushey Heath station giving scope for further projection. The Water Company had already realised that a straight extension of the railway would cause it to pass directly over the site of its proposed Hilfield Park Reservoir. The Chief Engineer confirmed that the Board did not contemplate extending the line westwards in a continuous line and confirmed that every endeavour would be made to ensure that any future extensions did not cross the new water storage facility.

The question of pollution was then raised with reference to the aircraft engine testing that had been undertaken by Napier during the war. Aldenham Reservoir had become contaminated from copious amounts of oil and aviation spirit that had been allowed to permeate the ground and various methods were being tried to remove it. An assurance was subsequently obtained from Croom-Johnson that everything would be done to protect the Water Company's interests.

After its successful passage through the House of Commons, the Bill came before a Select Committee of the House of Lords on 21st July. The Colne Valley Water Company again pursued its unsuccessful application made in the Commons regarding drainage and decontamination of the site. The House subsequently passed the Bill subject to the inclusion of a clause that the Board would take all reasonable steps to prevent its works from polluting Aldenham Reservoir. Royal Assent was received on 13th August 1947.

Another piece of legislation that was to have a major influence also gained Royal Assent during that summer. The 1947 Transport Bill received the King's signature on 6th August, and thus cleared the way for the British Transport Commission to be established, its inaugural meeting taking place just one week later.

Initially three Executives were established under the provisions contained in the Bill. The Railway Executive comprised the 'Big Four' companies established under the 1921 Act together with a number of smaller independents, which had passed to Government control during the war. Docks and Inland Waterways were the responsibility of the second Executive, whilst London Transport was considered to be large and complex enough to warrant its own. Lord Latham became the first Chairman of the London Transport Executive, having previously been appointed as Acting Chairman of the London Passenger Transport Board on 1st October 1947 following the retirement of Lord Ashfield.

In anticipation of a shift of power under the 1947 Transport Bill, the Board considered the implications of the Special Enactments of Time Act 1940, under which it had obtained extensions to expiring statutory powers by means of orders made by the Ministry of Transport under the Act. Applications for the extension of statutory powers could not be made earlier than six months before the date of expiry.

As the 1940 Act had been passed as an emergency measure and could be terminated at any time, the Board established a dialogue with the Ministry of Transport on 17th June 1947. The main discussion centred upon the likelihood of the Board suffering a major reduction in its powers upon the establishment of the British Transport Commission. With the Commission about to become an official body, there would be no means by which a Bill could be promoted in the 1947/48 session of Parliament should the 1940 Act be terminated, the Board's statutory powers expiring in 1948. Some reliance was therefore placed upon the Minister being prepared to consider an application for the extension of powers earlier than the prescribed period.

In response to the Board's concerns, the Ministry intimated that the 1940 Act would be terminated on 30th June 1947 but its Minister would consider an immediate application for a further extension of timc. Approval of the embryonic Commission was therefore secured and an application was made for a three-year extension of the Board's statutory powers, which included the Edgware to Bushey Heath line. On 9th October 1947, the Board received notice that the Minister of Transport had subsequently granted an extension of five years, with the stipulation that all aspects of the New Works Programme should be completed by 30th September 1952.

The Bushey Heath extension was the subject of further investigation in a report compiled during April 1948. At that time it was noted that £450,000 had already been expended on the line which would require £1,690,000 to complete. It was now estimated that work would commence in 1950 and be completed in 1952, just ahead of the deadline set by the Ministry of Transport.

Towards the end of 1948, the London Plan Working Party's Report was published. The uncompleted state of the 1935/40 New Works Programme attracted a comment which referred to the considerable sums already spent upon the various projects, including the depot at Aldenham. The Working Party therefore remained satisfied that all works should be finished substantially as planned, and the route to Bushey Heath was included amongst those in the first priority.

The report was received by the Commission in February 1949 and five months later, on 25th July; a meeting was convened at the Ministry of Transport for the purpose of preliminary discussion. It was anticipated that the report would receive ministerial consideration after the summer recess and the purpose of the meeting was to consider the findings of the London Plan Work Party. Significant interest was expressed concerning the order in which the works should be undertaken, should the Ministers agree to such a course of action.

Facing page top **The site of Brockley Hill station showing in the background the completed arches that would lead directly on to an embankment that would take the line towards Elstree. Supports for a further eleven arches dominate the foreground and have been constructed as far as springing level. This view was taken on 5th September 1957. Note what appears to be two tipper-wagons which, if the property of the original construction company (Robert McAlpine), would have been on the site for some eighteen years.**

Representing London Transport Executive was its Operating Manager (Railways), Mr Alec Valentine, who was asked to justify the high priority of works from the 1935–40 New Works Programme such as the Edgware to Bushey Heath extension. Valentine replied that considerable sums would be wasted should the works not be completed, although modification of the Bushey Heath extension was being considered having regard for the Green Belt.

The Executive's Chief Development and Research Officer F A A Menzler, submitted a report during August 1949 which, amongst its recommendations, concluded that the extension of the Northern Line from Edgware to Bushey Heath should be abandoned.

On 1st September 1949, Valentine produced a document entitled 'Future Policy with Regard to the Northern Line Extensions'. In his summary of the outstanding works, the Bushey Heath extension was considered in two separate sections. The construction of the line as far as Brockley Hill would carry it to an important road junction although it remained difficult to defend the extension unless, in addition, further housing development could be expected in the district. The current Green Belt proposals precluded further building but as the exact boundary for the area was only tentative, a final appreciation of the traffic value of a station at Brockley Hill could not be made.

The report then continued that there was no traffic justification for the remainder of the extension, the only consideration being the future policy for Aldenham Depot. By that time it had been established that adequate facilities could be provided by developing a satellite depot at Highgate on a site then owned by the Commission. Such action coupled with a few additional sidings at Morden Depot and relatively minor improvements at Golders Green Depot gave rise to the fact that there was no reason at all for the line to Bushey Heath to be built. Subsequently the report recommended that the line from Brockley Hill to Bushey Heath should be abandoned, to which the Executive gave its approval.

The estimate for the work undertaken beyond Brockley Hill was set at £380,000. However, this figure included £230,000 for the construction of Aldenham Depot, which would become a total loss if the land on which it stood was returned to agriculture should Town and Country Planning approval not be forthcoming for it to be put to other industrial purposes.

No public statement was immediately issued regarding the fate of the extension and it was not until 12th April 1950 that the subject was raised as part an informal meeting between the Executive and the British Transport Commission. It was then that Lord Latham suggested that an announcement should be made in view of the possibility of the point being raised in the Committee of the House of Commons that had been established to consider the Commission's 1950 Bill. The proposed line was still being shown on bus and Underground maps issued by the Executive and it was agreed that this feature should be omitted from all future printings.

The arches at the site of Brockley Hill station, 1958.

Below **Demolition of the piers for the viaduct on the south side of the Watford By Pass began on 9th March 1959 in preparation for a housing development by Sterling Homes, which were offering luxury flats starting from £3,250. When this view was taken some six months later, construction had commenced of the first house across the track formation, which is bounded by the rear gardens of houses in Glendale Avenue (left), and those of Hillside Gardens. Such was the width of the land allocated to the Elstree extension at this point that the developer was able to project a new road almost centrally between them which he unashamedly named Sterling Avenue. Shelley Close was constructed along the same path, its only means of access being from Purcells Avenue.**

This platform at Edgware was built on the site of five sidings and was completed after work had ceased on the remainder of the extension. In this view the platform serves as nothing more than a storage facility, its planned function having been to provide an interchange between terminating trains (on the left) and through traffic to Bushey Heath.

Consideration was therefore given as to what would be the most beneficial occasion for announcing the abolition of the project – either to the House of Commons Committee or by way of public statement. In fact, it was not until October 1950, some thirteen months after Alec Valentine's report, that it became official that there would be no further construction work on the Brockley Hill to Bushey Heath section of the extension.

Menzler's department issued a subsequent report in February 1952 regarding the extension to Brockley Hill. Since the Executive adopted the recommendations made by Alec Valentine, the Middlesex Draft Development Plan (1951) had become available. In December 1948, the population of the area that could be served by Brockley Hill station was placed at 7,700, which, under the Draft Plan could rise to 10,900 by 1971. The calculation was based on Edgware becoming a through station and that in so it doing would suffer a reduction in the 'population served'. Consequently, the estimated combined net gains for both stations was 2,000 in 1948 and 3,800 in 1971. The figures are shown in the table below.

Population Served

	December 1948			**Planned for 1971**		
	Edgware	Brockley Hill	**Total**	Edgware	Brockley Hill	**Total**
Present Layout (Edgware being the terminus)	27,900		**27,900**	29,500		**29,500**
Line Extended to Brockley Hill (Edgware being a through station)	22,200	7,700	**29,900**	22,400	10,900	**33,300**
Increase or Decrease through extension of line	–5,700	+7,700	**+2,000**	–7,100	+10,900	**+3,800**

In determining the figures, it had been assumed that there would be no further extension of the line from Mill Hill East towards Edgware. Surprisingly, the economic case for the short extension was considered slightly stronger than it had been in 1949 but there was a downside. The Ministry of Housing and Local Government was already strenuously opposed to any expansion in the Green Belt just north of Edgware. Any proposal made for an increase in population in the Brockley Hill area would require the Ministry's approval. The report concluded that there was no case for the extension and if an immediate decision was sought then it could only be in the negative. F G Maxwell, Operating Manager (Railways) commented 'it looks as though this supplies the final four screws for the coffin of this corpse – if it were not nailed down already'. On 26th November 1953 the project was officially abandoned by the Executive with a press release eventually being issued in February 1954.

Haymills' last involvement with the Aldenham site occurred on 15th August 1948 when the firm was awarded a contract for the demolition, restoration and alteration to various buildings. The plan was drawn up by Chartered Surveyors, A L Currie and Brown, who were destined to become heavily involved with the later development of the site. The project was undertaken in advance of the decision not to proceed with the extension. Thus, material from the excavations and demolitions was to be deposited on the spoil site, situated on the low ground to the north of the car shed. Anticipating the construction of the railway, the contract required spoil to be neatly trimmed and levelled with care taken to keep existing ditches clear of tipped material.

Although the Elstree Extension had been abandoned for almost three years by the time this photograph was taken on 19th June 1952, the erstwhile Underground depot had yet to be fully transformed into Aldenham Bus Overhaul Works. The housing development of 252 new homes adjacent to Elstree Hill was built on land originally owned by the LPTB, an exchange having taken place in 1939, the residents being within walking distance of the planned Elstree South station.

Another 19th June 1952 view, this time from the west. Additional buildings abound, all of which were erected by the three wartime occupants. London Transport retained a considerable number, which it used for the overhaul of the post-war RT fleet from 1950. The track bed at the rear of the depot can be easily discerned, although no work was ever accomplished at two stations at either end of the site. Buses awaiting overhaul can be seen together with the new RTs waiting licensing before their entry into service. The rash of buildings adjacent to Aldenham Reservoir was De Havilland's test facility for their overhauled Merlin engines.

Buildings to the right of this view, which still show traces of camouflage, are of wartime temporary construction, those in the foreground almost shrouding the car cleaning shed. This view taken on 30th June 1953 shows a concrete mat in the process of being laid, marking the site of the famous Aldenham Works high bay where bus bodies would be lifted clear of chassis and craned into special stands as part of the overhaul process.

Being the first of the two major buildings on the site to be completed, the car cleaning shed was equipped with provision for track to be laid. An all-over concrete floor topping was installed for De Havilland's occupancy in 1940. This was finally removed during its transformation from Underground depot to bus overhaul works in October 1954, revealing beneath the reinforced concrete running rail supports.

Facing page lower **The tunnel mouths south of Elstree Hill in 1965 shortly before being covered over during construction of the M1 motorway extension.**

With the abandonment of the line beyond Brockley Hill, little time was lost in issuing a contract to Kinnear Moodie and Co in November 1949, for the dismantling and removal of two tunnelling shields located beneath Elstree Hill. When work ceased on the line in 1939, the northbound tunnel had been driven a distance of 160 feet and the southbound 70 feet, both seeing later use by the Home Guard, presumably as rifle ranges. After the removal of the shields, the company was required to construct two concrete headwalls and build timber hoardings at the mouth of each tunnel complete with lockable access doors. Spoil from construction work at Aldenham was deposited in the area of the tunnels, all traces of their existence disappearing as a result of the M1 motorway extension towards London during the mid-1960s.

The two aerial views on this spread were taken on 12th May 1958 and 15th June 1962 respectively. Both show the Brockley Hill construction works intact but in between the two photos the piers south of Edgware Way have disappeared in connection with the building of Sterling Avenue, under way in the second view.

Demolition of the piers for the viaduct on the south side of Edgware began on 9th March 1959, although three were still in situ some five months later. Brockley Hill station arches survived into the 1960s, and their piers still survive today as does the base of a bridge support on the north side of Edgware Way.

Between Edgware station and the Edgware Way the former London Transport land has been built on. Following the route from Edgware a small single storey building and car park are behind what would have been a bridge over the railway in Rectory Lane, followed by two depressing rows of lock-up garages. Heronsgate extends into the next bit of land, followed by Campbell Croft and then Shelley Close, across Purcells Avenue where there is a slight prominence in the road surface. A garden separates Shelley Close from the next development, Sterling Avenue and its 1960s maisonettes. Perhaps appropriately, all the residential streets built on the alignment of the aborted extension come to a dead end.

This view, also dated 15th June 1962, shows the route from where Sterling Avenue is under construction to Edgware station. Campbell Croft has recently been completed but work has not yet started on Shelley Close.

The abandonment of the extension to Brockley Hill in November 1953 allowed a plan to be produced showing a revised track layout and associated works for Edgware station. Dated August 1954, the plan went through a number of modifications until it was finally approved over a period spanning August 1957 to January 1958. One noticeable detail was for the signal cabin built in 1939 to be brought into use, as indeed it was; but not until 1965.

The 1939 excavations under Station Road provided space for a very short extension of platform roads 2 and 3 at Edgware station. The work was undertaken during 1966 to improve safety margins following the introduction of programme machine signalling then under the control of Golders Green signal box. A scissors crossover, which had been sited at the London end of the platform roads could only just be cleared by 7-car trains until the platform roads

were lengthened and special track circuits installed to double-prove that trains had cleared the crossover points, as they self-normalised under programme machine operation

There was a final piece of irony to emerge after the Bushey Heath project was closed down. John Taylor, a firm of civil engineers for the Colne Valley Water Company, wrote to the Ministry of Home and Local Government in November 1951 regarding the Hilfield Park Reservoir upon which construction had just started. One of the first parts of the scheme was to be the construction of a reinforced concrete tunnel. At the time, it had been found impossible to obtain the steel for reinforcing. Fortunately, a number of cast iron segments that would have been used to complete the tunnel under Elstree Hill had been discovered near the site. The segments were deemed eminently suitable as a substitute material.

Documents Consulted

Archive and Records Management Service, Transport for London, 55 Broadway, SW1H OBD

The Pick File		*Wartime*
LT12/005	LT12/448	A0182
LT12/010	LT12/451	A0065/01
LT12/010/01	LT12/452	A0065/002
LT12/010/02	LT12/455	A0065/003
LT12/016	LT12/456	
LT12/019	LT12/458	
LT12/019/01	LT12/459	*Parliamentary*
LT12/165	LT12/465	A0050/008
LT12/166	LT12/466	A0052/005
LT12/137	LT12/472	A0053/007
LT12/178	LT12/488	A0053/010
LT12/193	LT173/002	
LT12/215	LT173/003	
LT12/253	LT173/004	*General*
LT12/302	LT173/007	LT232/283
LT12/306	LT173/009	LT243/005
LT12/313	LT181/002	
LT12/357/01	LT181/005	
LT12/381	LT181/006	*Contracts*
LT12/382/02	LT181/007	LT172/025/008
LT12/389	LT181/013/01	LT172/027/015
LT12/390	LT182/003	LT172/031/003
LT12/392	LT182/004	LT172/044/033
LT12/393	LT185/001	LT172/050/002
LT12/394	LT185/002	
LT12/395	LT185/003	
LT12/399	LT185/004	
LT12/418	LT185/005	
LT12/447		

London Metropolitan Archives, 40 Northampton Road, London EC1R 0HB

Minutes of the London Passenger Transport Board and the London Transport Executive and the reports relating thereto.

Minute Books of the Watford and Edgware Railway Company and the Union Surplus Lands Company.

Notes of Informal Meetings between LTE and BTC.

House of Lords Record Office, London SW1A 0PW

Deposited plans in support of 1861, 1897 and 1903 Watford and Edgware Railway Bills and Parliamentary proceedings relating thereto.

London's Transport Museum, Covent Garden, London WC2E 7BB

Plans and Photographs

Public Record Office Kew, Surrey TW9 4DU

AN13/360	HLG50/2404	RAIL796/1
AN13/484	HLG50/2405	RAIL1030/78
AN13/562	HLG50/2186	RAIL1062/95
AN13/563		RAIL1066/78
AN13/1082	MT6/1734/7	RAIL1066/365
AN13/1092	MT6/1980/1	RAIL1066/674
AN13/1093	MT6/2255/2	RAIL1066/969
AN13/1094	MT6/2927	RAIL1066/2909
AN13/1165	MT6/3384	RAIL1066/2910
AN13/1172	MT33/189	RAIL1066/2911
AN56/50	MT37/33	RAIL1066/2912
AN97/181	MT37/51	RAIL1066/2913
AN97/185	MT37/52	RAIL1110/295
AN97/206	MT45/400	RAIL1110/465
	MT45/402	RAIL1030/78
AVIA10/166 et seq	MT46/21	RAIL1124/217
AVIA11/64	MT46/142	
AVIA15/2321		T160/967/ F15252
AVIA15/3709	RAIL236/718/23	T163/66/3
AVIA15/3775	RAIL236/719/11	T163/66/4
AVIA15/3776	RAIL236/719/14	T163/135/2
	RAIL236/719/30	T191/71
BT285/268	RAIL236/722/15	
BT31/33563 /29412	RAIL236/1171	
	RAIL285/268	
CAB139/227	RAIL390/1101	
CAB139/228	RAIL390/2043	

These remnants of the arches that would have provided support for Brockley Hill station still exist on the north side of the Edgware Way. Now graffiti daubed, these monuments stand as a quiescent reminder of the tube line that never was.